THE CHILDREN IN ROOM E4

The Children in Room E4

AMERICAN EDUCATION ON TRIAL

by SUSAN EATON

ALGONQUIN BOOKS OF CHAPEL HILL 2007

Published by
ALGONQUIN BOOKS OF CHAPEL HILL
Post Office Box 2225
Chapel Hill, North Carolina 27515-2225

a division of
WORKMAN PUBLISHING
225 Varick Street
New York, New York 10014

Library of Congress Cataloging-in-Publication Data
Eaton, Susan E.
The children in room E4 : American education on trial / by Susan Eaton. — 1st ed.
    p. cm.
ISBN-13: 978-1-56512-488-2; ISBN-10: 1-56512-488-X
1. Discrimination in education — Connecticut — Hartford.
2. Discrimination in education — Law and legislation — Connecticut — Hartford.
3. Hartford (Conn.) — Ethnic relations. I. Title.
LC212.23.H37E28 2007
371.82900974'63 — dc22   2006045502

10 9 8 7 6 5 4 3 2 1
First Edition

For Eli, Will, and Mark

And for the children in room E4

There are things that cannot ever occur
with any precision. They are too big and too
magnificent to be contained in mere facts.
They are merely trying to occur, they are
checking whether the ground of reality can
carry them . . . An event may be small and
insignificant in its origin, and yet, when
drawn close to one's eye, it may open in its
center an infinite and radiant perspective.

— Bruno Schulz, *Sanatorium Under the Sign
of the Hourglass*, translated from the
German by Celina Wieniewska

A good head and a good heart are always
a formidable combination.

—Nelson Mandela

CONTENTS

AUTHOR'S NOTE

THIS IS A WORK of nonfiction. All the people presented here exist. There are no composite characters or conflated or "representational" scenes or invented dialogue. When a person is said to have felt, believed, thought, or recalled something, the emotion, belief, thought, or memory was explicitly described to me by the person to whom it is attributed. In the case of recalled events, I was nearly always able to contact others present to confirm that my subjects' memories were accurate. I've changed the names of all subjects under the age of 18 and the names of their parents or guardians, in order to protect their privacy, and in one case, I changed a parent's former occupation.

The material for this book was culled from thousands of hours of observation; lengthy, open-ended, informal conversations; and formal interviews, and from thousands of pages of government and public school district documents. In addition, I reviewed transcripts of court proceedings, conducted interviews, collected newspaper articles, and watched videotapes to reconstruct scenes from the first *Sheff* trial and other events in the early 1990s for which I was not present. (I attended every day of the third *Sheff* hearing in 2002. The entire *Sheff* trial in 1992–93 was videotaped by the American Civil Liberties Union, and I was provided unlimited access to those recordings.) I used statistical data within the public domain to calculate changes in test scores, dropout rates, and other indicators of school success and failure.

In the interest of full disclosure, a plaintiff witness in the *Sheff* case, Gary Orfield, was a professor of mine during my doctoral studies at Harvard and has been a frequent writing partner in the past.

INTRODUCTION

I STARTED THIS BOOK simply planning to write about a little boy we'll call Jeremy, his teacher, Ms. Lois Luddy, and, across town, some civil rights lawyers trying to open blocked corridors to opportunity. The stories driving this book, all of them set in Hartford, Connecticut, are straightforward accounts of specific children, schools, and lawyers. But taken together, they also assess the fate of a basic American conviction — a nationwide promise that we have our children say daily. It's the pledge of our flag: "one nation, indivisible."

The civil rights case at this book's heart, a crucial one you may never have heard of, is an 18-year-long, still-running legal battle. In *Sheff v. O'Neill,* 19 schoolchildren and their families sued the State of Connecticut, arguing that the racial, ethnic, and class segregation that characterized their schools failed to deliver the equal educational opportunity promised in the state's constitution. The band of civil rights lawyers behind the case hoped it might do more than help children in Connecticut's struggling cities. They believed it could revive the ideals inspired by *Brown v. Board of Education.*

Back in 1954, the U.S. Supreme Court unanimously declared in *Brown v. Board of Education* that "in the field of public education . . . 'separate but equal' has no place." *Brown* sparked the civil rights movement, which toppled enforced, intentional segregation down south. But after just twenty years, a more conservative Supreme Court set about curtailing *Brown*. By 1974, *Brown* would be unable to stop the segregation that was growing ever more extreme up north. The argument at *Sheff*'s core is that such de facto segregation, born not from explicit laws but from a variety of causes, is devastating too.

Like many Americans, I'd grown up inspired by the old civil rights stories of the 1950s and '60s. Suddenly, *Sheff* presented one for my generation. I'd covered the case in the early '90s, while I was a newspaper reporter. After finishing graduate school in 1999, I began investigating the *Sheff* story more deeply. *Sheff* was 10 years old by then. But I found that Hartford's educators, like their counterparts across the nation, had little reason to indulge in hopeful discussions about racial integration. Segregation was a condition they'd had to accept as a given. Many teachers and administrators seemed to believe that the only feasible remedy for inequality was to nudge up newly consequential test scores in their segregated schools. Most educators I met gave it their all, feeling that if only they worked harder, separate really could become equal.

In one Hartford school, they seemed to be succeeding. At the all-black-and-Latino Simpson-Waverly Elementary School, test scores had risen in recent years, often matching scores in the suburbs. I approached Simpson-Waverly's principal with a predictable, heartfelt, and naive inquiry: "How might we transfer your successful model to other urban schools?"

As I think readers will come to see, I'd asked far too narrow a question. I eventually found my way to a tougher, less fashionable one: Is what politicians call "school reform"—the contemporary, bipartisan goal of quantifiable standards and better test scores—a just, effective replacement for *Brown*'s and *Sheff*'s requisite integration and equal opportunity? Or is it actually a return to the "separate but equal" doctrine expressed in *Plessy v. Ferguson*, the Supreme Court decision that had held minorities in place from 1896 until the *Brown* ruling overturned it 58 years later?

In late 2003, when I'd nearly completed my reporting, the Bush administration awarded Simpson-Waverly Elementary School a Blue Ribbon and dubbed it one of six national models for urban education. Meanwhile, on the other side of town, *Sheff v. O'Neill* had been argued, decided, appealed and decided again, reopened, decided, reopened again, and settled, and would reopen yet again. As of late 2005, *Sheff*'s plaintiffs and lawyers planned to return to court for at least one more round, hoping to win access for more children to racially and economically diverse schools.

Over the years, I've come to understand why so many people in this story keep the faith and keep up the fight. Hearing my accounts of the *Sheff* battle, many friends have wondered if the continuing effort is "worth it." I'm confident that my readers will answer that question for themselves.

Susan Eaton
Boston, Massachusetts
2006

THE CHILDREN IN ROOM E4

PART ONE

Jeremy

The Scarecrow watched the Woodman while he worked, and said to him:

"I cannot think why this wall is here, nor what it is made of."

"Rest your brains and do not worry about the wall," replied the Woodman; "when we have climbed over it we shall know what is on the other side."

. . . The Scarecrow climbed up the ladder first, but he was so awkward that Dorothy had to follow close behind and keep him from falling off. When he got his head over the top of the wall the Scarecrow said,

"Oh, my!"

—L. Frank Baum, *The Wonderful Wizard of Oz*

"He Lived *Here*?"

ON A DRIZZLY, CHILLY LATE afternoon in 2000, eight-year-old Jeremy Otero snatched the sole remaining copy of *Harry Potter and the Sorcerer's Stone* from a library shelf in downtown Hartford. In the checkout line, he tapped his foot and glanced over his shoulder, as if expecting someone to swipe his good luck.

"Maybe someone put this book on the shelves but it wasn't supposed to be there," Jeremy said. "They're not going to let me have this."

The children's librarian smiled at him and said sure, he could take the book home.

"Really? Oh, thank you! Thank you!" he replied, hands clasped prayerfully. "You can't know how much this all means to me today!"

He positioned the book in a backpack, which he hoisted onto his broad shoulders. He was built like a half-size sumo wrestler. He grinned, anticipating the night ahead. "It's Friday," he said, leaping off the middle stair outside the library, landing unsteadily. "No school tomorrow. I can stay up late. I can read!"

Jeremy didn't always notice where he was walking. Stopping short, ducking to the side, he dodged a bronze leg. He looked up, taking in the sculpture that rose from its granite pedestal above him. He slid his pinkie along the statue's rain-slick shoe.

"Who's that guy?" he asked. "No. Wait. Wait. Don't tell me. Here. It says. Mark Twain? I never heard of him."

He read the inscription out loud: "One of the nation's most celebrated authors, Mark Twain lived in Hartford at the peak of his writing career, from 1871 to 1891. About Hartford, Twain wrote: 'Of all the beautiful towns it has been my fortune to see, this is the chief . . . You do not know what beauty is if you have not been here.'"

The city fathers of Hartford had long since claimed the American icon Twain. In the '60s and '70s, curators had transformed his 19-room mansion (with Tiffany interiors) into a posh museum. The statue, erected more than eight decades after Twain's death, returned him to permanent residence. In the new millennium, Mark Twain, famously short in real life, stood eight feet tall and stared solemnly down Main Street, along a block and a half of vacant commercial space and the bustling, battered front of a methadone clinic.

"He lived *here*?" Jeremy asked, puzzled. "In Hartford?"

Hartford, Connecticut—Jeremy's town too. The city his grandmother and mother had migrated to, fleeing Puerto Rico's poverty. Hartford, where Jeremy had been born in 1992, and where he has pretty much always lived—first, in a Puerto Rican ghetto, over a pager shop that catered to drug dealers. Hartford, where, just before dawn one morning, a bomb had flown into the pager shop and spat flames through the building in one of a rash of neighborhood arsons that year. Hartford, where Jeremy lived now with his grandmother, his aunt Nina, a brother, and two cousins, in a tiny, dark apartment in one of the city's black ghettos.

A century ago, Mark Twain's Hartford had been one of the nation's most prosperous cities. Jeremy's Hartford, ringed by suburban wealth just beyond its borders, was America's second-poorest big city.

"I don't understand something," Jeremy said, looking back toward Mark Twain. "With all the money he got from being famous, couldn't he have moved?"

Circumstance

FROM THE LIBRARY DOWNTOWN, it's about a two-mile walk to Westland Street, where Jeremy lived, in the eastern section of Hartford's North End.

"There's all kinds of shooting noises you can hear," Jeremy said that drizzly night, stepping out of my car, sweeping his hands out like a tour guide presenting his neighborhood. "The shots come from here and there and over there. And it just so happens that people do get shot around here. And everyone's seen someone get beat up for weird reasons, like for nothing. It's a pretty normal thing. And so, you kind of just stay inside and you just have to hope it doesn't come so close near you."

Jeremy lived with frequent gunshots and street slayings. He could watch daily drug dealing out his window. He also lived less than two miles from Windsor, Connecticut, the closest of Hartford's northern suburbs. Windsor—a town of modest ranch houses, standardized apartment complexes, and middling chain stores—was nothing fancy, but it was safe. And its high school had a fine reputation. To many of the families in Hartford's North End, Windsor, which annually hosted a dog show, a Fourth of July pie-eating contest, and a winter carnival and carol sing, represented an unreachable aspiration.

"Where *are* we?" Jeremy had asked me from the back seat of my car early one afternoon. I'd missed the turnoff for his street and ended up just over the city line, in Windsor.

"This is *not* where I live," he said. "I think we have to turn around."

Heading back south, toward Hartford, we passed a bent, faded rusty sign, marking the line between suburb and city. Jeremy read that sign out loud too: "Welcome to Hartford. Beautiful capital of Connecticut," he announced brightly.

Several blocks past the sign, men and women climbed the cement stairs of the welfare office. Four decades ago, the sprawling brick building had a different function. From the 1900s until the early 1970s, as many as 2,500 workers, many from the neighborhood, had arrived here in shifts. They'd twisted wire, fitted handles, packed boxes, kept the books, and collected steady paychecks when the welfare office had been the phenomenally successful Fuller Brush factory. Door-to-door Fuller Brush salesmen kept America tidy. During World War II, the Hartford plant had won a government "high achievement" award for making gun-cleaning brushes. But in 1968, the corporate giant Sara Lee acquired Fuller Brush. Four years later, they shut the Hartford factory and moved operations to Kansas.

It was still a busy place and old timers persisted in calling it the Fuller Brush Building. Inside, bureaucrats handed out government forms to citizens applying for help, not jobs. Thirty-one percent of Hartford's residents were officially poor; 41 percent of its children were poor. Welcome to Hartford. The poorest city in the wealthiest state in the richest country on earth.

CHECK-CASHING CENTERS, storefront churches, and, farther down, liquor stores lined Main Street near Jeremy's apartment. A much-loved little diner, Hal's Aquarius, had hung on for years, selling good, greasy food at fair prices. But the city had foreclosed on the property and its days were numbered. The old Hartford Jai Alai over on Weston Street had drawn bettors for a while. It was slated to shut down. A few dance clubs offered what nightlife survived. A barber shop and a few nail salons limped along. A jail—the Hartford Correctional Center—hid down around the corner. A school bus parking lot tacked a swatch of dusty yellow onto the gray landscape. Saturdays, a flea market set up.

Nearing Jeremy's house, a 20-something, muscular black man stood before an out-of-business car repair shop spying through binoculars. The young man told me he was on duty with a loosely knit crime-watch crew. He'd deployed himself after a local minister, galled by all the shootings on these streets, had challenged churchgoers to do something. The man was scoping out the parking lot of the liquor store across the way, ID'ing drug dealers. What does he do when he spots one?

"I dunno" he answered, binoculars fixed to his eyes. "I got kids. I ain't losin' 'em to this shit."

I'D MET JEREMY for the first time in September of 2000. His school principal, James Thompson, had pointed out a chubby, grinning third grader waddling up the corridor toward us. Too wide for little-boy clothes, Jeremy was also too short for bigger sizes. His pants fit at the waist but he'd rolled the cuffs up to avoid tripping. A teacher hurried Jeremy and his classmates along. Even walking fast exerted him. He stopped and huffed and drank from a fountain where his long shirt-sleeve dangled and got soaked.

"That little guy right there is exceptionally bright," Thompson said. Jeremy, lifting his head, drying his shirtsleeve on his pants, waved exuberantly.

"Good afternoon, Dr. Thompson," Jeremy shouted, moving speedily to catch the straight line of brown-skinned children winding toward the cafeteria. "Hey, nice tie! Very colorful!"

Thompson nodded and yelled after Jeremy, "Thank you, sir."

Jeremy saluted.

"Exceptionally bright, like I said," Thompson whispered. "And definitely a future candidate for the mayor of Hartford."

Thompson urged me to come back and observe "a great educator in action." Her name, he'd told me, is Ms. Lois Luddy. She taught third grade, up on the second floor, room E4.

I did return and discovered that Jeremy was the star teacher's star student. "I think I remember you," he told me. "You were with Dr. Thompson when he wore the tie with drawings of kids on it. I never forget a face."

He seemed to never forget a place either. He listed for me "everywhere I've been, ever": East Hartford (a working-class suburb, where he'd lived briefly); Philadelphia (he'd visited relatives); a farm for two hours (it was "somewhere," but he didn't know where), with a state-appointed, transient "mentor"; and Springfield, Massachusetts (20 minutes north, where he'd "sat in a room with other poor kids like me, ate nasty food, and played board games"). And three years earlier, he'd driven with a friend's family to a nearby amusement park. He'd zipped down a waterslide, tumbled over face-first, swallowed water, and "felt choky, like I was going to die."

Jeremy, beginning third grade, hadn't heard of West Hartford, the upscale suburb a few miles beyond his neighborhood. He'd never heard of the wealthier towns a bit farther out, Avon to the west, Simsbury to the north, Wethersfield just south.

Jeremy did know he wanted to live elsewhere. He said that often, but trying to conceive of a location beyond his place and moment, he had to summon back to mind pictures he'd seen in books. He had no firsthand knowledge of locales beyond his own. His world consisted of his apartment, his school, and the block he walked between home and classroom.

Late that fall, Jeremy issued big news.

"I saw it," he said cryptically, as if we were secret agents together.

"You saw what?" I asked.

"West Hartford." Riding in his social worker's car to visit his little brother, who lived with a foster family farther out, they'd driven through it.

"What did you think?"

"It's so nice out that way," he said glumly. "I couldn't believe it was really a true thing."

NEITHER JEREMY NOR his guardians would think to label their neighborhood and its school "racially isolated" or "disadvantaged." But more than a decade earlier, in 1989, a group of civil rights lawyers, parents, and political activists had set out to make these worn-in invisible social circumstances visible. The ambitious group attempted to repair the harm of what social scientists, in interchangeable lingo, call "concentrated poverty" or "racial isolation" or "class isolation" or "segregation." News of their major civil rights case, *Sheff v. O'Neill,* and of its aspirations to desegregate—maybe even merge—urban and suburban schools, hardly penetrated Jeremy's world. He and the adults around him concerned themselves instead with tangible harm closer at hand, such as stray bullets.

And anyway, not everything around them looked so bad. Take the report cards Jeremy brought home from Simpson-Waverly Elementary School. They showed perfect marks for behavior and homework. He read several grade levels ahead. Jeremy also scored well on the state's standardized tests. In fact, he scored amazingly well, considering that he was extremely poor (studies show a strong link between poverty and school failure); that he was functionally fatherless (kids from poorer single-parent families tend to do worse in school); and that he lived on welfare in the ghetto with his guardian, a grandmother who barely spoke English and hadn't finished high school (these are also dreary, much-studied indicators). In fall of third grade, Jeremy scored higher than the average kid in some surrounding suburbs and easily met the state's "mastery" standard in reading, writing, and arithmetic.

So far, he had beaten the odds. And so had Simpson-Waverly Elementary, where recent high test scores had prompted Hartford's school superintendent to invite the teachers to the common room to hear a short congratulatory speech and eat cake.

Character and Content

I N SCHOOL, JEREMY HAD attracted many adult fans with what Ms. Luddy called "his openness."

"The thing about science is, you get to really, really think," he said in the school cafeteria, his plate stacked with government-issue Tater Tots. He launched into one of his soliloquies: "You just think at the beginning and you kind of guess. And your guess is okay, because it's supposed to be a guess? I mean, you pretty much infer, which is a word I think Ms. Luddy taught me. Anyway, yes, you infer what might happen, like if you add dirt and water and sand and you want to know what will settle down where. Then you test it all out and then you see what happens and then you need to come up with some ideas. Like new ideas about the way things are. You think of a lot of other questions like, 'Okay, what does water do to other things, like after many, many years, like a century or something?' 'What's water do to wood?' And then, you know, you start thinking, 'Well, okay, how could I figure this out? What could I do?'"

Ms. Luddy had several of what she called "fully engaged" students. But Jeremy in particular—one of two Puerto Rican kids in an otherwise all-black class—was a little different from the others. He had none of what she called "that street attitude some kids present up front." In the lunchroom late one morning, two fourth-grade girls kicked at each other's legs, scratched, pulled hair. A teacher dashed over, peeled the girls apart, yelled, and, an offender in each hand, marched them out.

Jeremy, sipping milk from a straw, looked on. "Goodness!" he exclaimed. "Someone's upset today!"

Patrick, a classmate, looked at Jeremy disbelievingly.

Across from him, Kayla stuffed french fries in her mouth.

"You a pig," Patrick told her. "A ghetto pig."

"Yeah. You a fat ole pig. PIG!" Kayla volleyed back. "You's ghetto. Not me."

Rashida, Kayla's ally, burst out laughing.

"Pig," she said to Patrick's ally, Owen, who swiftly returned, "You skinny ass. Shut up."

Shasa rolled her eyes and looked my way. "Fools," she informed me, returning to her Bible stories word-search book.

"Oh," Jeremy said, sighing. "Let's call a truce, hey? Let's try being nice."

Shasa lifted her eyes. "You a good man, Jeremy. You know? You all should listen to that."

JEREMY BROKERED PEACE in the lunchroom. And in the classroom, he made Ms. Luddy feel happy. She delighted in his discoveries.

"Oh! I get it," he'd screamed one afternoon, sitting cross-legged on the floor, reading through a book of science projects. He'd just read a text that explained why, if you lay a string on an ice cube and sprinkle salt on it, the string will stick and you can pull the cube right up. (The salt briefly lowers the freezing temperature of the surface a few degrees so the ice surface remelts and the liquid saturates the string and refreezes, embedding the string.) Jeremy traced the explanation step-by-step, sliding his finger under the words. He whispered each sentence to himself. He penciled little check marks beside certain words. He'd chosen this ice project for the school science fair. "It's not an experiment," he conceded, but a "demonstration." He hoped other kids would repeat it at home.

"When I finally get it, when I get things like this, I feel things connect all together, like *whack, click, bing,* in my brain." Jeremy closed the book and stretched his arms overhead. "Then, I can't help it, it just gets me thinking like crazy all the time about what kind of other things I could do with salt."

Over at Waverly, though, Ms. Luddy, still a deft and indefatigable teacher after 28 years in Hartford's classrooms, couldn't indulge Jeremy often. Simpson-Waverly, like most of America's inner-city schools, had been pressed by city administrators and government bureaucrats who above all else had to keep test scores up. Ms. Luddy had to stick to an exacting, prescribed curriculum, patterned meticulously to mirror the state's annual standardized exams. Every school in the state had to release its scores for grades four, six, and eight. Kids took tests in third and fifth grade too. In 2002, President George W. Bush would sign the No Child Left Behind Act, requiring still more testing in third through eighth grades and potentially tough sanctions against schools that didn't measure up. Under the law, every state had to align curriculum with testing standards.

Educators, even before No Child Left Behind, put test results to many uses. Some teachers used them to identify kids who needed extra help. But in Hartford, as in increasing numbers of poorly performing, large urban districts, educators had come to use scores to decide which children to hold back. A principal's—and a school superintendent's—job security often depended upon the results. Eleven of Hartford's 33 schools carried "failing school" designations when I showed up in 1999. Two more would be added later to the federal list of schools "failing" to "make adequate yearly progress" under the No Child Left Behind Act. Under NCLB, such schools could be shut down. Or eventually, students in them could transfer. But there was a catch. Students had to stay in their school districts. In Hartford, that usually meant a student would only move to another poorly performing school. Hartford's tough-talking school superintendent, Anthony Amato, called

the Connecticut Mastery Test — CMT for short — "die on your sword"
exams.

So Ms. Luddy rarely taught science or social studies, which weren't
on the state test. With her own money, she still bought her kids books
about U.S. presidents, famous African Americans, state capitals, the
Civil War, and the organization of U.S. government. On Friday afternoons, she continued to convene her sacred "class council" meetings,
at which students practiced democratic decision making. She managed
to pull down colorful maps and work in stories about her trips to Japan,
Africa, and Guatemala. But she had to talk faster about cultures, tradi-
tions, languages, music. These mild, once-standard, mind-stretching
extras forced Ms. Luddy, a Catholic-school girl who'd always followed
the rules, to redefine herself as a subversive. She also "schemed" (her
word) about how to help the several obese children (including Jeremy)
in her class. The school had two inventive and cheerful phys ed teachers, though recess had been sacrificed for more test prep a year before
I'd shown up.

Ms. Luddy believed strongly in something she called "character
building." But she could almost never find time anymore for its core
exercise of having children wrestle with ethical dilemmas.

"I think we should see ourselves as children," Jeremy declared during
a rare session — this one about whether or not disrupting class more
than three times should trigger the loss of some yet-to-be-defined privilege. "Disrupting isn't showing consideration. But also, we are children
and some of us are working on behavior things and the rest of us need
to be kind of patient with that. We are all working on something."

Jeremy didn't see himself as perfect either. Consider his "baddest"
deed — faking an earache to get out of school and go on a doctor's visit
with his big brother, Raymon. Raymon, a year older, had long suffered
from what Jeremy called "a sneezing hive allergic reaction to the floor."
Jeremy knew that after doctor visits, their aunt headed to Burger King.
Jeremy loved their burgers and fries, but what he really craved was the

plastic woolly mammoth toy they handed out with each meal. Grammar drills lost out. Hand clasped to his ear, he told Ms. Luddy he hurt "real bad." She sent him down to the school nurse. Jeremy's aunt walked around the corner and fetched him. He'd felt victorious, briefly.

But he'd confessed the sin that same afternoon. Sitting on the couch in his apartment, under a framed color print of Mother Teresa, Jeremy turned the new woolly mammoth over and over. The move wasn't worth it, he said. He offered a hangdog smile. "Please," he begged. "Don't tell Ms. Luddy."

Odds

AFTER AFTERNOON DISMISSAL the following week, Ms. Luddy, in neat khaki pants, a well-pressed white blouse, and sensible blue shoes, sat atop a student's empty desk. I knew that she would probably admire Jeremy for his earache caper. She couldn't help appreciating the easygoing rule followers like him, but she had a soft spot in her heart for mischief makers too.

"Innocence has its limits," she said. "Especially around here." She swung her legs and munched cheese curls. With an impish grin and perpetually rosy cheeks, Ms. Luddy, in her late 40s, sometimes still looked like a kid herself. She hoped fervently for the children she taught. But there was little Pollyanna left to her. "That child," she said, referring to Jeremy, "he's amazing. He's like a mystery." She smiled sadly.

To Waverly's adults—because of his eagerness to learn, his obvious intellectual potential, his caring nature, even his ordinary little-boy traits—Jeremy represented their accomplishment.

"Jeremy is a joy to teach!" one of his report cards home read. But Ms. Luddy dared to consider Jeremy in context. She'd seen her share of Jeremys. Each year, many sweet, wildly smart, deeply good children left Hartford's apartment buildings, hacked-up multifamily tenements with bars on the windows, and garden-style housing projects. They walked the broken sidewalks past boarded-up businesses, into her constructive, organized, brightly lit room. Many school years began promisingly, but few children ever presented Ms. Luddy with happy endings. She figured that Jeremy's chances of "staying on track over the long term" hinged on two questions. One looked out: How on earth might this kid connect with the opportunities of mainstream society from which his neighborhood school and city were isolated? The other question, the one Ms. Luddy more often pondered, concerned his broken family: Could his aunt and grandmother shelter and nurture him adequately for another nine years?

That question led to others: Could Jeremy possibly reach beyond his few streets and actually get to college? Could he stay there? Could he then navigate in the world beyond the North End of Hartford? In hopeful moments, Ms. Luddy imagined a sequence of grown-ups, like herself, who'd spot Jeremy and lift him, in turn. But with thousands of high-potential Hartford kids sharing Jeremy's predicament, he faced low odds of staying a special cause.

"Not good," she guessed. "Let's be realistic."

The paths out from Waverly so seldom ended anywhere safe. After Jeremy finished third and then fourth grade with Ms. Luddy, he would indeed have two more years at his efficient elementary school. But come seventh grade, he'd most likely find himself at Fox Middle School. Fox pulled kids from the toughest, most destitute streets in the city—two-thirds of the kids there were officially poor, according to federal definitions. In 2001, only 9 percent of eighth graders would meet the state standard goal in every subject tested on the CMT—math, writing, reading. After Fox, Jeremy's next slated destination looked even less promising. Weaver High School had repeatedly received warnings and probation from its accrediting agency. Hartford had won some national attention for rising elementary school test scores yet would draw no such press in 2001, when the city's three high schools placed dead-last in math, science, and reading. Weaver was the city's lowest-ranking high school in science and math, with only 4 percent of 10th graders meeting the state's goal on both tests. (Three years later, in 2004—the same year two boys would get stabbed in a hallway brawl—only 5.5 percent of Weaver's 10th graders would reach the state's goal in reading and only 3 percent would in math.)

What contributed to the Weaver mess? The beckoning street life? Drugs? Poor, single mothers? Class injustice? Neglectful teachers? Lack of leadership in city hall, on the school board? Racism? Kids' crappy attitudes? Kids' untreated depression? Segregation? What came first? What caused what?

No matter where anyone came down on those questions, the numbers pointed to at least one truth: Weaver High School was unlikely to offer a rigorous educational environment that would prepare Jeremy for college.

"So really, then, we don't know," Ms. Luddy said, licking orange cheese-curl dust off her fingers. "And it's a sin that we don't know. There shouldn't be a question. But there are huge questions. The kid has so much going for him. But I worry about him. I worry about him a lot."

Home and Beyond

THAT SECOND QUESTION — about Jeremy's home life — also mattered a lot to Ms. Luddy. Early in his third-grade year, she wasn't sure how to call that one either.

Jeremy's home situation offered school officials people to blame for his uncertain future. The problem, a few of Simpson-Waverly's administrators suggested to me, lay with that chunky and disheveled lady waiting by the curb at dismissal time, the one with the perpetual frown, standing apart from other parents and guardians, shoulders hunched, eyes darting, hair dyed pomegranate red, hands stuffed into an oversize man's Windbreaker. Aunt Nina.

Jeremy had a grandma at home too. A tired, depressed grandma, it was said, who spoke little English and never came around. A grandma few people at Waverly had ever seen. In the North End of Hartford, adults rarely even asked the question I posed often in my first months there: "Where are the mom and dad?"

"Oh. Jail," Ms. Luddy said, as if it were merely a detail. Jeremy was hardly the only one. In Hartford, having a parent in jail was not extraordinary. Nothing to be ashamed of.

Ms. LUDDY AVOIDED THAT pop-psychology term *dysfunction*. She said it spanned a continuum and, at the low end, was a misnomer. Many nontraditional or serially improvised temporary arrangements

functioned pretty well under rough circumstances. School administrators lamented the children who got shuffled from one family member
to another. But the tsk-tsking ignored a prevalent, arguably positive feature of many poor African American and Puerto Rican families. Often,
not just the mother and father, but a range of relatives, related by blood
or history, felt responsible for a child. And for many kids, that collection
constituted a large, cozy, comforting circle.

Less comforting, however, was James Thompson's estimate that
slightly less than half of birth mothers and a far higher percentage of
fathers (upwards of 75 percent, he calculated) were not significant,
constant caregivers to their children. Many Waverly mothers had given
birth as teens. Their kids were often raised by grandparents, aunts,
cousins, friends, sisters of former lovers, big sisters, half sisters. In a
poor neighborhood, the security and duration of such arrangements
dipped and rose with the economy, with a caregiver's health, with the
comings and goings of other competing children, and with the terms of
new romance. A rent rise or layoff could easily fragment a family.

The fragility of many poor families in poor neighborhoods, Ms.
Luddy often complained, showed itself in classrooms as "inappropri-
ately expressed anger," "fear of failure," and a "profound insecurity" that
caused "nervousness . . . a jittery personality," an "inability to focus,"
and "a kind of child depression."

Only 3 of the 20 students in Jeremy's class returned home each afternoon to a mother and father together, reasonably solvent and married. Nearly every parent and caregiver worked (Jeremy's happened to
be an exception in this regard). Usually parents and guardians worked
at low-paying service jobs (chain-store cashier, hotel maid) or unreliable pickup construction labor, or off-the-books chores. Some of the
parents of Jeremy's classmates, for example, babysat during the day,
cared for a friend's elderly kin, sewed clothes, fixed electronics. Those
with cars ran informal taxi services (Jeremy's landlord did this) and
drove neighbors downtown or to the suburban strip malls or to Wal-

Mart in nearby Manchester. The Wal-Mart transport could net a driver $10 to $15 round-trip. The most reliable jobs held by Ms. Luddy's students' caregivers were prison guard, bus driver, postal clerk, and nurse's aide — steady work that elevated families to working class. Most Waverly families, though, were "working poor" and in tough economic times slipped to just plain poor.

Parent-guardian horror stories no longer shocked Ms. Luddy. She'd heard it all. Kids who, save for Waverly's free starchy breakfasts and lunches, survived on candy and sugar cereal. Kids who stayed up till 3 a.m. watching television, then nodded off in her classroom. Six-year-olds who roamed the streets, sometimes in their socks. Guardians who never bothered to pick up report cards. Mothers who let their nine-year-olds hop into strangers' cars. Fathers with no idea where their children lived.

After dismissal one afternoon, Ms. Luddy sadly watched a mother scold her daughter in the parking lot: "Tasha, why you wearin' those fuckin' shoes? I hate those fuckin' shoes. When we get in the car, you take those fuckin' shoes the fuck off your fuckin' feet."

Waverly's caregivers, though, were rarely so horrible. Most were stressed and overwhelmed. Nearly every year, at least one parent came in "poised for battle about everything." Ms. Luddy, never one to be rattled by aggression, was known around Waverly for her ability to win over seemingly difficult parents.

"A lot of these parents have been through hell in their lives, whether it was an abusive work situation or an abusive relationship, a dangerous street corner," Ms. Luddy said, a few days after a tense meeting with a mother who questioned why Ms. Luddy hadn't, for example, taught students that "God is black" and that "Jesus was black."

In Ms. Luddy's experience, such parents "come in expecting to be mistreated and expecting that their child will be mistreated because that's what they're used to. You need to do a little bit of standing in their shoes." In most cases, she sensed that "people are doing the best they can do."

Take T.J.'s father. He'd quit his second job, on a carpentry crew, to pick up his two sons after school. He escorted them to the library, helped them with homework, and volunteered as a Boy Scout leader. T.J. was one of her strongest students.

"I keep my kids close," T.J.'s father told me one afternoon outside Waverly. "My eyes don't come off of them. They ain't goin' outside, hangin' with the elements. I take 'em home, lock the door tight. We sit inside and we work."

WAVERLY'S SEASONED EDUCATORS told me that by Hartford standards, Jeremy's home life seemed only a little tougher than average.

Like many poor urban kids, he'd been shipped around. When he was a baby, his family had been burned out by the pager-shop arson. They'd moved to an apartment in East Hartford. Several years later, police found cocaine there. It may have belonged to Jeremy's mother's boyfriend. But they arrested Jeremy's mother, Christina, instead. It was her first arrest. She pleaded guilty and, under sentencing guidelines, got five years in the women's prison in Niantic, Connecticut. In flight from the boyfriend's beatings, according to family members, Christina had been shuffling between friends' apartments. She'd sometimes dragged her four kids with her. More often she left them upstairs with her mother, Anna, whom the boys called Mami.

"Mami was the one who brought the food around and cooked it nice and washed us up and kept things neat and talked with us real nice," Jeremy recalled. "She did all the mother things. The normal things a kid hopes a mother would be doing."

Jeremy had only faint memories of his father. "I know he did bad things to us," he said. "Smacking us and yelling . . ."

After Christina's arrest, the state placed four-year-old Jeremy and his three brothers in foster care. He ended up in the same house as his brother Raymon, then nearly six. His younger brothers, Pedro, a toddler, and the infant, Manuel, went elsewhere.

Grandmother Anna tracked down all four boys. The state awarded her temporary guardianship, supervised by its Department of Children and Families. Jeremy's aunt Nina, who'd recently moved in with Anna, shared responsibility for the four boys. Nina added her own baby boy, Carlos, to the household. Five years later, Nina would give birth to her second boy, Miguel.

Anna, a shy, portly woman with downcast almond eyes and long, thick, curly brown hair, willingly shouldered her new task of raising all those boys. She'd already raised her own three children, alone. But Mami, Jeremy remembered, began "feeling sad a lot and not sleeping right . . . Always, she was hurting in some way."

When Jeremy was about six, a doctor discovered elevated levels of lead in his and Raymon's blood. On the doctor's advice, Anna moved. In the North End, they gained one more bedroom at the cost of a rougher neighborhood. In the beginning, Raymon, the eldest, acted like a father. He cuddled, fed, and diapered babies with quick, confident hands.

On the street, in the living room, and in front of the Polaroid camera, Raymon's signature move was to drape an arm around one of his brothers, pull him close, and assume a look of wary defiance. Jeremy, unaccountably cheerful and giggly, warmed hearts. Raymon, inward, serious, lean, and handsome, played protector. They made an incongruous but inseparable pair.

The younger boys, Manuel and Pedro, though, were trouble. By the time he was four, Pedro, the third child, Jeremy recalled, "was just out of control—screaming, kicking, cussing," always "nervous and angry." Unprovoked, he hit classmates and, at home, clobbered his brothers. Pedro flew into rages over what Jeremy called "nothing . . . just out of the blue, just nothing." Soon, "Manuel followed his lead. It was hard for Mami. She tried. But it was very hard."

In addition to her headaches and stomach ailments, Grandma Anna continued to fight piercing neurological facial pain that felt, she said, "like needles all the time stabbing into my cheek." Her doctors believed they knew the source of the problem. In Puerto Rico, she'd suffered years of vicious beatings from her common-law husband. Doctors on the island had advised that she'd find better hospitals and medical coverage on the mainland. And she determined to escape the abusive boyfriend and find some way past the poverty that trapped the family in the home of a violent man. She'd half succeeded. In Hartford, there were no more beatings. And she found a doctor she trusted. But Anna no longer even imagined a life without poverty. She kept believing, though, that Raymon and Jeremy might escape it.

"In school, they do good," Anna told me in Spanish. "They work hard and I believe that they will do good things."

Jeremy's aunt Nina was only nine, the eldest of Anna's three children, when the family of four arrived in Hartford, directly from the small, once-rural, now-industrial city of Caguas. Anna, more hopeful then than now, had known a few families that had found jobs in tobacco fields near Hartford. She wasn't alone. Several thousand of Hartford's some 40,000 Puerto Rican residents had roots in Caguas, and Puerto Ricans are, of course, U.S. citizens.

Anna, despite surgeries, still lived with debilitating pain. Her medical problems worsened as she aged. She survived on monthly disability payments of about $500 and an allowance of $800 for costs associated with the boys. Each month, she paid $450 in rent. Utilities were extra. Routine chores—cooking, cleaning, washing, worrying—and the burdens of raising an incarcerated daughter's four energetic boys in a small apartment on a scary street wore her down.

On a hot summer night in 2000, with Pedro violently kicking and yelling, Anna had finally felt desperate, Jeremy remembered, "like she couldn't take it anymore." She'd dialed the social worker from the state's Department of Children and Families. She'd said she wanted help, wanted someone to take the younger boys for a while. Social workers arrived. Anna had a change of heart.

"The whole family cried and begged and screamed, 'Please, please, please, no, we can't let them go,'" Jeremy said. "We were crying, all of us." But Anna didn't yet have parental rights. DCF placed the two younger boys with foster families in the suburbs.

"It was a very, very sad thing," Jeremy said. "But," he allowed, "maybe their lives are better than ours now. Maybe they'll have more of a chance, which is what Mami tries to think about. I love them. I want them to be happy and to have their chances. You know, have their chances at life."

JEREMY'S APARTMENT TOOK up the first floor of a gray two-story house with a small concrete stoop and dusty windows. Torn-up chain-link fence ringed the yard. Inside, the apartment smelled of Anna's pungent stew and soup concoctions—of cinnamon spice and sweetness. Yard-high stacks of papers and clothes cluttered the boxy living room. An imprisoned uncle's weight bench took up one corner. Some plastic toys filled another.

The living room's windows faced the street, but Anna always left the shades drawn against neighborhood danger. Members of the West Hell gang hung just outside. Teenagers and junkies partied and slept in an abandoned apartment complex across the street. Anna kept the lights off because it saved money and because she liked the faint glow of the votive candles that illuminated a shrine by the TV. She'd mixed gold-tinged renderings of saints with Polaroids of the four boys. The TV was usually on, set just above a whisper.

Anna spent a lot of time in the stifling hot, spotless kitchenette, running water, scrubbing things. She often stepped out holding a dish towel or half-folded laundry. She let the boys eat a lot of junk food. She also served them traditional Puerto Rican dinners—rice and beans, fried meat.

The boys' social worker, assigned by the state, had said that she hoped to get the family into a safer neighborhood. But so far, Anna reported, "everything costs too much, she says."

Years after the social worker said she'd help, moving still seemed unlikely. Anna held a Section 8 certificate, a federal subsidy that covered
more than half her monthly rent. Section 8 regulations would allow
Anna to move elsewhere only if she could find a similar-size apartment
at the same or lower cost. Most affordable housing, though, was right
in Hartford's ghettos. In 2000, a full 40 percent of Hartford's housing
stock was classified as affordable. In suburban West Hartford, where
Jeremy said he wished to live, just 7 percent was.

While Anna cooked and cleaned, Nina supervised homework. She
also acted as the boys' intermediary with school.

Parents of other students had warned me early on of Nina's hot temper. She'd had some public scuffles, including one with the school
security guard. In the school's version, Nina had smacked the guard,
unprovoked, and pushed a child. Her rendition, though, filled in context. Two kids at Waverly had harassed and threatened to "beat on"
Raymon and Jeremy. The brothers had run home to her, panting, upset. She'd tromped over to Waverly. She'd glared. She'd yelled. She'd
shoved.

"But they do good in school," Nina said. "They come home, they say,
'We not going to school. The other kids, they botherin' us.' So I go. I go
stop them from gettin' hurt. I go so they keep goin' to school. You gotta
stand up for them. No?"

Unlike some guardians, Nina showed up for Jeremy's parent-teacher
conferences—though often hours late or early. She'd appeared 90 minutes early for one and haughtily told Ms. Luddy she'd leave if she had
to wait. Ms. Luddy stuck to her schedule.

"At first I thought, 'She's going to storm right out of here.' But she
didn't. She waited," Ms. Luddy recalled. Nina parked herself on the
floor right outside Ms. Luddy's door. They eventually had their conference. "And you know?" Ms. Luddy said. "Honestly? It went fine."

Nina's English was passable. She'd been in special education classes
at Hartford Public High School, and one former special-needs teacher

at Waverly had speculated that Nina "might have some mild mental retardation." Her wardrobe consisted of two pairs of jeans, two oversize T-shirts (one featuring SpongeBob SquarePants), a gray sweatshirt, and the man's blue Windbreaker with "New York" written on the back. She didn't own a bra. Nina also struggled with constant fatigue, debilitating migraine headaches, and severe backache. She was suspicious of everyone—of teenagers on the street, of teachers at Waverly, of police officers.

But surely Nina could bag groceries? Flip burgers? Push a vacuum? Perhaps. But she was the central guardian of Jeremy's fragile safety. To lift the family out of poverty, she would have needed at least two jobs at the state's minimum wage of $7 an hour. She'd have needed a new wardrobe and remediation of her adversarial, distrustful tendencies. Her entry into the work world would have stuck Grandma Anna with four little boys again—Jeremy, Raymon, and Nina's two kids, Carlos and Miguel. That hadn't worked last time they tried it.

Once I'd gotten to know her, I realized Nina wasn't simply the mean auntie others had described. She had bursts of temper. Jeremy was the target of some of these. But at home with the door triple-locked, the frown left her face. Afternoons, she often sat on the floor with Jeremy and Raymon and Carlos, her jumpy six-year-old. They drew with Magic Markers and crashed remote-controlled cars.

Ensconced in the darkened living room, Mexican soap operas playing in the background, Nina told me how much she hoped success in school would buy the boys' tickets out.

"They smart," Nina said argumentatively, as if I'd just called them dumb. She pulled two report cards from a pile and tossed them on the floor where I was sitting.

"See. See," she said. Nina tapped her foot on the papers. I inspected the boys' good marks.

"See? They smart," Nina said, grinning triumphantly. "They good boys."

A few days later, at lunch in the cafeteria, Jeremy squirted ketchup on a cold, gray hamburger. He looked me in the eyes, dead-on.

"I get a lot of love where I am," he said, unbidden.

A few minutes later in the hallway at Waverly, Jeremy's state-appointed social worker offered her assessment: "He's stifled in that environment," she said to Ms. Luddy. "It's not a good environment for his intellect."

It was true. Anna never drilled the kids on phonics and fractions. Nina never studied the weekend bus schedules or led the boys to the art museum downtown. They all stayed home. They watched terrifying R-rated movies, *Scream 2* and *The Rats*. They gorged on potato chips. Six-year-old Carlos pushed himself around the living room on a plastic tractor designed for a two-year-old. He crashed into his cousins, who got annoyed and yelled. Raymon played on his Game Boy for so many hours that his vision blurred and he had to go to bed. And amid the din, Jeremy read. Often, though, he gave up and watched TV too.

Still, Nina got on the boys about starting homework. She checked that they'd completed everything. She walked them over to the tiny public library branch on Barbour Street once in a while. Along the way, drug dealers plied their wares and junkies shuffled among the few shoppers. One of Ms. Luddy's former students, a 20-something minor-league thug, had been gunned down near the library recently. But it was the only proximate commercial center.

Nina and Anna surely were not noble urban heroes full of grace. They weren't traveling on the mythic American path of transformation. They seemed stuck and suffering from the sort of chronic health and emotional problems that plagued the inner city. But they did protect Jeremy in a place where bullets hissed through the streets.

Connecticut's Department of Children and Families had deemed, perhaps accurately, that Nina and Anna needed help and supervision. So every now and then Jeremy got phone calls from a social worker checking that he was at home. Once or twice a month, a social worker drove Jeremy and Raymon to visit their little brothers in the suburbs.

Soon after the state took the younger boys from the Otero home, DCF officials determined that Jeremy and Raymon would benefit from attending a horseback-riding camp with other "DCF involved" kids. The camp was just down the block on Vine Street, snug up against the sprawling Keney Park. Keney, with lush greenery, swaying tall trees, paths, ponds, even a golf course, was used by many people, including murderers dumping bodies. A mile from the camp, where Vine met Albany, loomed one of the heaviest drug-trafficking areas in the city.

"We did some good stuff. We did!" Jeremy told Raymon the following fall. Raymon, shaking his head in evident disgust, disagreed. "But the thing I remember most is that I shoveled manure and there were these big flies around my face the whole time."

Jeremy spent the following summers not at camp but sealed inside his apartment, safely reading the science books that teachers donated to him. One hot summer day, around the corner from Jeremy's apartment, a former student of Ms. Luddy's stabbed his girlfriend, his daughter, and a police officer. A few days later, Jeremy watched a man repeatedly back his car into a nearby house until the porch collapsed. The car screeched away.

"*That* was weird," Jeremy said afterward. "It's the sort of event that can't be explained by reason."

A week before Jeremy's birthday that July, Nina undertook the hour-long bus ride (with transfers) and visited a big suburban department store at sale time. She bought him a black bike at a quarter its regular price. He only rode it—in tight half circles—right outside the apartment.

Even though the summer had been quiet by Westland Street standards, and even though other parents, optimistic about the dip in the frequency of shootings and murders, let their kids ride freely, Anna forbade Jeremy to pedal even an inch out of her sight. She was wise.

Late in the summer, a young man pulled a gun in the early afternoon sunlight a few buildings away from Jeremy's apartment. He fired several times, killing a 22-year-old ex-con known as Teddy.

Teddy's friends and family built a plywood display box with a slanted roof. They painted it white. They hauled the box to the weedy lot near where Teddy had fallen and lifted it atop a cement slab. It looked like a puppet theater. They filled the box with candles, fresh flowers, neatly typed prayers, scribbled remembrances, and a recent photograph of Teddy, who'd had alert, steady eyes and a slight, weary smile — a handsome young face. No one smashed the makeshift memorial. The flowers decayed. Inside the propped-up box, the candles burned, renewed faithfully, their light flickering along Westland Street far into winter.

Jeremy and I passed by the box one afternoon in my car.

"He died, that guy. It happens all the time," he said, pointing. "Bang, and just like that a someone, a somebody, is gone."

PART TWO

How We Got Here in the First Place

One area of Hartford you need to try to avoid is what is called the North End. If you need to travel through that area, or if you're lost and end up there, just keep driving. It is NOT advisable to get out of your car, or to even roll your car window down to ask for directions. Keep the car doors locked as this is a high crime area. You're an easy target if you look lost or don't take these precautions.

—www.VirtualTourist.com

Vision

JOHN BRITTAIN HAD MOVED out of Hartford in 1999. He was visiting, in 2000, to speak at the University of Connecticut, to see friends, including Simpson-Waverly's principal James Thompson, and to review the sort of misfortunes Jeremy Otero lived with every day.

"Yup!" Brittain said snappily, driving a new green rental car past the familiar, messy streets, the abandoned houses and apartments, that damn blonde plywood nailed up where windows and doors are supposed to be. "Nothing much has changed. " He managed a slight laugh, but it came out sounding sad.

His prominent chin jutting over a fine silk bow tie, John Brittain, lawyer, professor, and civil rights activist, parked in the lot of the Simpson-Waverly Elementary School. Just getting out of the car, he looked regal. The business suit was tailored. His leather shoes reflected the afternoon sun. He was grandly dressed for the humble setting and his schedule of mostly social rounds.

He'd learned early to dress well. Back in the '60s, some of his professors at Howard, the historically black law school, had dressed elegantly. John Brittain had watched them carefully. He was a neophyte then, a lawyer-in-training for a supporting role in the civil rights movement. His legendary mentors had told him that down south, a black civil rights lawyer's courtroom moves had to be, like his wardrobe, impeccable,

beyond reproach. Two habits learned in the South—aristocratic clothing and refined courtroom manners—endured long after he'd come
back north.

John Brittain stayed formal even while pursuing his less dramatic
good works. Over at Simpson-Waverly, people still talked about the
day, several years earlier, when in full academic regalia John Brittain
had addressed graduating sixth graders. He'd worn the cap and gown in
which he'd graduated from law school, he'd told students, to show them
the sort of costume they'd be wearing at their high school, college, and
medical and law school graduations.

Draped in the shiny blue gown, he'd stood ramrod straight on Waver-
ly's small stage. A sash of black velvet and silk hung around his neck.
A braid of gold dangled off the side of his eight-point black velvet tam.
Teachers and parents had stared up at him, nodding and smiling.

"There he was—very dignified, at a little elementary school graduation," Ms. Luddy said. "People remember that because it sent a message. The way the man carries himself. I mean, whoa. Look out! He
had a way of telling the kids: 'Pay attention. Take this seriously. Be
proud.'"

John Brittain moves like a 20-year-old bantamweight boxer. Nearing 60, he is muscular still and lean. His skin is taut, polished-looking,
his cheekbones high and sculpted. He stands about five foot seven. To
study John Brittain, to regard his conduct and movement, is to study
the anatomy of charisma. Most charismatic people in his accomplished
league gravitate early to politics and big business. John Brittain stuck
with moral causes. Perhaps that's what's vested him with the power to
transform cynics into idealists, and even hard-bitten journalists—just
about anyone he meets—into at least temporary fans.

"Well, maybe it's worse here now, but, well, you know me," he said,
squinting in the sun in the Waverly parking lot. "I'd need more data to
conclude, but I could bet. I could guess what it's going to say. Hartford's
not getting any better."

He was well installed in Houston, Texas, as dean of the Thurgood Marshall School of Law. But he'd still felt dismayed reading in the *New York Times* that Hartford had recently been named one of America's five "fastest shrinking" big cities.

Hartford might have been first on the list of fastest-shrinking cities if the Census Bureau hadn't counted the 2,500 college kids in the dorms at the University of Hartford. U of H's administration buildings and official address stand in West Hartford, but the dorms, city hall officials had argued in a publicized tussle with the Census Bureau, sat over the line, in Hartford proper. The college students were counted and the city qualified for more federal money. And city officials softened an embarrassing headline. A few months after dodging the "fastest shrinking" ranking, Hartford officials accepted an image consultant's advice and took to calling the city "New England's rising star."

Municipal workers hung festive blue and yellow banners downtown, trumpeting the slogan, with a white star shooting upward. John Brittain had shaken his head when he'd seen them.

"Very nice looking," John Brittain allowed, but "mostly," he added, "they're distracting."

AROUND HARTFORD, PEOPLE PRAISE John Brittain fondly for his wit, warmth, smarts, style, big vocabulary, and funky silk bow ties. But mostly they associate him with that big legal case, *Sheff v. O'Neill*. He was a leader on the civil rights dream team that had filed the case more than 10 years ago. Brittain and another prominent lawyer had donated years of labor on *Sheff*. National and local civil rights groups had seen in the case both high hopes and long odds. They'd financed it and dispatched staff attorneys.

In *Sheff*, 19 plaintiffs—students and their families, led by a black fourth-grade boy from Hartford named Milo Sheff and his mother, Elizabeth—sued Connecticut in its state courts. The families claimed that extreme racial and class segregation in schools enabled and sustained by state-enforced school district boundary lines, denied them the equal educational opportunity guaranteed by Connecticut's constitution.

Sheff challenged those school district boundary lines, which, lawyers argued, cordoned off kids like Jeremy, separating the middle class from poor children, and white children from black and Latino children. Those official borders outlined long-standing housing segregation and enforced separate, unequal educational systems—overburdened, beset, minority city schools on one side and smoothly functioning, academically rigorous, largely white, suburban ones on the other. The *Sheff* complaint alleged that Connecticut compelled Hartford kids—forced them—to attend racially separate, inherently unequal schools. School district boundaries that ran right along suburban town borders with Hartford, the *Sheff* lawyers contended, corralled poor black and brown kids into a handful of overburdened educational institutions offering no exposure to the powerful social networks, unwritten rules, expectations, academic rigor, and opportunities that every kid in mainstream America experienced. The white middle and upper classes, meanwhile, sheltered themselves in the highest-achieving, best-connected schools money could buy. In other words, the lawyers argued, the game was rigged and Connecticut's constitution said it should not be.

The case had been filed some 11 years before I'd run into Jeremy and his classmates. But in 2000, Jeremy and his friends were in the same fix that *Sheff*'s original (presently past-school-age) child plaintiffs had complained about more than a decade earlier. The metropolitan region was diversifying slowly because of demographic shifts, but 93 percent of Hartford's students were either Latino or black, while the more elite suburbs nearby remained mostly and disproportionately white.

As John Brittain had discovered while working so long on the case, challenges in fighting segregation and inequality lay not only in the courtroom but also within neighborhoods and schools like Jeremy's. Inequality and separation had been a given for as long as any current Hartford schoolkid could remember. To a lot of folks, the situation of blacks and Puerto Ricans living in cities while whites lived elsewhere seemed natural and normal—a fact of life sustained by personal choice and housing costs, not by mandated structures and systems. Segregation was hardly an "issue" anymore. To the teachers and administrators at Waverly and to local politicians too, segregation had evolved into a largely accepted reality, a seemingly immutable, if chronic, condition, with no insidious cause and no feasible cure.

But the conundrums at the core of *Sheff* had fermented in John Brittain's heart, mind, and soul for decades before the case even existed. Just days after first moving to Hartford, back in 1977, he'd driven around the impoverished black and brown city, taking in every detail of the physical evidence in depressingly clear relief. Brown children had poured from the huge brick junior high school into the bleak bustle of Albany Avenue. Every last kid, he'd noted, was black or Latino. So was each man, woman, teenager, and child hanging out, waiting for a bus, pushing a stroller, crossing the street. The buildings, a lot of them, looked bombed out following riots that had erupted nearly a decade earlier.

He'd driven those few minutes north, over the line to the suburbs. "White," he'd whispered to himself. Then he'd driven that route over the city line to the south. "White," he'd said again. West? "White."

Unlike his friend and longtime jogging partner, the principal, James Thompson, Brittain had never engaged the minutiae of running a school. So Brittain had the privilege of seeing Hartford in broad, complex terms—caught in a web of history, politics, poverty, racial discrimination, wealth, habits, and economic change. He didn't have to worry, as Thompson did, about the arrest of a particular student's mother, about the third-grade nonreader who threw down his textbook in tears or the shrinking pool of adequate teachers. Brittain had always taken a wide view, always longed for "structural change" to connect kids at Waverly to the opportunities "out there, " the "out there" where John Brittain had always positioned himself.

To many citizens, the very fact of armed guys on street corners, children running wild, heartbreaking makeshift memorials to young murder victims, trash strewn about, sagging roofs, and too-young, single mothers suggested that Jeremy's neighbors caused their own woes. John Brittain thought otherwise. He was a lawyer by training, but one who'd always seen past locating blame and pointing fingers. One of his tasks, he'd said during our first phone conversation, in the summer of 1999, was "to help others hold in their mind's eyes a vision" of "a nation — or at least one measly metropolitan region — truly indivisible." In lectures and in conversations, Brittain often started by telling the well-documented yet forgotten story of Hartford.

"One of the problems is amnesia," he said. "The families of Hartford did not create the city of Hartford."

In other words, even if Jeremy's grandmother had somehow learned how to try harder — if she and Nina had bought piles of children's books instead of a hallucinatory Game Boy, if they'd miraculously begun spouting studied observations of Simpson-Waverly's math curriculum — they'd still be unable to exert tangible influence over their social environment, which had been shaped over decades.

"See," John Brittain said, glancing around the Simpson-Waverly neighborhood, "it's a challenge, because people forget how we got here in the first place."

Here

HARTFORD IS COMPACT, its borders enclosing just 17.5 square miles. Jeremy's neighborhood, Northeast, is one of five disparate black and Puerto Rican neighborhoods that Hartfordians lump together and call the North End.

The western corner of the North End includes the mostly well-tended middle- and working-class black enclave called Blue Hills—John Brittain's old neighborhood. Blue Hills claims a scattering of mansions, pristine single-family homes, streets filled with tiny starter houses, and duplexes cut into rentals. Ubiquitous white and red BLOCKWATCH PROTECTED crime-prevention signs have sprouted along sidewalks.

In the '60s and '70s, middle- and upper-middle-class black families, including the Brittains, migrated into then predominantly white Blue Hills. In those years, even prosperous blacks suffered discrimination in the booming suburban housing market. Blue Hills, with its backyards, cozy commercial village, and decent neighborhood elementary school, was, for blacks with the means, a prestigious address.

But soon, Blue Hills "tipped," as demographers of urban change put it. White home owners, alarmed by the black influx, sold their houses and moved out. Many blacks, including John Brittain and his family, had moved in by choice. Investigations, though, eventually confirmed that real estate agents steered blacks in and encouraged whites to move away, pointing them to nearby developing suburbs such as Glastonbury,

South Windsor, and Simsbury. By the 1990s, Blue Hills had its own severe crime problems, although it remained separated from Jeremy's far-rougher ghetto by the woods and green of Keney Park.

South on Main toward downtown is Clay Arsenal, another ghetto. On this neighborhood's portion of Main Street stands the prettiest, most modern of the city's elementary schools. The $11.5 million SAND (South Arsenal Neighborhood Development) School has a clean brick facade and wide floor-to-ceiling windows that face the street. A bright American flag flaps on a pole out front. For several consecutive years SAND had been on the state's list of failing schools. It's next to Albany Avenue's blatant drug-trafficking pockets and vibrant commercial strip. There are bodegas, Jamaican restaurants, a bakery—and the police station's there too, identified by an enormous blue and yellow sign. The enterprising bail bondsman's shop next door advertises: CALL 860-229-JAIL!

Three Puerto Rican enclaves dominate the city's lower and central sections. Along Park Street in Frog Hollow, Latin love songs float from a record shop, and the heavy, homey scent of fried meats wafts from restaurants in the Mercado, a small mall. Women buy food in a crowded corner market that features fresh mangoes and chorizo sausage alongside jars of Velveeta spread. Teenagers push well-dressed babies in cheap strollers. Amid the bustle sprawls the jail for juvenile offenders. The beautiful buildings of Trinity College stand on a hill, behind a well-patrolled spiked iron fence, along Broad Street. Junkies roam the lower end of Park. If they turn left onto Main Street and walk up a block, they're at the methadone clinic.

Farther up Main, in Hartford's middle, stand the public library and the Mark Twain statue. Downtown, mirrored office windows block the view in. Guards man the entrances. A cluster of good restaurants serve office workers. Many don't offer supper and close on weekends. Within the Old State House Museum, tour guides stroll about in colonial garb. Outside the dramatic, fortresslike art museum, the Wadsworth

Atheneum, parents laden with toddlers and workers clutching lunch boxes await buses. Only on weekdays, and only during the day, do men and women in business suits cross streets hurriedly, talking on cell phones. At about 4 p.m. the streets start to empty. Renters in some of Frog Hollow's old six-family tenements can glimpse the ornate, Gothic State Capitol building—the center of Connecticut's government, crowned with its gold leaf, decked with curlicue detailing. At the top of Bushnell Park, the Statehouse is a fairy-tale movie set. Down the hill, an old-fashioned carousel spins, fountains shoot water, and kids slide, crawl, and run on a small playground. Carp swim in a constructed pond's black water.

To the north is the West End, the wealthiest and most identifiable "white" neighborhood. Even Hartford residents confuse it with adjacent West Hartford.

EVERY ONE OF JEREMY'S classmates aspired to leave the North-east neighborhood. Like other American kids, they hoped to follow their interests, gain status, find peaceful home lives, economic security.

"I want to see something new," Jeremy said, eyeing a corroded moped in a weedy brownfield near his house. "Pretty much anything new, I would take. Just to see it."

Jeremy imagined "meeting a nice girl who I can respect, settling down real nice, and having a few kids."

"I'd like," he said, "to be able to make enough money so my wife can stay home with our children. That's if she wants to, and I hope she wants to. Because that's the most important job of all. And so maybe I will work at two jobs."

Jeremy's classmate Shasa, a bright, dutiful, rail-thin girl, always with her frantic hand up high to answer Ms. Luddy's questions, hoped to become "a trauma surgeon." At suppertime, she always turned on to the surgery TV show and watched genuine ER docs treat genuine gunshot wounds.

"Some nasty stuff," Shasa's mother, Kara, said, shivering squeamishly. "There's my Shasa, just eatin' her dinner, watchin' this gooey, bloody . . . Ew! She eats while she watches this! And then she comes to me, says, 'Mommy, Mommy, tonight they took off somebody's arm and saved his life. I wanna be able to do that!'"

The sensitive, broad-shouldered Patrick, as chubby as Jeremy, had the most elegant manners of any child I've seen, right along with a fierce volatility that scared off adults. But Ms. Luddy had peered beyond Patrick's anger. He was trouble in the early months of third grade—muttering angrily to himself, refusing to do his work. He'd thrown a chair clear across the room. By early spring he was her hardest worker, respectful and appreciative.

Patrick wanted to be a college football coach or "a counselor who helps kids do better in school" or perhaps "a business manager for a music group."

Petite, soft-spoken Naia, who wore glittery T-shirts (one read "Hottie") and pastel fleece sweatshirts, wanted to "write about the news in the newspaper."

T.J., dead-serious, deeply proud, and reliably high-achieving, hoped to be a police officer or, he said, "if I can't do that, a lawyer."

Rashida, wiry, boisterous, sassy, rebellious, who often wore her pink, blue, and yellow teddy bear sweater with velvet pants and once a necklace (saying "Sexy") that Ms. Luddy confiscated, wanted to "be a lawyer who works to help people who get unfairly arrested."

Keesha, heavy, happy, quiet, and shy, with sympathetic eyes, loved "swings and swinging high to make the wind hit my face" and "the idea of horses." She said she'll be either a person "who teaches in college" or "a doctor for little kids."

Hamilton wanted to be a pediatrician or a "doctor for dogs."

Martin, artistic, dreamy, and poetic, wished to study insects and work in a rain forest "that I saw in a book Ms. Luddy gave me." "There are people who get paid," he told me, "to find butterflies and to maybe draw pictures of butterflies. That's for me, that job right there."

Most children of Hartford's Northeast neighborhood unflinchingly called the place exactly what it is: the "ghetto." But it was their ghetto. Few of them had ever lived in any other sort of neighborhood, so the ghetto seemed a normal world, a natural place.

But the ghetto isn't natural. It is man-made. And at many points in history, those with the power to do so could have halted its construction.

Before, During,
and After the Ghetto

IN THE MID-19TH CENTURY, Hartford's thousand or so African Americans, about 2 percent of the population, made shoes and dresses, cooked, cleaned, and chauffeured for the aristocracy. They laid bricks, built buildings, and lived all about the city. In 1850, more than half the city's black residents had been born in Connecticut. Others, urged by relatives, had come north from Virginia and Maryland and either boarded with their employers or rented apartments near the State Capitol building, near downtown. Jeremy's Northeast neighborhood was mostly farmland back then.

Most black social life—churches and a segregated "African" school—stayed downtown. Until about 1860, blacks had a hold on low-level employment and service positions. Some, who'd been around for a while, owned property in what would become the mostly white South End. By the late 1850s, nearly two million Irish immigrants had sailed to America. Studies indicate that factory owners and whites seeking domestic help preferred them, so African Americans went to the back of the line and grew poorer. Industry owners, meanwhile, contributed to improvements, linking the southern neighborhood, home to many African Americans, to the town center. Property values increased as Hartford prospered. By 1880, 800 factories with 21,000 workers operated in the city.

Climbing rents and discrimination drove African Americans from this newly valuable southerly section. Speculators bought out black

owners. Most landlords refused to rent to blacks. In the North End —
increasingly home to working-class Jewish and Italian immigrants —
landlords responded to their limited options by setting high rents for
cramped quarters.

JEREMY FOUND IT TOUGH to imagine that Italians and Jews had
long ago settled on his street.

"Really?" he asked.

"There used to be a bakery around here somewhere and a furniture
store," I told him.

"Really?"

"Yes, really. I found a picture of the bakery at the library."

"Cool," Jeremy said, "or, well, I guess, not cool, you know, since it's
gone and everything."

FOR DECADES, NORTHEAST STAYED racially mixed. In the early
1900s, about 60 percent of Hartford's blacks lived elsewhere. A Jewish cemetery — with graves for the Schloss and Gordon families — sits
steps away from Jeremy's school.

Factory whistles called. Farmland shrank, except on the prime tobacco fields along the Connecticut River valley. The American North
shifted from an agricultural toward an industrial economy, and Hartford too belched smoke. Trolleys clanged through the city's busy streets,
between previously isolated neighborhoods and centralized shopping.
Downtown sidewalks grew more crowded.

Hartford's insurance industry was already more than 100 years old
when the city adopted its accurate, dull motto, "Insurance capital of the
world," in the 1900s. Connecticut River water power ran huge mills and
gave them inland shipping access. World War I upped industrial production. Warehouses lined the river shore. War manufacturing brought
big profits. Connecticut became the nation's most industrialized state,
and Hartford had become one of America's wealthiest cities.

Around this time, the federal government, responding to security concerns and overcrowding, restricted immigration. Factory owners found themselves short of workers. Newer white immigrants, who'd toiled, backs bent, poorly paid, in the region's tobacco fields, took the new, steadier industrial jobs. But they still didn't satisfy industry's demands. And tobacco farmers grew even more desperate for workers.

Connecticut's tobacco farmers asked the National Urban League, a community-based civil rights group, to help recruit Southern black college students to work summers in the fields up north. Factory owners followed tobacco's example but recruited Southern blacks for full-time, year-round work. Several companies sweetened the deal with offers of free transportation north. Some historians, in fact, suggest Hartford recruiters may have pioneered strategies that spurred the great migration of Southern rural blacks to Northern cities.

For Southern blacks, the North must have looked mighty attractive. They eagerly packed up and boarded trains. Southern agricultural jobs had declined drastically. The South's racial discrimination, expressed in legalized segregation and racial violence, had consigned many blacks to marginal lives. Southern black migration to Hartford nearly tripled from 1900 to 1920, when 4,119 blacks lived in the city.

"It was discovered that there was, at that time, plenty of work and at good wages, but the universal complaint was the lack of homes suitable for proper living and the extortionate prices asked for rents," Emmett J. Scott wrote in his 1920 book, *Negro Migration During the War*. Describing an investigation by a Hartford Chamber of Commerce committee, Scott wrote: "They were obliged to live in poor tenements and under unhealthful conditions because accommodations of another class were withheld from them. Negroes in Hartford were suffering from the cupidity of landlords . . . It appeared for the first time in many years Hartford had a race problem on its hands."

As Scott noted, African Americans did indeed find industrial work, especially during stepped-up wartime production, though those with higher skills got the unskilled and semiskilled jobs. Blacks with trades, including masons and carpenters, were shut out of union jobs.

According to Charles S. Johnson, an urban sociologist who studied black employment patterns during this time under commission from the Urban League, Hartford employers used African Americans as a "reserve labor supply." A black man, Johnson calculated, had a one-in-three chance of rising to steady employment. "They may be hired if the unions don't object, if the non-union white workers don't object; and if the employer happens not to object," Johnson wrote.

DURING THE BLACK MIGRATION up to and after World War II, the National Association of Real Estate Officials openly acknowledged a policy that restricted African Americans (and other new arrivals) to a few outlined areas. The article in its 1924 charter read: "A Realtor should never be instrumental in introducing into a neighborhood . . . members of any race or nationality . . . whose presence will clearly be detrimental to property values in that neighborhood."

Brokers wouldn't revoke the order until 1950 and would unofficially stick to it for decades more. Hartford's newly arriving African Americans continued to crowd the North End. By 1941, 80 percent of the city's blacks had been concentrated in a 40-square-block area in North Hartford. The city population was still more than 90 percent white.

Even before Pearl Harbor, industries in Greater Hartford had undertaken war-related production. Fifty-two companies looked to hire 11,000 more workers. The continuing migration of Southern blacks to the North was crucial to this war effort, even as housing discrimination continued.

In 1950, African Americans made up 7 percent of the city's population. Puerto Ricans had begun migrating to Hartford in ever larger numbers too, during and after World War II, attracted by the jobs that were opening up as working men went overseas to fight.

Agricultural jobs in Puerto Rico declined during the 1950s. American sugar companies had taken over huge swaths of land, displacing small farmers. Bigger but more mechanized growers had left fewer jobs for Puerto Rican farmworkers. The displaced farmers moved to the island's burdened cities, hunting for work. Puerto Rico—only 100 miles long and a third as wide, with little arable land—couldn't provide work for its own displaced rural population.

In coordination with American industry, the federal government set about reducing the island's population. The U.S. Department of Labor set up a Migration Division that placed thousands of Puerto Ricans in mainland jobs. Hartford became a major destination. American employers, including the Shade Tobacco Growers Association in Greater Hartford, hung signs in rural areas, shouted through bullhorns, and spread leaflets enticing workers. The poorest of Hartford's Puerto Rican migrants traveled up from rural, isolated mountain regions to earn about 50¢ an hour harvesting tobacco. Some Puerto Rican women cleaned chickens at Hartford Live Poultry. In 1950, that paid 75¢ an hour. Slightly better-off Puerto Ricans migrated from cities and gravitated to custodial and factory jobs and restaurant work.

By 1960, 6,000 Puerto Ricans had come to Hartford. They settled in downtown neighborhoods abandoned by earlier immigrant groups, as well as in the North End's Clay Arsenal neighborhood. During this time, city fathers expended energy, money, and hope on a huge downtown development project, Constitution Plaza. Twenty years later, many otherwise adversarial factions in town agreed on one point: Constitution Plaza was a debacle. Its anchor building was mostly vacant. Retail plans had fizzled.

At the same time, an economic downturn in Puerto Rico propelled 10,000 more poor migrants to Hartford. By 1990, Hartford's 38,000 Puerto Ricans would make up 27 percent of the population—the greatest concentration in any American city.

• • •

As early as the 1950s, black and Puerto Rican migration — or more exactly, whites' exclusionary acts in reaction to that migration — had strained North End housing beyond its limits. Hartford officials responded the way other cities did — by developing public housing. Federal government housing policies guaranteed that the poor stayed where they already lived. It was simple: Federal policy based local housing authorities in individual cities or towns, not in states or counties. In turn, local authorities sited each housing project within its borders. (Suburban applicants for federal housing money usually built low-income housing for the elderly, especially after 1959, when subsidies encouraged it.) Hartford's first housing project, Nelton Court, built in 1940, accommodated 146 families in the North End. The next year, the city broke ground on the huge 500-family Bellevue Square housing project, again in the North End.

In 1951, the city opened the 600-family Stowe Village in Northeast, a series of identical, rectangular brick buildings. Some political representation came with the increasing population. Hartford elected its first black city councilor, John Clark, in 1955. An all-black-and-Latino elementary school in the North End would later be named for him, although he'd spoken out against housing segregation and had called North End landlords "vicious rent gougers." The next year, a *Hartford Courant* reporter, Robert Rotberg, investigated this charge — a decade before the rising civil rights movement emerged in full force.

"Hartford's version of the South's legal segregation finds its manifestation in the so-called north end of the city . . . predominantly one of overcrowding, dilapidation and deteriorated neighborhoods," Rotberg wrote. "As in nearly every northern city, the Negro population is concentrated in one general area. There is little intrinsically good or bad about the north end as an area, but the Negro must usually live there if he wants to work in Hartford. He must rent his room or buy his house in the north end because there is no place else he may go."

By the late 1960s, 94 percent of the region's low-income, subsidized housing was inside Hartford. On some North End streets, there was "dilapidation," as Rotberg had noted. But furniture stores, markets, a deli, bakeries, churches (the churches remain), lined what were mostly safe streets.

"People thought of it as the black neighborhood, but," recalled Waverly's principal, James Thompson, who'd grown up in the North End then, "living here, you understood it was actually a racially diverse place. On Sunday we walked over to the black church to attend services and then maybe you stopped in at the Jewish bakery. The neighborhood in the fifties had a very alive, very, very healthy feeling. There were poor areas, but generally the neighborhood felt safe and sustainable."

Northeast's elementary schools taught black, Jewish, and a few Italian and Irish kids. Weaver High School in the 1960s enrolled a mix of white and nonwhite students. Residents worked steadily at decent jobs — rarely high-status jobs in offices, but jobs that supported families. Industry had yet to abandon Hartford. One didn't yet need a college degree or even a high school degree to get decent work.

Alan Green, a black local lawyer and adviser to nonprofit foundations, grew up on Westland Street in the 1950s and '60s near where Jeremy would live almost a half century later. Green had strolled the streets unsupervised. He'd often visited his friend Mike, whose mom cooked traditional Italian dinners for neighborhood kids. He also frequented a Jewish friend's house, where he first encountered matzo ball soup. Alan's buddies heard jazz for the first time at his house. "It wasn't all racial harmony all the time," Green stressed, but "the white kids in North Hartford were having the experience of the true America. The true, ideal American experience. It seemed like it was natural for them, for white kids, to be my friends, to hang out, walk to school. I'm not sure you find that in Hartford anymore, not very often anyway. You certainly aren't finding it up on Westland Street."

"Who the Hell Would Want
to Live in Hartford?"

W HEN *DID* IT HAPPEN?" Ms. Luddy asked late one afternoon as we left Waverly. "It's not something you really
think about, but I've wondered whether or not anyone saw it coming."

The first clear alarm signaling the city's eventual decay and demise
sounded about half a century back, when Hartford's middle-class population began its decline. (Census data showed that between 1950 and
1960 alone, about 56,000 people—mainly poor—moved into Hartford.
And about 95,000 people—mainly white and middle class—moved
out. Overall, the city's population dropped by about 15,000 people.)

After that, statistical alarms rang steadily. Hands occasionally wrung
too. Movements to halt the region's free fall toward segregation flick-
ered but always faded.

THE TRENDS PROGRESSED: In 2005, blacks and Latinos made
up nearly 80 percent of the city's population. The city's 49,000 Hispanics—largely Puerto Rican—outnumbered blacks, composing 41
percent of the city's population. Ninety-five percent of the students
in Hartford's schools are either black or Latino—about the proportion found in the public schools of many other great Northern cities:
Milwaukee (76 percent), Detroit (96 percent), Newark (91 percent),
Chicago (88 percent) Washington, D.C. (93 percent), Cleveland (80
percent), New York City (73 percent), and Boston (77 percent). More

than two-thirds of Hartford's students are poor, again, about the poverty figure for America's other large urban districts. A typical poor child in Hartford attends a school where 72 percent of the students are poor.

In the nation at large, poor blacks remain our most segregated racial minority group. For ghetto residents, economic segregation is increasingly intense.

As for class segregation, Georgetown University professor of law Sheryll Cashin notes that the "overall direction of census trends since 1970 . . . has been one of growing economic segmentation of American life space." Demographers explain that most measures showed a small decline in class segregation during the 1990s, likely a result of a particularly robust economy. The total number of residents of high-poverty neighborhoods dropped from the 10.4 million peak in 1990 to 7.9 million in 2000. It looked like — and was — progress of a sort. But the level of concentrated poverty in 2000 actually represents an increase from 1970 levels. Since 1970, the number of census tracts (a rough approximation of neighborhoods) with 40 percent poor residents has nearly doubled, from about 1,300 in 1970 to about 2,500 in 2000.

In other words, Sheryll Cashin explains, the change during the 1990s "didn't effect a reversal . . . All it did was avoid a further deterioration of our separated condition." During the 1990s, more than half of America's largest cities became, like Hartford, what demographers call "majority minority." During the 1990s, America's largest cities lost about 2.3 million white residents.

Public school mirrors and magnifies trends in the larger society. Statistically, children of all racial groups are generally more segregated than adults. And while some racial minority children might not live in technically high-poverty neighborhoods, they would still, in many cases, attend high-poverty schools. This is because childless white people are far more likely than white families with school-age children to live in urban, integrated settings. As of 2003, a typical black or Latino student attended a school where nearly half the students are poor — more than twice the share of poverty found in the school of a typical white student, where 80 percent of his or her classmates will also be white. Asian American children, our most integrated group, both by race and class, are most likely to be living the multiethnic American reality.

THESE TRENDS TOWARD isolation by race and class weren't inevitable. After World War II, Hartford and the dozens of cities like it might have gone a different way. Hartford in 1950 was a major employer in a prospering region. It had good hospitals, a solid liberal arts college, the legacy of Mark Twain, a pretty river, architectural gems (some now demolished and replaced by parking lots), industry, a solid middle class, cohesive neighborhoods with strong characters, a beautiful art museum, and the nation's oldest continually published newspaper. But the federal government steered white folks to another place.

In order to spur home ownership, create construction jobs, and help veterans, the government offered families favorable home mortgages. The government, beginning in the 1940s, guaranteed more than 90 percent of the value on mortgage loans; banks suffered little risk, and in turn, they lowered interest rates. The American dream—a house on a plot of land—was at hand for a mere 10 percent down payment.

The problem was this: Bank loan regulations strongly favored the purchase of single-family *suburban* homes. And that's just where blacks, steered away by means both direct and subtle, had been prevented from moving. Loan regulations also discouraged construction or purchase of the multifamily houses common to urban areas. Terms for fixing up older homes—which obviously predominate in cities—weren't nearly as favorable. The kicker: Every loan required an appraisal. As part of the determination of value, an appraiser rated the neighborhood. The history of such ratings stretched back to a government-invented risk-evaluation system that first institutionalized the banking and real estate practice known as "redlining." The highest ratings on the spectrum went to neighborhoods that were "new, homogenous, and in demand in good times and bad." Identifiable, poorer black neighborhoods were rated "hazardous" and placed in the lowest possible category, making them ineligible for loans.

Millions of white families across America found the government's incentives to leave the city irresistible. Financial disincentives to staying in the city, especially in a low-rated area such as the North End, increased.

These loan programs, offered when minorities, because of discrimination, simply could not move to suburbia, "completely reshaped" the residential housing market of the United States, sociologists Douglas Massey and Nancy Denton wrote in their 1993 book, *American Apartheid*. The loans, Massey and Denton say, "were a major impetus behind the rapid suburbanization of the United States after 1945."

Because of the loan programs and coincidentally declining home-construction costs during the 1950s, buying in the suburbs grew less expensive than even renting in Hartford. Lenders, appraisers, and insurance agents redlined whole neighborhoods of central cities—where blacks and Puerto Ricans remained stuck—making them ineligible for loans. That practice may have seemed like smart business. But it didn't simply reflect a neighborhood's deterioration. It fueled further decline.

Italian Americans left the Northeast neighborhood and moved southward to Wethersfield. The Jewish population found its way first to Bloomfield and Windsor and then to West Hartford. Later, Avon, Simsbury, Glastonbury, and Suffield grew.

In 1962, the Citizens Committee of the North End, a neighborhood advocacy group, issued a housing report describing a persistent situation: "In the North End, second rate housing costs more to live in, more to rent, and much more to buy in comparison with other areas that are just as old . . . Families continue to stay in a rut financially because they must have a place to live and are forced to accept sub-standard conditions."

Hartford's economy, meanwhile, had begun to sag. This same pattern also befell other like American cities. In 1960, manufacturing jobs still accounted for 21 percent of employment—23,100 jobs. But by 1970, the black population had climbed to 30 percent of the city, and manufacturing jobs had declined to 15 percent. By 2001, manufacturing jobs would account for only 5 percent of the city's jobs. Out in the suburbs, cloned single-family Colonials and ranch houses grew on former farmland. Strip malls, giant grocery stores, bargain outlets, superstores—the infrastructure of suburbia—sprawled, chasing these expanding markets.

In 1967, suburban legislators lined up at a podium in the Statehouse and orated against a bill proposed by a Hartford state representative. The bill would have established a regional Housing Authority, shifting and spreading the burden of public and affordable housing beyond Hartford. Opposing legislators, though, preached about "erosion of local government" and the "denial of home rule." State Representative Elmer Mortenson, a Democrat from nearby Newington, declared that his town had "its own problems." Public housing, he said, would "just invite these type of people into town." The movement died.

Around this time, the Greater Hartford Chamber of Commerce sponsored research on regional cooperation. Their report echoed the activists' report of 1962. It said that North End housing was crowded and overpriced. It observed that the neighborhood's streets and sidewalks weren't safe. Retail stores and banks were fleeing. The report said that "a gap exists between their life expectations and their current life situations." "In short," it continued, "these families constitute one of the bases of what has come to be called the 'Negro revolt.'"

As predicted, about a half dozen of what the police first termed "disturbances" flared in the warm months of 1967. Young men tossed rocks and bottles from rooftops, marched angrily through the streets, looted stores, and set small fires. Officials called the men into city hall to explain what had riled them. The men claimed white business owners in the North End jacked up prices and wouldn't hire them. Ghetto workers, the men complained, didn't have equal access to union jobs.

After the assassination of Martin Luther King Jr. in 1968, Hartford's neighborhoods again erupted in anger, with looting, burning, and marching. Even worse riots raged in 1969 for five days and nights. The riots didn't open up jobs or unions, but they did push most of the remaining economically stable families and the businesses out.

With no one else to take on the task, neighborhood-based groups and churches, usually with little money and little expertise in urban planning or fund-raising, established self-help and beautification programs. They took on "revitalization" projects.

In 1968, Congress had passed the Fair Housing Act, prohibiting "discrimination in the sale, rental, and financing of dwellings." It still didn't adequately address the problem. The U.S. Commission on Civil Rights concluded, in 1974, for example, that banks in Greater Hartford remained biased against minorities and women looking for mortgages.

"Mortgage lending traditionally has been—and continues to be—a closed community," the study's director, Sally Knack, testified at a public U.S. Department of Housing and Urban Development hearing. "It is operated largely by white male decision-makers, and its standards are geared to facilitate service to white male customers."

Through the 1970s, a Hartford-based research and advocacy group, Education/Instruccion, investigated housing discrimination too. In one study, 60 teams of Hispanic, black, and white undercover EI researchers posed either as potential home owners or tenants in more than 100 test situations. Real estate agents made disparaging remarks about blacks and Puerto Ricans to the white researchers. They warned whites off racially mixed neighborhoods. And they steered blacks and Hispanics into developing ghetto neighborhoods and suburban enclaves populated by minorities.

EI's taped transcripts caught agents describing the racially transitioning Blue Hills section of Hartford to a white home buyer as a "slummy and high-crime area," "not safe," "a bad investment," "a depressed area." To whites, agents described the Northeast neighborhood as a "tough place," with "vandalism" and "people on welfare." One agent asked a white home buyer, "Who the hell would want to live in Hartford?" Another said, "I throw listings for Hartford homes away."

In response to EI's findings, the U.S. Department of Justice filed lawsuits against eight of the nine largest real estate firms in the area. The firms settled out of court, promising to adopt a program to market more effectively to prospective minority home buyers.

Meanwhile, insurance corporations, including some with national headquarters in Hartford, redlined too. It was difficult to get favorable financing for house purchases in the North End. Anyone who did manage, paid exorbitant insurance premiums—that is, if they could get insurance.

EI researchers used five homes as fronts in their investigation. The homes were of like construction and age. Owners of each house had updated the heating, electricity, and plumbing, making location the only variable. Three were in the black and Latino North End. One was in the white South End. The fifth house was in suburban West Hartford. EI researchers made 36 contacts posing as insurance policy customers. Agents refused 23 times to do business on urban properties, and all but one of those denials was for a property in the North End. Insurance agents denied policies just over the phone, after hearing a North End address. "On Williams Street? I'm sorry, we couldn't write in that area, we couldn't," a Travelers agent, whose company headquarters were a mile away, told a caller. Agents offered a policy on the West Hartford property five out of six times.

Local banks also disinvested in Hartford. Education/Instruccion found that the 10 major banks in the region took in most of their deposits from the city but invested the money in suburbia, with the average bank's mortgage loan portfolio 91 percent suburban. In 1975, for example, Hartford National took 86 percent of its deposits—more than

$1 billion—from Hartford-based sources. But 96 percent of its mortgages went to suburbanites.

The government continued to subsidize projects that made suburban living more convenient. With the help of federal money, state officials had completed work on Interstate 91, heading north-south, and an east-west highway, Interstate 84.

Soon after the highways were finished, a local economist, Andrew Gold, studied the interdependence of Hartford and its suburbs. He found the relationship strong but asymmetric. Hartford employers relied upon a suburban labor pool, especially for jobs in finance and insurance. Suburban residents relied upon professional jobs located in the city. But city residents, Gold concluded, were at "a severe disadvantage" in getting suburban jobs.

The current racially segregated and isolated urban-suburban structure, which defines Greater Hartford, was firmly established by the early 1970s. Government officials regularly built schools, as few as 15 years after *Brown v. Board of Education,* that were 100 percent racially segregated from day one. All-white schools, funded in large part by the state government, went up in expanding suburban neighborhoods and still do. Jeremy's elementary school, Simpson-Waverly, did not *become* segregated over time. The day its doors opened in 1970, it was a black school.

No one could assert that government officials set out to "create" segregated schools. But they abetted their creation simply by siting and building schools to fit the racially and economically separate setup that discrimination had created. Even though segregation wasn't desirable, it became a given in the education of thousands and thousands of the city's children.

How the Suburbs
Sealed the City's Fate

HARTFORD'S BULKELEY HIGH SCHOOL class of 1955 held its 20th reunion in white, suburban Glastonbury in 1975. The dislocation wasn't lost on Nicholas Carbone, a member of the class and Hartford's deputy mayor at the time.

"That was appropriate," Carbone wrote ironically in a *Hartford Courant* editorial. "Of the 289 classmates who were accounted for, only 10 percent still live in the city that provided their education."

In the mid '70s, Carbone, a fast-talker with working-class roots, had started a one-man educational movement that examined regional inequality. He'd complained persistently that the city was losing out to the suburbs and that culpable local suburban governments set policies that penned in the poor behind the city line.

State-sponsored investigations backed Carbone's assertions. Suburban governments, official reports said, excluded low-income families through zoning, by limiting multifamily units, by requiring large house lots and high minimum square footage, by prohibiting condo developments, and by imposing strict reviews on multifamily housing.

"Many towns in Connecticut practice forms of zoning that have had the probable effect of excluding large portions of the State's population from residence within the boundaries of their towns," one report commissioned by the state read. "Connecticut, by its zoning enabling legislation, has made possible the practices which, together with other public and private discriminatory acts, increase the degree of separation between higher and lower income groups and between whites and minorities."

Nick Carbone gathered audiences in suburban meeting halls and church basements. He asked that officials help shoulder the burdens of concentrated poverty that he and other city officials had borne alone for decades. He held up graphs depicting the disproportionate share of social service programs, drug treatment programs, police protection, low-income housing programs, that Hartford bore while large numbers of suburban commuters earned their paychecks in Hartford.

"I was so optimistic," Carbone recalled more than a quarter century later. "I thought that all people needed was a better understanding of what was happening. So I made charts." In 1974, Congress had passed the Housing and Community Development Act, an antipoverty program consolidating housing and neighborhood stabilization programs. One stated goal was to reduce "the isolation of income groups . . . through the spatial deconcentration of housing opportunities for persons of lower incomes." Carbone thought the act might entice his new suburban friends to share Hartford's challenges.

In the following years, suburbs did line up for the money—but not to help the region's poor. Suburban officials described "urgent" needs in their communities (a broad and vague lesser purpose of the law). West Hartford officials requested money for street construction. In Glastonbury, officials asked for money to develop a downtown commercial center. Farmington wanted more sewers. Vernon wanted more parks.

Hartford applied for money to fix curbs and streets in poor neighborhoods, to paint and repair dilapidated housing, to buy social services and legal aid. Grant applicants in each community also had to outline plans for affordable housing and indicate the number of low-income people "expected to reside" there. Six towns near Hartford failed to draw up such plans and either left blank the space for the "expected" number of low-income residents or frankly wrote, "0."

In Hartford, resentment soared. Carbone argued that either the suburbs should use the money as intended—to meet needs of the poor within the region—or the money should be reallocated to Hartford. City officials outlined Carbone's argument in a lawsuit they brought against the federal government. After many twists and turns, Hartford lost.

By 2001, only 14 percent of the population of Hartford County lived in the city itself. Yet as of 2002, more than 41 percent of the county's subsidized housing stock was there. Retail stores had followed the middle class out of the city. Between 1980 and 1985, 11 of 13 chain supermarkets inside the city borders closed.

AROUND THE TIME of Deputy Mayor Carbone's disappointments, West Hartford's mayor, Ellsworth Grant, made clear that he didn't welcome Hartford's poor.

In a 1976 interview with a West Hartford newspaper, Grant said Puerto Ricans "should remain in the core city or go back where they came from" and not burden West Hartford taxpayers. "They don't belong here," Grant said of Puerto Ricans. "I think West Hartford—the Hartford area—has been a port of entry too long for these types of people."

Puerto Rican activist groups demanded a public apology, and Grant eventually complied, saying, "West Hartford welcomes . . . anyone who can find a rent here or make a down payment on a house."

Yet in 1986, a state commission discovered that for blacks and Latinos, finding, renting, or buying a house in a town such as West Hartford was tough. Researchers echoed earlier findings, declaring, "Discriminatory steering and screening practices prevent minorities from renting property in predominantly white neighborhoods." Landlords, the report said, discriminated by screening out rental applicants over the phone "who sound black or Hispanic" and that "blacks who are able to get through the various screening devices are often rejected on site."

Three years later, *Hartford Courant* reporters investigated housing discrimination again: Posing as home buyers, they tested 15 real estate agencies. Eight discriminated against black testers, giving extra scrutiny to blacks' financial qualifications. Seven steered testers to areas based upon the testers' race.

The economic picture for residents in the city's poorest neighborhoods worsened. Between 1980 and 1990, for example, Hartford had lost 17,000—more than 25 percent—of its remaining manufacturing jobs. An increase in employment—about 41,700 jobs—came in the "service" sector. These low-paying, irregular jobs include those of waitress, waiter, hotel maid, front-desk clerk, and cashier. Jobs in finance, insurance, and real estate increased by nearly 15,000. But such jobs require education—a bachelor's degree certainly and, usually, specialized training. Work in new fields popped up in the region, including jobs in photonics and biotechnology. These jobs require college degrees and often a master's or a PhD. According to the 2000 census, about 12 percent of Hartford residents have bachelor's degrees. About 40 percent don't even have high school diplomas.

More than 8,000 black residents left Hartford between 1990 and 2000. By 2001, the *Hartford Courant's* page one headline CITY LOSES BLACKS TO SUBURBS described what city planners had long feared: Just about anyone who could was getting out. In 2000, for the first time since before World War I, Hartford's black population dropped. Federal antidiscrimination laws, coupled, perhaps, with suburbanites' more welcoming attitudes, had helped open markets previously closed to nonpoor minorities, who, like their white counterparts, went in search of a higher standard of living.

Population increases in the suburbs and corresponding declines in the city forced legislators to draw new districting maps for the state legislature, increasing suburban clout. The cities lost out again. In 2001, the population drain forced two of Hartford's most effective Democratic state representatives—Barnaby Horton and Ken Green—to run against each other.

• • •

As MANUFACTURING JOBS melted away, drug culture and related crime rose. There aren't many drug dealers relative to the population, but their circles of bored, rambunctious teens and 20-somethings took over much public space in the North End. Most misbehaviors in the North End were undramatic "crimes against property"—burglary, auto theft. And most days in Jeremy's North End neighborhood went by unremarkably, although violent crime remained a realistic and constant fear. The unceasing sequence of murders, armed robberies, and assaults captured headlines and shaped the area's internal and public images.

One crime event generated months of publicity about the North End. On July 4, 2001, a stray bullet from a drug dealer's gun flew into the cheek of a pretty seven-year-old girl named Takira Gaston. She'd been riding a scooter along Garden and Mather streets. The bullet shattered Takira's jaw, pierced her tongue, and exited her right cheek. Surgeons at Yale–New Haven Medical Center stabilized Takira, removed fragments of bullet, bone, and teeth from her throat, and reconstructed her face.

Takira's shooting followed a rash of street slayings of black and Puerto Rican teenagers and men. But her maiming inspired John Rowland, the populist Republican governor at the time, to call a press conference: "I call them the junior varsity, the gang wannabes. But the JV still sells drugs and kills people. So I don't care who they are, gangs or otherwise. We're going to play hardball," Rowland told reporters.

The crackdown didn't help for long. That August, 17-year-old Gary Little was shot in the head playing chess on a friend's front stoop. In 2002, another spate of deadly shootings brought state police back to the North End. The following year the youth gang West Hell fought against another gang, the Ave, for status and a lucrative corner. In May 2003, a 15-year-old boy was shot and killed near Quirk Middle School. A few months later—three years after Takira was shot—a stray bullet slashed the leg of 12-year-old Martin McClendon, who was pedaling a bike near his house.

Little Takira (who did recover) and Martin (he's okay too) bear the scars of a recent drug turf war. That deadly war grew from a less conspicuous, century-long swirl of historical forces that concentrated poverty and segregated races in the neighborhood. Politicians didn't tend to talk about that.

Connecticut governor John Rowland, for example, supported a familiar solution to Hartford's woes, one that had been on city-planning agendas since the late 1960s and that had failed in the past: a really big downtown development project.

They called this one Adriaen's Landing. Rowland pledged that the $1 billion plan would reinvigorate the city. It included a giant convention hall, retail stores, a parking garage, pricey condos for the middle class, and a science center. The state handed over to private developers $29.9 million in tax credits. The Connecticut Development Authority gave Marriott Hotel a $2 million sales-tax exemption. Only about 28 percent of the cost of Adriaen's Landing came from private sources , but promoters said the new project was to bring 330 jobs to the city, mostly low-wage service positions.

PROFESSORS AND POLICYMAKERS refer to people like Nina and Anna as "the underclass." This dispassionate shorthand defines men, women, and children who dwell within America's borders but aren't connected to, have little firsthand knowledge of, the customs, protocols, and opportunities that materialize up the social ladder. It's in middle-class suburbia that the headwaters of the American "mainstream" begin.

The mainstream flows by the places where middle-class families live, work, shop, hang out, talk, trade tips, favors, and networks, and, most consequentially, go to school. School is where suburban kids soak up "mainstream" culture—the sets of unwritten codes, shared understandings, and rules that engage them with opportunity. Expectations—about behaviors as intimate and revealing as body language and grammar and cadence of speech—are deeply installed and hardly noticed, except when they're unwittingly violated. Generally, from wealthier suburban schools children paddle into the future on a wide river toward a safe and visible horizon. Knowledgeable guides, experienced in the arts of applying to college and getting jobs, usually pilot them.

Meanwhile, on the other side of the border, a place of disinvestment and resource draining and deterioration, residents of the Northeast neighborhood did what American blacks and Latinos have had to do for centuries—they've resourcefully created cultural and social communities of their own. Some residents, for all their complaints, remained committed to the area. Despite Northeast's isolation and inequalities, the neighborhood feels comfortable to many people, even though they're also intimidated walking down the street.

"I don't see us movin'," said Shasa's mother, Kara, a single mother who is a guard at a nearby prison. "But just 'cause I'm comfortable, that doesn't mean I don't want better for them. I know they gotta see stuff that's out there."

Like many parents in Northeast, Kara did what she could to "help my kids understand the North End of Hartford isn't the whole world." On weekends she often put her kids into her old Chevy and cruised, radio up, around the rich suburbs. Kara pointed to big houses, inched slowly around quiet cul-de-sacs. Her three kids picked out their favorite homes.

"I tell them, 'You want that? You keep yourselves in school.' It's not like I'm sayin' they gotta have that, that that's all there is to a good life, but livin' here it's maybe harder for them to know what else is there, and I guess I'm just sayin' I would like my kids to have a choice to have it if they want. Like, keep the option open."

Jeremy's classmate Patrick built himself fine homes in his imagination.

"Yellow," he said, "with a fence all around, one of those nice wooden fences and a little yard where we could play football. I like it quiet like, not all loud with all the screamin', the shooters."

Patrick longed for but didn't expect to encounter that halcyon place, one that "wouldn't have all these bad influences on me."

For Patrick's grandmother (and the four kids she raised in a garden-style housing project across from Simpson-Waverly), moving away would require both the patient and systematic provision of outside information and a pretty big psychological leap.

"Yeah, I'd like to get out of here," Patrick told me, a bit accusingly. "Definitely, I think, more than you know. But my grandma, see, she's been here her whole life and where's she gonna go with us is the question. She don't know. Sometimes she say Enfield Street maybe." That was around the corner.

"Our neighborhood isn't the type of place you say you like livin' at. It's bad, bad, bad where we live. But I'm used to it," Patrick said. "The way I see it, this is the place we got and I can live with it fine."

BLACK CHURCHES REMAIN Northeast's anchor. Many have taken over the old shops along Main Street. The churches offer the standard spiritual fare of renewal as well as substance abuse counseling, support groups for domestic abuse victims, financial management workshops, health care referral services, and adult education classes. Sundays, Northeast's bleak streets burst with life. Men dressed in suits and ties and women in fine dresses and hats stroll to church with their children.

In 2001, the city's Housing Authority toppled the worst of the North End's housing projects, Stowe Village, three decades after its construction. By 2002, the Housing Authority had built about 150 single-family and duplex houses on the old Stowe Village site in Northeast. The houses whisper the American dream: they're painted cheerful yellows, blues, and greens, have small front lawns, driveways. The hopeful development, though, runs seamlessly into crime-ridden Barbour Street, named after a former president of Yale, who lived nearby way back when.

"So it's really bad here, isn't it, where I live?" Jeremy asked me from the back seat. I'd driven him to the library for the afternoon, where he'd fallen in love with Google and a Web site on atoms and another on Madagascar.

Bad? I'd been trained to think in relative terms. His neighborhood was better than the bleak, squat housing project along Hartford's southern edge, where I'd done some reporting the previous day. The litter problem was worse in Frog Hollow. And there seemed to be fewer drug dealers in Jeremy's neighborhood than several blocks away on Garden Street.

Unlike Jeremy, who had visited hardly anywhere for long, I'd often visited Hartford's suburbs to the north of here, the downright posh ones to the west, and others a few minutes down the highway south. Six minutes away, in West Hartford, lived a friend from my first newspaper job, with her husband and two children. In its town center, a neon FURS sign lit the sky. At the entrance of a shop called Reigning Cats and Dogs stood a $300 scratching post for kitties. Upscale restaurants and expensive clothing stores lined the main shopping street. West Hartford is known as a progressive, welcoming little place. Still, West Hartford's school superintendent had recently dropped plans to seek state money for a middle school that would have enrolled Hartford students *and* West Hartford's more privileged kids.

Middle class and formally educated, I wondered about the appropriateness of applying my standards to Jeremy's environment. Who was I to issue a verdict? Wasn't Jeremy asking a terribly complicated question? One that would elicit only subjective answers? One I'm sophisticated enough to know how to evade?

Jeremy's teacher, Ms. Luddy, fielded questions like this all the time. She managed graceful, optimistic, attentive answers such as, "If there's love in your home, you are in a good place," and "If you want something different for yourself than what you see around you, stay focused on your goals; don't ever give up."

Yet each day after the kids went home, she told me, her tiny class-room always felt so quiet. The difficult questions echoed. She couldn't really answer them either, not completely, not in a way that would reveal as much as she knows.

So she prayed a lot. She kept trying to imagine ways to make it all better. She never ceased inspecting the world for hints of ways out for her kids. She came up with few answers. Beyond her classroom—beyond the neighborhood and the little city whose kids she loved, beyond the modest suburb where she lived without children of her own—she knew that the immense obstacles that block most dreams are, in ways she sensed but hadn't framed clearly, "built deep into our society."

"Grrr," she growled one day after dismissing her students. Her hands clutched the sides of her head, as if trying to hold it steady. Her freckled face flushed red.

"What's the solution?" she asked a bulletin board scattered, by coincidence, with appropriately grim vocabulary words: *barren, deserted, perilous, grueling.*

PART THREE

A Feeling That We Can Do Better

A little boy planted a carrot seed. His mother said, "I'm afraid it won't come up." His father said, "I'm afraid it won't come up." And his big brother said, "It won't come up." Every day the little boy pulled up the weeds around the seed and sprinkled the ground with water. But nothing came up. And nothing came up. Everyone kept saying it wouldn't come up. But he still pulled up the weeds around it every day and sprinkled the ground with water. And then, one day, a carrot came up. Just as the little boy had known it would.

—Ruth Krauss, *The Carrot Seed*

Expert Witness

JOHN BRITTAIN'S PERSONAL HISTORY helped him to envision solutions for urban problems that tripped up Ms. Luddy and her kids.

The year Brittain began his education, 1949, the states of the old Confederacy still barred blacks from white schools. But in Norwalk, Connecticut, five-year-old John walked right in and sat right down, no questions asked, in the kindergarten of the otherwise white Winnipauk Elementary School. Nearly a decade before, his Georgia-born parents had moved clear of the South's segregation and enforced poverty. As John continued his journey through a white suburban elementary school, his parents told him stories about life under segregation. In 1954, the year he turned 10, by unanimous decision in *Brown v. Board of Education,* the U.S. Supreme Court barred intentional school segregation. His parents put that in context for him. Brittain felt lucky to live up north. From the start, though, he regarded himself as absolutely entitled to be where he was. Always a full, hearty participant, he still lived slightly outside the frame.

"The four musketeers, they called us," Brittain remembered. "My friends. Peter, he was Jewish, from Israel. Gary? Straight from Italy. And there was Edward, from England. We were different, each of us. Add us up, we figured we'd been called every epithet in the book. So we stuck together. We'd have been more vulnerable alone."

BEFORE JOHN BRITTAIN'S FAMILY came to Connecticut from rural Georgia, John's father, John Sr. (Jake to everyone), and his mother,

Ardessa, had been domestic servants to a white Coca-Cola executive. In the early 1940s, the boss moved, with his "help," up north to a seaside mansion in elegant Westport. Jake, Ardessa, and their little girl, Marge, moved into the estate's comfy servants' quarters. Marge enrolled in public school and each year was the only black child in her class. When John was about to turn five, Jake sought a place of their own. They bought a classic New England Colonial in a quiet working-class neighborhood, a seaside town away. Jake and Ardessa were early suburban pioneers to Norwalk. Neighbors showed "surprise," John Brittain remembered, the day his family arrived, "but there were no problems, none at all."

Jake started fixing Chevys at a local dealer. Ardessa worked full-time as nanny and housekeeper for Lawrence Wein, who owned the Empire State Building.

By seventh grade, John Brittain had constructed a socially comfortable world for himself at West Rocks Junior High. He had a lot of friends. He played baseball and soccer. He earned A's. One of just a handful of black kids, he began to feel the weight of national events more heavily, he imagined, than did others around him.

Walking to school each morning, he watched yellow school buses carry wealthy white children right on past the more racially mixed school closer to their homes in the posh Norwalk beachfront neighborhood called Rowayton. The buses took those white kids to the richer, whiter West Rocks Junior High, where John happened to be a student. The junior high it passed by, John knew, enrolled far more of Norwalk's black kids — including the black kids from a nearby housing project. Brittain recalled squinting in at the white faces through bus windows. He was about 12, he said, when he first discerned the meaning of those circuitous routes. He felt the insult. He filed the information away.

Around 1960 — five years after Rosa Parks sparked the bus boycott in Montgomery, Alabama — Norwalk was changing too. More black families had moved in. Brittain enjoyed his racially mixed crowd of high school buddies. The white boys got into hockey that year. The black kids didn't, but Brittain laced up skates, gave hockey a try, and surprised himself by being a natural. Recruiters from hockey colleges dangled scholarships. He dreaded leaving his high school sweetheart, Sondra, come fall. But something else about those schools didn't feel right. His big sister, Marge, helped him define the problem.

"You already know how to deal with white people," Brittain remembers her saying. "You need to learn how to be around black people. That's what you need." Marge, eight years older than John, hadn't made many friends in the Connecticut suburbs. After high school graduation, she'd opted for the historically black Howard University in Washington, D.C.

John sacrificed hockey. At Howard, he majored in political science, collected more A's, and kept the flame burning for Sondra back home. He began to imagine a future as a rabble-rousing preacher. But his professors, impressed with his analytical mind and with his moral leanings, ushered him toward the university's law school.

Civil rights law had been more or less invented at Howard Law School. Its most famous graduate, Thurgood Marshall, had finished first in his class a generation before John Brittain, in 1933. During Brittain's years, the stars in the field were on trajectories that passed through Howard to deliver lectures, teach, recruit young lawyers, consult, and attend parties. One of those stars, Herbert O. Reid, took a shine to John Brittain almost immediately. Reid had graduated from Harvard Law School in 1945. He wrote for big-name law journals, litigated high-profile cases, but remained devoted to Howard students. Reid's "exactingness," and his Hulk-like frame wrapped in fancy suits, John Brittain remembered, "plain scared people — and attracted them too."

Reid lightened his rigorous Legal Method and Constitutional Law class with tales about his own revered and feared mentor, Charles Hamilton Houston. As vice-dean, in the 1930s, Houston had fashioned Howard

Law School's unapologetic social justice mission. He'd brought in the nation's best black legal scholars, who, at the time, would have been denied professorships at white universities. With his students by his side, Houston had argued seminal segregation cases in graduate school admissions and employment, both crucial preludes to *Brown*. Houston's most promising mentees—Thurgood Marshall was one—worked on real cases, filing briefs, doing research. As Houston had trained Thurgood Marshall, so Herbert O. Reid trained John Brittain to research every case ever decided on any issue, to perfect procedure and decorum as well as argument.

"There were to be no missteps," Brittain remembered. "Not one. He told us straight out, 'You are going to be a black civil rights lawyer. They are going to be waiting for you to trip up.'" John Brittain planned to do exactly what Herbert Reid told him to do. He'd go south. "If you were serious," he said, "that's where you went."

Brittain had already taken some months off from college and worked as an election observer in Mississippi in tense times. He'd been shoved, thrown across a room by white election officials, and inspired by black people who'd gone right ahead and lined up to vote, often for the first time.

After graduation, Brittain returned north to Norwalk, married Sondra, passed the bar and packed up his racing green MGB convertible. He and Sondra drove straight toward what Brittain called "the heart of the problem": Mississippi.

At 25, Brittain won his first school desegregation case, based on the *Brown v. Board of Education* precedent. He continued to litigate desegregation and discrimination cases, first for the U.S. Justice Department in Oxford, and later for the Lawyers' Committee for Civil Rights Under Law, in Jackson. He learned how to preach—Sundays from the pulpits of black churches and weeknights from the floor of civil rights meetings. The parishioners took a liking to him. A few asked if he'd considered becoming a preacher. He had been an altar boy at St. Paul's

Episcopal in Norwalk, swinging a chalice, smoking up the congregation with incense. But he'd long ago dropped what he called "organized religion's subjective beliefs," while staying enamored of secular sorts of good-works idealism. Civil rights became his church. And if indeed there were a God, Brittain remembered deciding, civil rights was surely his work.

Jake and Ardessa felt proud of their son. They also told him straight out that they thought him "a little crazy." Word of John's work reached friends all over Connecticut.

"I used to get phone calls, you know, 'We're proud of you for fighting the good fight down there,'" he recalled. "The sentiment seemed to be that I was working to improve a very backward place—which was true. But the South allowed a lot of people up north to avoid looking at their own problems."

In the mid-1970s, John and Sondra, with a son and a daughter to feed now, worried some about money. A friend asked John to join his private practice in San Francisco. He bided his time jogging up and down the city's hills, training for marathons. Sondra tired of six-hour flights to see family. She longed to be home in Connecticut. Brittain applied, sensibly, for a teaching job at the University of Connecticut Law School, in Hartford. Within months, at 33, he hopped on the tenure track.

The family settled into a big Colonial on manicured, tree-lined Ridgefield Street in Blue Hills. From the living room, John looked onto running trails in shady Keney Park. The Brittains' neighbors included other black professionals—doctors, lawyers, academics, leaders in state government—and stay-at-home mothers like Sondra.

"We felt calm," Brittain remembered. "It was quiet, less dramatic than the South."

But one September night, in 1977, the phone rang. An investigator from the U.S. Department of Justice wanted to know if John and Sondra had ever looked for houses in the predominantly white suburbs. Had real estate agents informed them of available houses there? Had

John sensed that agents had "steered" him to Blue Hills because he was black? Brittain remembered laughing at the suggestion. He'd deliberately chosen his well-to-do black neighborhood. And anyway, no one, he assured the investigator, could ever steer him where he didn't wish to go.

"But I had a strong feeling it was a good idea someone was digging," Brittain said. "Pieces came together. I turned the tables, I asked the questions."

He asked the investigator how many real estate firms had been implicated in discriminatory practices. Which neighborhoods were changing? How fast? Was the population dropping, and by how much? When was the last time a lot of white people had lived in the North End?

"I'd seen within minutes, driving up Albany Avenue, that this place was extremely segregated and unequal. I know my history. These things don't happen by accident. I suppose, for me, that phone call is what started it all."

Around this time, people discovered John Brittain. They called from colleges, civic and business groups, legal organizations, and media outlets and found him eloquent and approachable. He moderated panels, delivered speeches, led symposia. He accepted every call, and when he got there, he pushed his issues — racial inequality, school and housing segregation, poverty. He noticed that whites in his audiences, whether in law classes or public forums, resisted the idea that Connecticut was "segregated." The very word *segregation* seemed to imply lynch mobs and piggy-faced Southern governors blocking schoolhouse doors.

He'd dazzled congregations in Mississippi's churches, and he dazzled audiences in Connecticut's lecture halls. He connected morality to case law, Connecticut to Mississippi. His conclusion, often, was that Northern de facto segregation remained as damaging as the freshly eradicated Southern segregation. Both constricted lives, eroded humanity. He could win over crowds and make audiences feel, if only briefly, that there was no other way but his to think about these matters.

But a tougher challenge lay ahead. A semantic tussle summed it up. Since law school, he'd engaged in polite academic discourse over the appropriateness of two related yet distinct legal terms that students of civil rights law learn—*de facto* and *de jure* segregation.

De jure, "of law," refers to racial separation enforced by laws or statues. De jure segregation—the segregation of the Jim Crow South—is unconstitutional. *De facto,* "of fact," is visible racial separation deriving from and sustained not by explicitly racist laws, but by a mix of social forces, not all of them initially and directly sinister. Brittain, though, found this "de facto" label simplistic. It let government off the hook. He knew that government policy and action in housing, zoning, and defining school district borders contributed to—and sometimes was the primary reason for—the construction and maintenance of segregation.

"*De facto* has come to translate, incorrectly, as meaning 'no one's fault,'" Brittain told his Connecticut audiences. "Truthfully, it's in all probability at least partially de jure. If you go back far enough, given unlimited time and resources, one might very well be able to prove that what we call de facto is absolutely de jure." Connecticut's segregation was "of fact," he opined, "but hardly ever is it not also de jure. It's just not been proven to be de jure. But no one's proven it's only or mostly de facto either."

Even Brittain's fans didn't always get it. After his talks, people of every sort urgently needed to compliment him on his principled stances. White suburbanites approached, shook his hand. "They said to me, 'We don't segregate our children in Connecticut. We don't even know how to do that.'" When he heard that familiar ring of Northern self-assurance, the old image of those wealthy white kids from Rowayton busing past a racially mixed junior high in Norwalk flashed into John Brittain's mind. His patience wore thin.

"Don't tell me anything about that," he'd told them. "I know all about that." In the months to come, he'd learn even more.

Discovery
1977–85

THE HIGH, CURVED CEILING at the Connecticut State Library was painted sky blue, with cumulus clouds. The library's genteel patrons — lawyers, legislative analysts, historians — were absorbed in documents and seldom looked up. John Brittain settled in at one of the library's long, dark wooden tables for an hour each week.

He unfolded maps. He measured distances from Hartford to Windsor, Hartford to West Hartford, Glastonbury to Hartford. He broke down census data to the block level. He tapped calculator buttons. For each tiny corner of the city, he penned answers to a list of queries: How many poor people? How many on welfare? How many with college degrees, jobs, cars? How many black, white, Hispanic? He went back through several decades of Hartford records. He did the same with the suburbs.

He charted the schools' racial changes. What he saw matched what had happened in other Northern cities. Government officials and scholars had issued warnings about segregation, even shaken shaming fingers. But over and over, John Brittain discovered, people in charge had barely responded.

In 1965, he found, the U.S. Civil Rights Commission had documented the "widespread existence" of racially segregated schools. Their report urged state action. The same year, the city had hired Harvard consultants who'd concluded that the intense racial and economic segregation in the region—which they were sure would worsen—diminished the "life opportunities" of minority kids. Tragedy could be avoided, the consultants had said, by redistricting students within the city and by state-funded voluntary transfers of minority children to suburban schools.

Officials had responded mildly in 1966. They'd developed a small program that would allow some Hartford students to attend suburban schools. The program, Project Concern, Brittain read, had been popular. Its waiting list by the 1970s had grown to several thousand kids. But there were no plans for expansion beyond a token 1,500 students—about 2.5 percent of Hartford's nearly 30,000 students.

In 1970, Brittain discovered, a group of local attorneys working for the local NAACP had filed a class-action lawsuit in federal district court on behalf of racial minority families in Hartford. The complaint, *Lumpkin v. Meskill,* had charged that the state maintained segregated schools in violation of the U.S. Constitution. Two years later, the City of Hartford itself had filed a similar complaint.

The first constitutional violation, according to *Lumpkin,* was that Connecticut—like most Northern and Midwestern states and unlike much of the post-*Brown* South—had established each town or city as a separate school district and required students to attend school where they lived. "Numerous" schools within Hartford, the lawyers had pointed out, had minority group enrollments "in excess of 90 percent." Soon, the lawyers contended, desegregating schools within Hartford's borders would be futile. A true remedy to segregation, Lumpkin asserted, would fold suburban communities into a regional desegregation plan, a configuration that had become common and no longer novel or controversial down south. Lawyers suggested starting with two contiguous municipalities: Windsor and West Hartford.

In 1973, with *Lumpkin* and Hartford's parallel complaint still unheard in court, Hartford's general counsel filed an amicus curiae (friend of the court) brief in the Detroit case, *Milliken v. Bradley,* before the U.S. Supreme Court. Detroit's conundrum, brought to light in *Milliken,* was almost like Hartford's—and matched trends in dozens of other American cities. Post–World War II white suburbanization had persisted through the 1960s and 1970s, leaving urban school districts with steadily expanding proportions of minority students. Two decades after *Brown,* the job of simply integrating urban schools was stymied, even in cases such as Detroit's, where intentional segregation had been proven. There weren't enough white students left in town to go around.

In response, a federal court in Detroit in 1973 had approved an interdistrict desegregation plan that included white children from adjacent suburbia. Hartford's general counsel had prophetically written, "The decision [*Milliken*] here will have an enduring and critical effect upon metropolitan areas in this country and will shape and structure the future relationships between city and suburb, between black and white, between poverty and wealth." The brief had continued, "State school officials have not merely acted to sanction and passively condone interdistrict segregation: rather, state boards have fostered, promoted and actively participated in the establishment of racially dual systems of public schools within the metropolitan areas of this nation."

John Brittain agreed with every word. But he knew what was coming.

In a 5-to-4 decision, the Court, with the votes of four Nixon appointees (and one Eisenhower appointee), ruled that absent a finding that suburbs had intentionally helped create the segregated patterns in the city, no federal court could force them to participate in desegregation. The Supreme Court's overriding decision in *Milliken* rendered the local case moot. The Hartford cases died.

The Court invoked the overriding virtue of "local control." The suburbs were sovereign. Urban schools, rapidly becoming segregated with all black and Latino and heavily poor students, were on their own. *Milliken* reversed the glory of *Brown* and crushed hopes for remedying Northern segregation and ended *Brown's* 20 useful years. In his *Milliken* dissent, Thurgood Marshall, the civil rights lawyer turned Supreme Court justice, called *Milliken* "a giant step backwards."

"Today's holding, I fear, is more a reflection of a perceived public mood that we have gone far enough in enforcing the Constitution's guarantee of equal justice than it is the product of neutral principles of law," Marshall wrote. "In the short run, it may seem to be the easier course to allow our great metropolitan areas to be divided up each into two cities—one white, the other black—but it is a course, I predict, our people will ultimately regret. I dissent."

JOHN BRITTAIN STUDIED Hartford's urban epic. It provoked his anger and stirred his imagination. He spread this history out on his desk in the state library. There sat piles of esoteric charts, obscure statistical tables, and horrifying commission reports expressed in dense, dull, depersonalized language. Each piece in isolation was hardly compelling. Still, he connected dots, built the story, not into a tragedy, but into a cliffhanger in need of resolution. Back in his office, he'd made up his mind; he picked up the phone, called lawyers from the Connecticut Civil Liberties Union, activists from the Puerto Rican Political Action Committee. He also called a local labor lawyer who'd worked on the *Lumpkin* case. Finally, he called the president of the local NAACP chapter.

He got everyone into a conference room. The group decided to start a "watch," old civil rights jargon for a systematic attentiveness that might lead a group toward action—a lawsuit, a boycott, a really big march. Concerned watchers collect data. Brittain and his watchers started going to public meetings. They took notes. They clipped newspaper articles, assembled files. They recruited others to join in. They networked phone numbers, traded business cards, made call lists. They conferred about what they'd gathered.

"Basically, we were watching the school system decline, become overburdened by the year," John Brittain recalled. "Documentation wasn't enough. You start to think about action. You keep your eyes open, manage to keep something alive."

Rebirth
The 1980s

JOHN BRITTAIN KEPT SPEAKING to crowds, kept clipping, kept watching. He labeled his files by author and by subject and dedicated a special beige cabinet to them in his UConn office.

But, he remembered, "there was a feeling that in terms of action, our watch was stuck—stuck in *Milliken* quicksand." He knew *Milliken* would lock regional school desegregation cases out of federal court. He'd always been an idealist, though never a fool.

Through most of the 1980s, as he taught classes, he referred now and again to notes he'd taken in his old mentor Herbert Reid's seminars. From his office window, he watched students pass, harnessed into heavy backpacks. He acceded to the realities of an academic's life and did his bit on departmental committees. He couldn't avoid the collected evidence rattling in the file cabinet in the corner of his office, though. He sustained a vague hope that he'd find a way to put the papers, the reconstructed history, all that damning evidence the watch had gathered, to good use.

Individual civil rights lawyers such as John Brittain, not attached to big and solvent organizations, could only lay low in the 1980s. The federal courts, affected by Ronald Reagan's judicial appointments, rendered more and more conservative decisions. (After eight years, Reagan would appoint 378 judges, including three Supreme Court justices.)

But lawyers at the NAACP Legal Defense Fund in New York, which

Thurgood Marshall had founded back in 1940, did have a tradition of soldiering through challenging terrain. In the 1980s, LDF's 40 or so lawyers and a handful of selected interns understood how unfashionable their causes had become. Theirs were all uphill struggles. They mapped the steep terrain.

"So we had to do something because, well, the alternative was to just sit there," said Jack Boger, who in the late 1980s had become director of LDF's new Poverty and Justice program, whose mission is to "enlarge the legal rights of the minority poor."

Boger, with a quick smile, slight build, wispy blond hair, and faint mustache, came off like a professorial Mr. Rogers. It was as easy to imagine him teaching first grade as arguing before the Supreme Court, which he'd actually done. By 1987, Boger was following his attraction to education law.

He'd recently led an exhausting journey as LDF's lead counsel in the U.S. Supreme Court case *McCleskey v. Kemp*, in which lawyers had argued that racial discrimination manifest in the criminal justice system rendered the death penalty unconstitutional. Boger represented Warren McCleskey, a black death-row inmate who'd been convicted of killing a police officer during an armed robbery in Georgia.

McCleskey's team of lawyers argued by assembling statistical models that controlled for nonracial factors such as the nature of the crime, criminals' past records, and the type of weapon used. The studies showed that black perpetrators with white victims were far more likely to get death sentences than were either white perpetrators with white victims or black perpetrators with black victims. Boger argued that the statistics proved that the laws weren't applied equally to all citizens — a violation of the 14th Amendment of the U.S. Constitution. But in a 5–4 decision, the Supreme Court disagreed. Justice Lewis Powell wrote that a decision for McCleskey, "taken to its logical conclusion, throws into serious question the principles that underlie the entire criminal justice system." That, of course, was exactly Boger's point and the same

kind of argument he'd go on to make about the public education system. Boger, unlike Justice Powell, imagined fixing the system. Prison
officials electrocuted Warren McCleskey in 1991.

"I was at the end of the process of unequal opportunity with *McCleskey,*
in the sense that my client was intelligent but had few opportunities
education-wise. And here he was on death row. His life could have
been different," Boger said. "I'd started to think more about how one
might affect factors at the *front* end. Looking toward education was a
way of trying to find an avenue of hope."

But for lawyers working on racial equality cases, avenues of hope
seemed hard to locate in those years. In 1984, Ronald Reagan had won
a landslide second term. In 1981, Congress had cut more than $25 bil-
lion in benefits, including child nutrition programs, food stamps, and
job training. They had cut $20 billion more during 1982 and 1983. In
1984, a congressional study revealed that welfare reductions had pushed
more than a half million people — mostly children — into poverty.

The civil rights community especially regretted Reagan's nomination
of William Rehnquist as chief justice of the Supreme Court. Rehnquist,
a Nixon appointee, had been a justice since 1972. Rehnquist's Senate
confirmation hearings in 1986 swept out a pile of dirt, some of which
had previously shown up 14 years earlier after Nixon's nomination.

Back in 1951, when the Supreme Court was hearing arguments in
the *Brown v. Board of Education* case, William Rehnquist, a first-year
law clerk for Supreme Court justice Robert Jackson, had written, "I
fully realize that it is an unpopular and unhumanitarian position for
which I have been excoriated by liberal colleagues, but I think *Plessy v.
Ferguson* was right and should be reaffirmed." *Newsweek* had published
the memo in 1971, during the earlier confirmation hearings. (*Plessy* had,
in 1896, affirmed the constitutionality of "separate but equal" facilities.
Brown, in 1954, had overturned it.) Rehnquist had then claimed the
words reflected Jackson's views, not his.

The memo resurfaced in 1986 during the new nomination hearings.

Rehnquist again claimed the memo reflected Jackson's opinions. Oddly, Justice Jackson, who'd been appointed by Franklin D. Roosevelt after having served as his solicitor general, had a long record as a pragmatic, middle-of-the-road Democrat. Jackson had grown up, gone to college, and been active in Democratic politics in New York. There'd never been even a whispered suggestion that he was a closet segregationist. In 1954, Jackson, sick in a Washington, D.C., hospital bed and undergoing treatment for a serious heart condition, had left against doctors' advice and voted formally with his eight fellow justices in the *Brown* case. He died five months after the *Brown* decision, in October 1954.

The memo was right in line with Rehnquist's politics, however. In 1964, Rehnquist, testifying as a citizen of Phoenix, Arizona, against an ordinance that would have banned segregation in public accommodations, said that integration would result in an "unwanted customer and the disliked proprietor . . . glowering at one another across the lunch counter. It is, I believe, impossible to justify the sacrifice of even a portion of our historic individual freedom for a purpose such as this." Rehnquist had been the only justice to dissent in a 1983 decision upholding a federal policy that denied tax-exempt status to Bob Jones University, which had banned interracial dating.

Nevertheless, in 1986, the U.S. Senate confirmed William Rehnquist's promotion to chief justice of the Supreme Court. The vote was 65–33.

At LDF, JACK BOGER opened his first Poverty and Justice program staff meeting the following year, 1987. He glanced at the handful of lawyers around the table and asked, "So, how are we going to solve the problem of poverty in America?" In any other place, the question might have sounded arrogant or naive.

"Oh, it was inspiring, really!" said Marianne Lado, Boger's intern from Berkeley's Boalt Law School. "He transferred the feeling of possibility to us."

Boger and the other lawyers took the mission seriously. They set about crafting a new docket of cases in housing, health care, and education that would challenge the limitations of existing law such as *Milliken*. The attorneys surveyed narrow, untrodden avenues of argumentation that reached beyond damaged tools such as *Brown*. Their ambitious Poverty and Justice initiative reflected the mission of LDF's director-counsel Julius Chambers. Chambers is known for his representation of black families in the 1971 Supreme Court case *Swann v. Charlotte-Mecklenburg Board of Education*, which authorized busing in school desegregation cases. *Swann* had inspired violent protest but by the mid-1970s had evolved into a brag for Charlotte, North Carolina, where press and politicians lauded "the city that made desegregation work."

During a 1984 campaign stop in Charlotte, Ronald Reagan had said busing "takes innocent children out of the neighborhood school and makes them pawns in a social experiment that nobody wants . . . and we've found out failed." But as the local writer Frye Gaillard reported, even the heavily Republican crowd had met Reagan's attempt to stir resentment with an uncomfortable silence.

In the late '80s, Julius Chambers had witnessed the spectacular civil rights gains of the 1960s slipping away. But there would be no clinging to past glory in LDF's work. He spurred his team on.

Marianne Lado recalled, "Julius wasn't shy about asking questions like, 'How can we make our vision a reality?' He made it very clear that at LDF we were guided by values, a vision. We were to stick to that even given the present environment. Julius pulled everyone together. Julius thought big. He gave all of us permission to do the same."

Soon after Marianne Lado had started her internship, Chambers summoned her to his office.

"The *Rodriguez* case," Lado remembered him declaring to her. Just that.

"I know *Rodriguez*," she'd answered.

Civil rights lawyers often mention the 1973 *San Antonio Independent*

School District v. Rodriguez and *Milliken* in tandem. The cases are different, but complete each other.

Rodriguez's plaintiffs were Mexican American parents from a poor section of San Antonio called Edgewood. Their case, built on *Brown's* precedent, challenged Texas's property-tax-based funding, which had allocated fewer education dollars to property-poor districts and more to rich ones. But the Supreme Court, asserting that education was not a "fundamental" right in the Constitution and invoking the importance of "local control," ruled that Texas's unequal school-funding scheme was constitutional.

Taken together, *Rodriguez* and *Milliken* read the U.S. Constitution as providing no guarantee of "equal" schools and no bar against racially separate ones either. In his *Milliken* dissent, Justice William O. Douglas argued that as a pair, these decisions represented a "dramatic retreat," even from the discarded 1896 *Plessy v. Ferguson* decision, which had said that blacks could be segregated so long as their facilities were "equal." *Brown* had shone up that notion as racist nonsense. Justice Douglas argued that, following *Rodriguez* and *Milliken*, minority kids might very well be better off with *Plessy*, when at least that "but equal" requirement was in there.

It had been 15 years since *Rodriguez*. But Chambers asked Lado to write him a memo imagining how *Rodriguez* could be overturned.

"There was something about Julius, the way he thought about things, that made you say, 'Well, certainly it's possible to develop a strategy that would overturn a Supreme Court decision . . .' If you look not far back in history, to the civil rights movement, Julius had been there. This had happened. The country had changed."

The research memo she delivered bolstered a 1987 article by Chambers, "Adequate Education for All: A Right, an Achievable Goal." The article had argued, among other things, that new "educational benchmarks" developed by states present an opportunity for lawyers to freshly define a right to a "minimally adequate education." Forty-eight state constitutions, Chambers wrote, "recognize a right to education." *Rodriguez* would stand, but the attorneys were on to something.

Lawyers at LDF had always been oriented toward federal court, yet faced with the "*Milliken* and *Rodriguez* quicksand," as John Brittain termed it, they wondered whether state courts might be the more promising venue. A parade of lawyers following *Rodriguez*, for example, had successfully sued in state courts to equalize lopsided property-tax-based school-funding formulas.

The trouble was, working on state-based litigation was piecework—a far less efficient battleground, sometimes fifty times the effort. A federal court ruling applied to a region or "circuit"; state court rulings applied only in that state. But after the negation of *Brown* by *Milliken* and by *Rodriguez*, repeated litigation across the nation was the costly, energy-sapping, inefficient, but still navigable road to wide-scale racial justice.

The school finance reform movement, while often successful in courts, had yielded incomplete remedies. Huge differences in per-pupil expenditures remained, even in states that had passed equalizing legislation. State legislatures often moved slowly or simply didn't comply. What's more, lawyers such as Jack Boger and Julius Chambers insisted, the larger difficulty with finance reform is that equality isn't achieved simply by giving the poor the same amount of money as the well-to-do. Urban schools, overwhelmed by huge numbers of poor children, in fact needed *more* money than their suburban counterparts.

And the lawyers also considered a collection of generally overlooked cases that had provided stepping-stones to *Brown*. Such cases, inspired by Howard University's Charles Hamilton Houston and argued successfully by Thurgood Marshall, had established that nonmonetary qualities abundant in predominantly white settings—prestige, power and social connection of alumni, and practiced interaction and argument with future colleagues—were lacking in segregated environments and therefore compounded segregation's inherent inequality.

The American Civil Liberties Union's associate legal director, Helen Hershkoff, and Chris Hansen, a staff attorney, filled a thick notebook with a copy of each state's constitution. Hansen, Hershkoff, and john powell (he doesn't capitalize his name), ACLU's legal director, scoured documents for specific phrases—"equal opportunity," "equal education," "adequate education," "equal protection"—for anything resembling a broken promise. The trio conferred with Jack Boger, threw ideas around, worked fast.

"There was a bit of a feeling of panic," john powell recalled. "There was a lot of fear about going down a new path. But if we didn't, we'd just have to watch everything get stripped away."

They talked it through and decided that Connecticut's constitution might offer potential ground for an end run around *Milliken* and *Rodriguez*. The lawyers imagined tackling the paired, intertwined problems of inadequate education and de facto segregation there. They'd found that Connecticut had established clear educational standards and had even been measuring progress toward them by means of the Connecticut Mastery Test. And boy, was it a segregated state.

"It was tiny . . . easy to manage," Boger recalled. "And it had a great precedent."

The precedent, in fact, was one of the nation's earliest school finance equity cases, *Horton v. Meskill,* which had been waged in Connecticut's state courts in the early '70s. It had been crafted primarily by a prominent local attorney, Wesley Horton, who at the time sat on the school board in the Hartford suburb of Canton. Horton had been shocked to learn of Connecticut's school-funding formula, which provided per-child $250 flat grants to every municipality. This, Horton told his fellow board members, obviously ensured unequal school spending. Districts with more taxable property would always have more funds to supplement the grant than property-poor ones. This boring detail about a per-pupil funding formula had immense practical consequences—huge district-by-district disparities in per-pupil spending. Horton had signed on his own little boy, Barnaby, as lead plaintiff in 1971.

Horton v. Meskill was about providing more money, not to poor children, but, rather, to property-poor districts. Canton is a white, economically mixed, though mostly middle-class, town. Since the state—not the local school districts—bore the constitutional obligation to provide public education, the state, Horton argued, was responsible for the funding disparities that had engendered unequal conditions. A proper reading of the state constitution, he believed, guaranteed equal educational opportunity. And in 1977, the Connecticut Supreme Court had ruled in Horton's favor, striking down the state's education-funding system.

Legal scholars all across America immediately understood that the decision was a big deal. In *Horton,* the court had established a new right to "equal educational opportunity." Years later, Boger and the other lawyers, meeting in New York, speculated that perhaps they could extend the legal principle established in *Horton* to other educational matters.

Another detail of the Connecticut Constitution encouraged them. Section 20 of Article 1 expressly prohibited "segregation or discrimination" on the basis of race or color. The phrasing had yet to be defined by a court. But with that clause thrown in, a path around *Milliken* looked passable.

JACK BOGER ASKED A new intern, a Yale Law School student named Nina Morais, to poke around the state for potential allies.

"All I wanted was for her to get a lay of the land," Boger recalled, "come back with names, phone numbers. The idea was she'd write up a memo." Memos were big at LDF. Memos charted the developing plan of action, detailed what was possible or not possible, where to stop and where to keep going.

John Brittain's name came up early. Nina Morais rode the train up from Yale to UConn Law School to see him. He shook her hand warmly and told her the story as he saw it. She'd struck gold. He offered strong theories. She took notes. He'd also collected useful names and phone numbers—plenty of them. He handed them over. Then he opened that well-ordered beige file cabinet. He pulled out documents and gave them to her.

Brittain didn't know what to expect afterward. Many students from many colleges and law schools had wandered into his office for help over the years. His memory of those earnest kids had blurred. And this Nina was so young, still in law school. But something about her made John Brittain deal with her more as a colleague than as a student.

"The way she asked about things and what she chose to write down. She was really engaged. She knew what she was doing. She was headed somewhere. This was not an academic exercise to her. It was a mission."

Nina Morais took the train home. She wrote up her memo and delivered it to Jack Boger. There were indeed possibilities, he decided. The LDF lawyers folded John Brittain into their plans and kept going.

Gift

1987

B Y THE SUMMER OF 1987, a legal team had defined itself. Boger and Brittain had both spoken often with Martha Stone and Phil Tegeler, the staff attorney at Connecticut Civil Liberties Union (CCLU), an ACLU affiliate. The two ACLU lawyers, Chris Hansen and Helen Hershkoff, signed on. LDF and ACLU budgeted some funding, and John Brittain donated his time and services and long-accumulating cache. Phil Tegeler and Marianne Lado, the youngest members of the team, emerged as the case's initial workhorses. The team usually gathered on the first floor of the Connecticut Civil Liberties Union's scruffy offices in Hartford.

The faded three-story brick-front CCLU building sits in the heart of the Puerto Rican Frog Hollow neighborhood, squeezed between tenements at the corner of Grand and Hungerford streets, a few blocks and a world away from the grand State Capitol. Along Hungerford, young men fix and polish old cars, drink beer; women socialize on stoops. Little kids scamper about. Old men push shopping carts of redeemable cans and bottles. In summer, salsa music, laughter of families, hoots of street football, and the hiss of skidding bicycle tires float in through the lawyers' open windows.

The CCLU office is a no-frills, cash-strapped operation. There are no couches, potted palms, or corporate niceties. The rug is worn and needs a shampoo. Rooms are drafty. The haphazard decor and drab

walls signal its heads-down way. The conference room on the first floor
is crammed with law books, lots of chairs.

Gathering there, the lawyers began by pondering whether it was
even plausible to address the educational inequalities between cities
and suburbs in Connecticut. A second big question soon came up: How
should lawyers involve members of a given community—the educators, parents, grassroots leaders? The thought of tackling such a case
excited John Brittain. Doubts still tugged; he remembers wondering,
"How can we be sure people even want us lawyers around?"

He'd already had enough informal chats with parents, teachers,
grassroots organizers, college students, and many sorts of citizens to
gauge their hearts. He sensed that many would be right there with him.
Still, ordinary people couldn't do much about "the structural problems,"
as Brittain termed the ghetto trap and the entrenched inequality of his
home state.

FOR A YEAR, before his alliance with Boger and LDF, Brittain
had spoken to people who might place segregation onto a few political
agendas. He'd even sent out formal invitations to politicians, community leaders, and education bigwigs to talk. He'd been especially eager
to reach out to the state's education commissioner, Gerald Tirozzi.

Gerry Tirozzi had grown up in a blue-collar Italian neighborhood
in New Haven. His father had dropped out of high school. Gerry was
first in his family to go to college; he began his career as a high school
science teacher, eventually becoming a principal in New Haven. He
was magnetic and talented, and after several years he became school
superintendent.

Leading one of the state's largest districts, Tirozzi found he had the
ears of state officials to whom he often complained about a law that, he
said, "I very strongly supported on principle" but "resented in practice."
The law required him to redraw attendance zones within New Haven
every few years to keep his increasingly black and Latino schools ra-

cially balanced. He'd complied, angered that the school superintendents in the rich, white suburbs ringing his city had no such obligations. In most cases, the towns had no races other than "white" to mix.

"I told them, 'Come to New Haven with me and stand on any rooftop and you'll see these white, rich communities two, three, five miles away that have no obligation,'" Tirozzi said. "In between the time that law was passed in the sixties and the time it was finally fully enacted, not until the eighties, it was already irrelevant for urban districts. We hardly had enough white kids left. I'd go up and people would tell me, in private, they appreciated my commitment. But nothing ever changed."

In 1986, Tirozzi opened a note inviting him to come chat with John Brittain. He marked the date on his calendar and anticipated it with curiosity. They met at a neutral location, the offices of a local foundation. Tirozzi uncharacteristically asked few questions. He recalled feeling that he'd have felt rude, unnecessarily adversarial, if he had inquired exactly who John Brittain would sue and for what and when.

"Some of that was just John—this respect people had. He'd call people at the State Department of Education. He's a civil rights lawyer! And he's calling you up, wanting to ask you questions? But people say, 'Oh, sure, John. Yes. When's convenient for you?' And then there was another thing. Most people go into education because they have a moral commitment." An education bureaucrat's daily grind was not the stuff of righteousness, Tirozzi said, but of forms, monitoring, placating, protecting turf. "But John could remind people of why they went into this business in the first place. He moved people."

ABOUT A YEAR LATER, around Christmas, 1987, only months after the lawyers had begun meeting, John Brittain received an unexpected gift.

Each January, under its commissioner's direction, the State Department of Education filed a report. For many years it had been perfunctory and carried the same dry title: *A Report on Racial/Ethnic Equity and Desegregation in Connecticut's Public Schools*.

But this year, the report made the front page of the *Hartford Courant*. A mysterious source had leaked it two weeks early, just before the Christmas holiday, to the *Courant's* education writer, Robert Frahm. For the first time in the report's history, this one actually advanced a position.

"The premise underlying this report . . . is that segregation is educationally, morally and legally wrong," the new report began. "A trend is developing in Connecticut's public schools that is causing, according to the dictionary definition of segregation, the 'isolation of the races' with 'divided educational facilities.'"

The report posited "two Connecticuts." One Connecticut, the report maintained, was affluent, white, and fully participating in the state's economic and educational opportunities. The other was poor, black or Latino, and shut out.

The most controversial pairing of words came midway through. Under the subtitle "Recommendation One," the report read, "That the state, through administrative and legislative means, endorse the concept of 'collective responsibility' for desegregating the public schools of Connecticut." The report recommended dividing the state into several parts. In each, officials and citizens would draw up plans to reduce racial isolation.

The document—which the press quickly labeled "the Tirozzi report"— ignited indignation. Philip Robertson, a Republican state legislator from suburban Cheshire, called for Tirozzi's resignation.

"This is a preposterous plan designed by people living in an ivory tower," he told the *Hartford Courant*.

Another Republican, Thomas Scott of suburban Milford, wrote to the Democratic governor, William O'Neill, saying Tirozzi was "out of control . . . it is time for you to rein him in."

Even the cochairman of the legislature's Education Committee, a West

Hartford Democrat, Kevin Sullivan, called Tirozzi "cavalier." Sullivan didn't think much of the report either, describing it as "an example of how not to achieve what you want to achieve." Gerry Tirozzi, most likely with good intentions, had been impolitic.

"But see? I had been talking about this problem since 1977. People might ask why the chairman of the Education Committee wasn't looking at this issue, why, after watching segregation grow and grow, there's not even a discussion," Tirozzi told me years later. "When's a good time to bring this up? What's a politically acceptable method for bringing it up?"

In response to Tirozzi's report, the Connecticut Education Association, the Christian Conference of Connecticut, and the Connecticut Federation of School Administrators called for action on school integration.

Hartford's contingent of state legislators expressed thanks. "The school systems are segregated," said Frank Barrows, a state senator. "I would definitely support Tirozzi." Taking on segregation, Barrows said, "it's like trying to take on a big, big monster."

The morning of the above-the-fold, page one scoop, John Brittain spread out the *Courant* in his office at UConn and picked up the phone.

"Good news," he told his new lawyer colleagues. "In the newspaper. We have very good news this morning."

Mandate
1988

AFTER THE HOLIDAYS, in January, it looked as if Gerry Tirozzi might have sacrificed his career by forcing segregation and inequality onto the political agenda. Segregation had become an issue. "It was convenient for us," John Brittain said. "It was a spark, it felt like, to start our fire."

The Tirozzi report renewed debate among black and Latino activists and educators. The lawyers understood they had a rare and probably brief opportunity to build upon the momentum. But they also knew that they should proceed cautiously.

It "just didn't feel right," Jack Boger said, "to come into a place as complex as Connecticut, into a community with which I, personally, had little experience and say, 'Hello. Here's a lawsuit to desegregate your schools.'"

Brittain had agreed: "Even if we knew there had been documented harm over decades, we had a lot of listening and learning to do, consciousness raising."

To further that mission, they created a rather nonlawyerly umbrella nonprofit called the Connecticut Coalition for Educational Equity. They hoped it would mobilize citizens and educate lawyers and residents. And it would also allow them to find plaintiffs for their cases. Commercial lawyers are prohibited from such solicitation, but nonprofits are not.

Brittain and his colleagues decided to gather 100 or so educators, longtime activists, lawmakers, ministers, priests, and rabbis together in an auditorium and lead a discussion about the Tirozzi report. John Brittain would follow with a quick history of the construction, maintenance, and continuing harm of segregation. Someone would outline the achievement disparities between the rich and the poor. Then they'd lay out the legal options.

"What we were looking for, really, was the community's blessing," Brittain said. "Were we going to get a green light or a red light? We were there humbly to offer our services and to say, 'We may be able to help here. Do you want our help?'"

Nina Morais, the LDF intern who'd scoped out and identified state leaders, assembled the invitation list and mailed announcements of a Saturday morning meeting in early January. Brittain booked the UConn Law School auditorium.

On Thursday night—two days before the meeting—snow began to fall. Superintendents declared snow days; government offices opened late, if at all. UConn Law School stayed closed up tight. Plows opened trenchlike paths between buildings. The storm would not let up.

"It looked like it might wipe out the meeting—that all that momentum from Tirozzi was going to be lost," Brittain said. "But we decided to stake our chances on New England hardiness."

Come Saturday morning, Brittain drove his Peugeot the 10 minutes from Blue Hills to the law school in the West End. Driving down Ridgefield Street, across to Woodland and onto Asylum, he saw fewer cars than usual. The main streets were snowy, but it was sunny. From his car window he saw residents knee-high in snow, at curbs, in driveways, shoveling out.

He chose to act as if it were a normal morning. He went to his office, hung his coat, looked out the window at snow piled high. Would people glance out their windows and decide that shoveling out or sledding with the kids beat adding their two cents at some meeting about abstract ideals?

A few minutes before starting time, Brittain gathered his papers and walked to the auditorium. The refreshments were there. The place was empty. Just him, coffee urns, little sugar packets, milk, cream, plastic stirrers, and pastry.

At 9 a.m., the room was still empty. A few minutes after, a handful of people, dusty with snow, slush on their boots, stomped in. At 9:15, the auditorium held a small crowd, not even a quarter of the invitation list. Nina Morais came. Phil Tegeler and Martha Stone from CCLU arrived. And Ed Vargas, from the Puerto Rican Political Action Committee, had sauntered in. Hernan LaFontaine, the city's school superintendent, showed up. These were the die-hard allies. Diehards do not a movement make.

"Maybe it's just not there anymore," John Brittain permitted himself to wonder. "Maybe civil rights *is* dead."

Brittain prepared himself for disappointment. Outwardly he remained expectant. "I think we'll start a little late today on account of the snow," he announced. "We'll get going soon enough."

He glanced at the door, at his watch, and back at the door. At about 9:20, he exhaled. A steady stream of people, in boots and heavy coats, flowed in through the auditorium doors as if they'd all arrived on the same bus. He counted 20. Then 40. At 60, John Brittain stopped counting and smiled.

The crowd shook hands, hugged, laughed. John Brittain loved that sound of laughter. That hum of good feeling, he'd long found, was a predictor of a strong, long alliance. His optimism returned.

"Nothing's dead," he thought, watching the hearty crowd fill up on pastry, charge up on caffeine. "Nothing. It's all still there, waiting to be tapped."

The lawyers had invited Charles "Chuck" Willie to give the keynote talk. Willie was a Harvard professor and prolific sociologist. And he could also preach a hell of a sermon. That day, he combined talents.

"I wanted to get people going, and it wasn't hard," Willie recalled years later. "There were the intellectual issues, the legal issues. And then there were the moral issues. That meeting was about all of these things."

Feet stomped, people cheered, clapped, chanted. The lawyers asked the crowd: Should we pursue legal action?

"It was a resounding yes," Brittain recalled. "No hesitation there."

For Brittain, the meeting brought back memories. The sense of outrage and determination and the raucous, positive mood reminded him of the old civil rights rallies back in the South.

"People in the North were conditioned to living separately," he said. Inequality "was something everyone knew about. But once we got people talking, right under the surface was a feeling that we could do better, that it didn't have to be this way."

In Brittain's mind, the lawyers had received a mandate from the varied group of influential Connecticut educators, religious leaders, parents, and labor leaders. Come Monday the team would have to leave behind the inspiring speeches and get back to the less glorious work for which they'd been trained. Moral conviction had forced these lawyers to the underpaid margins of their profession, but good hearts and righteousness didn't win in court.

They hadn't even formulated a clear legal theory, much less a lawsuit, yet. Nevertheless they felt supported in starting to build both. The lawyers suspected that this could be a towering case, even though federal Supreme Court decisions had forced it down onto the lesser stage of Connecticut's state courts. Going toward the next stage, Brittain felt that all of them would be carrying precious cargo.

Finding Good Mommies
1988

EXHILIRATED BY THE community meeting in January, the lawyers still weren't quite sure an accounting of disparities or gaps in achievement and opportunity between city and suburb would be persuasive in court. They began to question whether they could, for example, plausibly lay the huge suburban and urban achievement differences at the feet of the state. Doubts remained about whether they could argue that the inequalities, though starkly manifest in test scores, proved state wrongdoing. They struggled with the question of how to make vivid the harms of segregation and concentrated poverty.

Marianne Lado, the rising-star LDF intern, had become a rising-star LDF staff lawyer and the youngest member of the new legal team. She worked the front lines in the community, talking with activists, parents, and educators. Her complex job changed daily. She had to shore up support for the cause within the community and at the same time get information from ordinary people "on the ground," as she put it, about how they perceived the quality and problems of their children's schooling. The information would shape the legal case. The most articulate, sympathetic, compelling interviewees could end up as trial witnesses.

Lado relished her part in developing the new case, in part because of childhood memories. She'd grown up in two places—the affluent suburb of Brighton, outside Rochester, New York, and the superwealthy

Connecticut suburb Westport, where John Brittain's parents had been domestic servants. Westport sat near, but apart from, the poor, heavily black and Latino city of Bridgeport. Lado grew up feeling uneasy about the contrasts between her Connecticut hometown and the big city around the bend.

"In physics class we got on the subject of SAT scores. And this one student was arguing that the high SAT scores in Westport prove people in Westport are smarter than people in Bridgeport. But it was more than that. He was saying that we lived in Westport because our parents are smarter and that people in Bridgeport aren't as smart and that's why they are where they are. As if this were a kind of natural selection. I'd laughed because I thought he was joking, making fun of that point of view. But he was serious. I was constantly amazed by the ease with which that logic thrived in that environment. It sounds naive now, but I remember being shocked—after the sixties and Martin Luther King—that people my age would think like that. It always stuck with me."

One interview stuck with Lado too. Early in 1988, she had listened to a middle-aged African American woman, Marge Little, tell her story. In the 1970s, Little told Lado, she and her husband, a Hartford police officer, had been raising their family in the vast housing project Stowe Village, in Northeast. Little had "always wanted the best offered" for her children and was "very active" in the Parent-Teacher Association in the city. Her children had been offered places in the state's small, voluntary school desegregation program, Project Concern, which arranged for black children to attend public schools in predominantly white suburbs. She'd worried that her children would face too much discrimination "out there," and so she'd quite proudly kept them in Hartford, near home. Her oldest boy had steadily earned good grades since elementary school. The year her son began ninth grade at Weaver High School, Little took a new job as a classroom aide in the nearby suburb of South Windsor. On the first day of school, the elementary school principal assigned Little to a remedial fifth-grade reading class. The teacher asked Little to hand out reading textbooks. Little picked up the first small pile of books, looked at the cover, and quietly began to cry. The remedial fifth-grade text in South Windsor was the same one her son was using in ninth grade at Weaver.

The next day, Little put all her children back on the Project Concern waiting list. They all finished their educations in the suburbs. Project Concern, Little had told Lado, "gives children higher aspirations. It's not about sitting next to a white person . . . It shows the kids that they don't have to live in Stowe Village their whole lives. Children also learn how to deal with other people." Little's son who'd had the fifth-grade text went through Project Concern, graduated from college, and was working toward a master's degree.

Soon afterward, in the mid-1970s, Little said, black parents with children in Project Concern started getting together with parents in Hartford to compare urban and suburban curricula. Project Concern's waiting list grew. The two sets of allied parents took to attending local Hartford Board of Education meetings together. Hartford parents asked board members tough questions. The parents wanted to know why the suburban kids were doing more advanced work, reading tougher books, taking more field trips, learning richer material. Why were the schools safer there? Why were special services, like help in reading, easier to get?

"The board didn't want to hear it," Little told Lado, "but it's the truth."

That same day, Lado talked with Project Concern's director, Mary Carroll, a white, socially concerned, middle-aged Catholic woman who'd overseen the program since its conception in 1966. Carroll told Lado that, sadly, in part because of these confrontations between black parents and the Board of Education, Project Concern had quickly become unpopular among the city's education administrators, who, rather inconveniently, oversaw Carroll and her staff. The black parents, Carroll said, decided it might be best if they stopped "downgrading" the city schools in their discussions about Project Concern. That may have calmed local politicians, but it also meant that gaping—and, Mary Carroll suspected, "continually widening"—inequalities between urban and suburban schools would have no route onto the city school board's agenda, or any agenda anywhere at all.

Mary Carroll resignedly saw that dropping the particular issue of "urban-suburban inequities" was a sacrifice she and the parents had little choice but to make for the survival of her program. Now, more than a decade later, Mary Carroll saw in young Marianne Lado and the new legal effort she'd mentioned a means to revive a "central discussion" that she'd had to forsake.

After more than 60 interviews, Lado felt that the "way people think about racially integrated schools" was too "fine-grained and complex" to be broken down into for-and-against talk show sound-bite categories. Lado heard from many African Americans, for example, who resented the implication that "black children needed white children to learn." But once she got past that surface-level feeling of insult, "their problem wasn't with racial integration itself at all," but "their fear that came from a knowledge that there had been white resistance to integration and that whites hadn't tried to make integration work the way it was supposed to."

After her interviews, she sensed "no naive optimism" about the miracles of integration, but, within Greater Hartford, "far, far more anger and resentment over the fact of separation." "People here," Lado reported to her fellow lawyers in late 1988, "are terribly angry about the fact that things break down along racial lines and that they are forced to go to school where they live. People did not think that the racial lines happened by accident. Not one person told me that the race and class lines should just stay in place, that things were working out well under the current system. That was not an acceptable idea to anyone."

• • •

SEGREGATION WAS NOT an acceptable idea to a woman named Elizabeth Horton Sheff, a local nurse and mother of two, who'd grown up in Hartford's sprawling Charter Oak housing project. During Sheff's childhood in the '6os, the project had been racially mixed, scruffy but safe. That was difficult to recall in 1988. By that time, Charter Oak meant drugs, violence, and squalid conditions. (The city finally razed it in 1996.) Sheff's basically positive experiences with racial integration there in Charter Oak had shaped her worldview, which accommodated, she said, "faith in humanity" and the "transformative power" of "diversity and empathy."

Sheff discussed her personal philosophy often and articulately with neighbors in her housing project, Westbrook Village, which spread neatly and depressingly in the city's northwestern section. She was an activist, a Peace and Justice Minister at the United Church of Christ. A neighbor in Westbrook Village came to Sheff and invited her to a community meeting to be held at a local church. The neighbor had wanted to go herself but knew that lawyers involved with the Connecticut Coalition for Educational Equity would be comparing resources and performance of urban and suburban districts. She had children participating in Project Concern and worried that her involvement in the meeting might cause her children to be singled out.

And so Elizabeth Sheff came at 7 p.m. on a winter weeknight in 1988, tired after a day's work, to a meeting room in Hartford's Horace Bushnell Church. She sat on a metal foldout chair, feeling testy. Before leaving home, she'd checked her son Milo's third-grade homework. Her older daughter, Tanya, in high school, would make dinner. But there hadn't been time to tidy up or catch up on some church-related work she'd wanted to do. Perhaps coming out was a mistake, she'd thought.

Up front some well-dressed gentleman greeted the crowd and started rattling off numbers and statistics and throwing charts onto an overhead projector. Right then, right there, they had her. They had her outrage, her protective maternal instinct, and, she said, her "faith." To Jack

Boger, John Brittain, Phil Tegeler, Martha Stone, and the other lawyers, the presentation had become routine, a dog and pony show they'd given in church basements, living rooms, school auditoriums. In each place, they'd lay out the extent of both racial segregation in the state and the achievement gap between cities and suburbs. To Sheff, the analysis helped articulate a central problem in her universe.

Up went maps. "Well, there were little areas all colored in or not. And if it was colored in a certain shade, it meant you had twenty percent or so minority kids in your schools. But most of the suburbs, those weren't colored in," Sheff recalled. "They were white, which was the appropriate color for them."

Nearly 91 percent of Hartford's students, Sheff learned that night, were members of minority groups, compared to less than 4 percent in Avon, 3 percent in nearby Canton, 4 percent in Suffield, 6 percent in Simsbury, and 5 percent in Glastonbury. Sheff knew the region was segregated. She hadn't known all these extreme numbers. The lawyers continued: About 48 percent of Hartford's kids' families were poor, compared with 2 percent in West Hartford, 1.5 percent in Glastonbury. That was the shape of Northern segregation.

Sheff felt bewildered by the lawyers' dispassionate manner. They revealed scandalous statistics, but did so in such an ordered, unemotional way. "Where's all the outrage?" she wondered. "I figured they are lawyers and it's not their job to get up there and rabble-rouse . . . But these numbers!"

In 1988, Brittain told the crowd, 70 percent of Hartford's fourth graders scored below even the lowest, "remedial" level in reading. By comparison, just 19 percent of children in West Hartford, 9 percent in nearby Avon, and 9 percent in Simsbury did as poorly. In math, 57 percent of Hartford's eighth graders scored below the remedial level, while 8 percent in West Hartford, 3 percent in Avon, and 5 percent in Simsbury did that poorly.

But there was a possibility, Sheff heard the lawyers say that night, that they could change things. The state, John Brittain told the crowd, had an obligation to provide equal educational opportunity because of that old case, *Horton v. Meskill,* which, oh, yes, Elizabeth Sheff recalled. Even though many factors affected a student's performance, lawyers wanted to go to court and argue that the segregation of minority children (among other harms) overwhelmed schools with the problems of concentrated poverty and thus exacerbated the unconstitutional condition of unequal educational opportunity. Just looking at the huge gap in test scores, the lawyers said, led either to the conclusion that Hartford students had a congenital inability to learn—which the lawyers, of course, did not believe—or that the education they got was flat-out inadequate.

The lawyers said they were looking for strong, committed mothers and fathers to sign on as official plaintiffs in a future lawsuit. The case was bound to be controversial, Brittain warned. Standing for it, he cautioned, wasn't for the faint of heart.

Before she headed home to Milo and Tanya back in Westbrook Village, Sheff walked up to Brittain and Boger. She caught Boger's eye. "I'm with you," she told him. She scribbled her name and number on a scrap of paper, and he smiled, thanked her, and took it.

Sheff got home around nine. Milo asked where she'd been.

"Baby, I went to this meeting of some good people trying to improve things for the students in Hartford," she remembered telling him. "There might be more meetings like it. Maybe next time you can come along."

Elizabeth Sheff suspected that Milo sensed where she was heading. When he was six, he'd marched against South Africa's apartheid right alongside his mother. Milo had been to United Church of Christ meetings and had heard his mother complain and explain about "income gaps." He'd held his own candle at a vigil for AIDS victims.

"He got this wise little, proud smile on his cute face and he said, 'Sure, Mom.'"

One weeknight, not long after, she got a call at home.

"It was the lawyer. That one with the nice clothes, is how I remembered him. He and Jack Boger. They wanted to talk." Hanging up, Elizabeth Sheff steadied herself and thought, "Okay. Okay. Get ready. Because here we go now. Here we go!"

"SHE WAS PERFECT," Brittain recalled thinking upon meeting Elizabeth Sheff. Brittain and Boger also soon met Milo. "He was, for his age, articulate," Brittain remembered. "And you couldn't help but notice, just this handsome kid, like a little angel."

She knew that this case would win her nothing tangible for Milo. Elizabeth Sheff signed herself and her son up as lead plaintiffs. The lawyers that first day told her this would be a long-running case. Perhaps in a decade, a remedy might come through. In the meantime, she'd have work to do. She'd have to speak from church pulpits, at high schools across the state, to professors and activists, inform them about the case, and ask for support.

"That's okay by me," Sheff remembered telling Brittain and Boger. "I understand what you are saying and I'm not in this struggle for myself."

Elizabeth Sheff had finished high school in Hartford. But she'd never finished college. Still, Brittain sensed that she'd teach the lawyers a thing or two. They all met often, planning next moves. She crystallized complexities. She pointed out that while suburbanites used the city for jobs, hospitals, the Atheneum, they gave nothing in return. She went on about the millions the state spent ("our tax dollars, ladies and gentlemen") building segregated, posh, exclusive suburban schools that offered "advanced placement courses the city didn't." Elizabeth Horton Sheff hit the moral center when she spoke out.

"We listened to her," Brittain said. "And we suddenly felt lucky."

Logic
1988–89

THE LEGAL TEAM got lucky again that year. Wes Horton, the locally famous architect of *Horton v. Meskill,* wanted to have a part in the new equity case taking shape around the corner from his law office. In 1988, Horton ran a lucrative private practice. For fun he taught a Monday night class on the Connecticut Constitution at UConn—where Brittain also taught. At UConn one afternoon, Horton approached Brittain and Martha Stone of the local ACLU affiliate and asked about the case. It was so early on that it had yet to acquire a name or a definitive central argument.

"Hey, look, if you think I can help out, call me. Count me in," Horton said. Wes Horton didn't then and wouldn't ever call himself a civil rights lawyer. He didn't style himself a self-sacrificing do-gooder, although his *Horton v. Meskill* had expanded educational opportunity and educational policy more than any other state-level legal case in Connecticut. He drove a silver BMW convertible, kept private about his politics, which (he told me) certainly should not be characterized as "liberal." He'd represented the National Rifle Association. He is white, a native of suburban Connecticut with edge-of-working-class roots, stands about six foot two, and bears a mild resemblance to the former British prime minister John Major. Still, as a school board member in suburban Canton, he had lobbied to bring Project Concern to town and won. He and his wife, Chloe, a Hartford schoolteacher, had gone against the flow in the 1970s suburban boom. They'd moved from Canton into Hartford. They'd sent their kids to the city schools.

Brittain and Martha Stone jumped at Wes Horton's offer to help. He was the undisputed expert on the state's constitution. (At the time, he was writing a book on it.) Adding him to the team was a major coup. Like Brittain, Horton donated his time to the case. He too was a tenacious overpreparer, morally certain, and a little obsessive.

IN SPRING OF 1989, a crisp 17-page legal complaint emerged from the often tortuous group process. After joining them, Horton had pressed the group to simplify its complaint. It would be most effective, he said, merely to point to Article 1, Section 20, in the state constitution. They could quickly and painlessly argue that (a) the constitution prohibits de facto segregation and (b) there was indeed de facto segregation in the schools.

It was spare, elegant, and creative. But the civil rights lawyers on the team wanted to do more. They'd gotten together essentially to find a way around *Milliken,* not merely for kids in Connecticut, but for the entire country. To Brittain this was a last-chance case, potentially the only legal wedge left that could open up mainstream opportunity for children schooled and housed a world apart.

And so the lawsuit, as finally filed in Hartford Superior Court in April 1989, combined Horton's simple approach with a more ambitious civil rights analysis. The case, *Milo Sheff, et al., v. William O'Neill,* named the Connecticut governor, William O'Neill, Gerald Tirozzi, and several other state honchos as defendants. Officially there were 19 plaintiffs, including black and Latino Hartford families and even some white families from the suburbs. The lawyers, though concerned principally with poor, minority children, had included the white plaintiffs to represent an argument they believed to be true, although at the time, it hadn't yet been validated by research—that racial isolation deprived white kids too, by failing to prepare them for an increasingly diverse society.

"The defendants have recognized the lasting harm inflicted on poor and minority students by the maintenance of isolated urban school districts," the complaint began. "Yet . . . the defendants have failed to act effectively to provide equal educational opportunity to plaintiffs and other Hartford schoolchildren . . ."

"Equal educational opportunity," the complaint continued, "is not a matter of sovereign grace, to be given or withheld at the discretion of the Legislative or the Executive branch. Under Connecticut's Constitution, it is a solemn pledge, a covenant renewed in every generation between the people of the State and their children."

Sheff's claims were simple and direct. One: Segregation *itself* rendered education unequal. Two: Through this segregation, the defendants discriminated against the plaintiffs. Three: Hartford's school system, because of concentrated poverty (racial segregation's twin) and overburdened schools, failed, as recent tests scores showed, to provide a minimally adequate education to students.

At their most optimistic moments, Brittain and his colleagues believed their case might breathe new life into *Brown* and travel across the nation. There were a hell of a lot of Hartfords out there. The same story line applied to schools in dozens of metro areas: Detroit; Newark, Trenton, and Camden in New Jersey; Rochester, New York; Gary, Indiana; Chicago; Providence, Rhode Island; Boston; Miami; Philadelphia; Baltimore; St. Louis; and Minneapolis—just to name a few.

They presented it by hand to the court. And they waited to be heard—for three and a half years.

PART FOUR

Trials

Once there, Joe tried the door, but it was locked.

"Stand back everyone," he ordered. "I'm going to try something."

He took a few steps back, raised his leg, and slammed at the door with the bottom of his foot. The door moved a little but didn't open. Gritting his teeth, he threw his leg out in another tremendous kick.

This time the door flew open.

—Franklin W. Dixon, *The Smoke Screen Mystery,*
the Hardy Boys Mystery Stories

Simile

Jeremy Otero was six months old when the *Sheff* case finally commenced in late December 1992. His family had just been burned out by the Frog Hollow pager-shop arson. Jeremy's mother, Aunt Nina recalled, was barely "making it through the day" caring for two little boys.

Over the course of eight weeks in the courtroom, the lawyers hoped to improve the educational prospects of Hartford kids like Jeremy as well as the tens of thousands like him they'd never meet and the hundreds of thousands not yet born.

The morning of the trial's opening, John Brittain put on his nicest blue lawyer suit and a crisp white shirt and drove to Wes Horton's office. They walked in together, as they'd planned, team cocaptains.

The mill of justice turns slowly. But *Sheff* had been delayed for a particularly long while. State's lawyers had twice tried to block it right after the case was filed. They'd argued that the segregation, such as it was, had not been created intentionally and thus the state should not be held liable. The judge in the case, Harry Hammer, had ruled that the plaintiffs should at least be heard.

It was late December. Gray snow lay around the courthouse. Elizabeth Sheff led an impromptu prayer vigil. Supporters sang "We Shall Overcome." Reporters surrounded them. John Brittain and Wes Horton convened a spirited press conference. In between press interviews, the case's articulate, attractive, now-adolescent symbol, Milo Sheff, whipped snowballs at his buddies. Walking into the courtroom, John Brittain laughed to himself about the setting. Ordinarily a case from Hartford merited a city courtroom. But a scheduling conflict had pushed *Sheff* into a suburban courthouse out in West Hartford. The legal team was trying to crack open access to these very suburbs. John Brittain decided it was an omen—he was partway there, waging battle on West Hartford's elegant turf.

THE COURTROOM WAS STERILE, painted beige and faded yellow. A crude green garbage bag lined a metal trash barrel. The heat malfunctioned, making the room swelteringly hot. Marshals opened windows, and winter air mediated the climate. Then the room cooled too much. The marshals shut the windows.

The lawyers settled behind their respective tables. At the plaintiffs' table sat John Brittain, Wes Horton, Martha Stone, Phil Tegeler, Marianne Lado, Chris Hansen from the ACLU, and an LDF lawyer, Ron Ellis, who'd stepped in when Jack Boger moved away to teach civil rights law at the University of North Carolina. The assistant attorneys general for the state, John Whelan and Martha Watts, sat at the other table, whispering and moving papers around.

"All rise," the uniformed court officer snapped. Judge Harry Hammer clambered up into his chair. In his late 60s, he wore big eyeglasses and, through eight weeks, would rarely show fatigue and always seemed attentive.

Wes Horton began, efficiently outlining the legal claims. He sounded authoritative, smiled ebulliently.

Then it was John Brittain's show.

"May it please this Court." He bowed his head.

From the podium, his voice was startling, jolting.

"This is a case of a dream deferred," he said, starting right off with a quote from the black poet Langston Hughes. "What happens to a dream deferred? Does it dry up like a raisin in the sun . . ."

It was John Brittain's last chance, before the numbers, the heavy reports, the charts, analyses of variance, and debates over the significance of statistical significance. Soon the clear moral center would submerge as a river of necessary details flowed by. If not tomorrow, then soon, John Brittain knew, this packed courtroom would empty. Only the lawyers, the judge, and a *Hartford Courant* reporter would stick it out. On days she could free herself from work, Elizabeth Sheff would come. He suspected that on some days, she'd be sitting on those hard wooden benches alone.

"Nineteen children . . . filed this lawsuit three and a half years ago, because the school district boundary lines have created a minority enclave of disadvantage in virtually every measurable category of education," he said, resolute, preacherly. "Black school lands in the city of Hartford and white school lands in the surrounding suburbs is to education what the South African Bantustans or homelands are to South African apartheid."

"The Hartford School District reached this condition through twenty-seven years of neglect by state defendants," John Brittain said, voice rising. "There have been so many studies in this state that you could stack them as high as this podium . . . The state defendants have studied the educational disparities to death. Their empty promises . . . merely perpetuate the dual system of education."

The opening went well. John Brittain realized that was the easy part.

JOHN WHELAN LED for the state. Whelan, tall, slow-moving, with a seemingly accommodating demeanor, had parted brown hair and a bushy mustache that drooped like a giant frown.

"There is no past or present segregation to undo," Whelan said matter-of-factly. "The Court will have no evidence of wrongdoing on the part of the state."

As the state hadn't "caused" segregation, Whelan argued, there was no "segregation." According to the state's theory, any so-called segregation that did exist wasn't of the unconstitutional sort. For segregation to be unconstitutional, Whelan argued, state officials would have had to knowingly and willfully construct it in the first place (as state officials had in the old South). What's more, Whelan argued, whatever problems existed in city schools were caused by the poverty of individual families, which the state couldn't cure.

Whelan's presentation was cogent and efficient. Even Wes Horton, whose opening role was to lay out straightforward, unemotional legal claims, barely muted his excitement. John Brittain's passion had turned his argumentation into a morality play.

Whelan, by comparison, seemed only to have recited his lines.

JOHN BRITTAIN CALLED his first witness. David Carter, the tall, commanding black president of Eastern Connecticut State University, walked briskly through the thigh-high swinging door that separated spectators from lawyers. He settled into the witness box, below and to Judge Hammer's right.

After the Tirozzi report hoopla and *Sheff*'s filing in 1989, the state's governor at the time, William O'Neill, had responded by convening another commission to develop recommendations for reducing racial isolation in the schools. O'Neill had appointed David Carter cochairman.

"I can say to you, at the end of seventeen months, you had a group of one mind, who felt strongly that something needed to be done in the State of Connecticut," Carter testified.

But the report had gathered dust.

"If the question is, am I pleased with the progress that's been made to date, the answer is no," Carter declared.

Right there at the start, Assistant Attorney General John Whelan's insistence that the state was "dealing" with racial isolation was countered by the very man the state had put in charge of its most recent official effort to assess and address the problem.

"There's one thing called change and there's another thing called *dynamic gradualism,* where you have much motion but no movement, and I think that's what we've had," Carter wryly told the court.

Brittain felt grand when he heard Carter's apt phrase "dynamic gradualism," which struck at the heart of the state's defense.

"So, is it your belief that, without a court order, the recommendations that are contained in the Governor's Commission Report will not be effectively implemented?" John Brittain asked witness number one.

"I have no reason to believe otherwise at this point. And, believe me, I would like to believe. But based on the lack of action to date," Carter said, "I can't."

THE LONGTIME PRINCIPAL of Hartford's Betances Elementary School, Edna Negron, testified next. Brittain asked her to describe her school.

"This year I think we have approximately four white children in the school," she said.

"Four white children out of approximately 580?" John Brittain asked again. He appeared shocked, eyes widening, pausing midbreath for her response.

She had plenty to complain about. Space was limited. She'd reluctantly let her reading specialists go after recent budget cuts. She'd had to open her school library with 4,000 books, even though a school that size usually had 16,000. She'd tried to launch a health clinic to treat asthma, depression, and festering dental problems that took kids away from instructional time.

"I've had three attempted suicides in the last three years," Negron told the court. Then she added, "Two of them were third graders . . . You know, I really don't believe that people understand the depth of deprivation of our children."

Brittain let the silence hang for a few seconds.

Negron swallowed hard.

"I'm sorry," she said. "Someone said to me this morning, 'Yeah, but your children are doing well compared to a third world country.' But we don't live in a third world country. We live in the richest state in the nation."

On cross examination, Assistant Attorney General Martha Watts asked Negron, "Would they be better off in different schools?"

"For some, that may be the case," Negron answered. "The concentration of poor students in my school does not provide them with the kind of atmosphere that would allow them to rise to their fullest potential."

The next morning, John Brittain rose early, picked the *Hartford Courant* up from his stoop. Things had gone well. On page one, the headline read, "SCHOOL SYSTEM LIKENED TO APARTHEID."

Steady Drum

O N DAY TWO, a stream of sincere-sounding educators, one after another, sat in the witness chair, banging a steady drumbeat. The teachers, counselors, principals, were, they testified, doing all they could. But the grown-ups and kids were sinking under the weight of poverty piled upon poverty.

"We have a large number of students who come in from the criminal justice system," testified Elizabeth Brad Noel, a white-haired, cherubic-faced former guidance counselor and administrator at Weaver.

Each day, Brad Noel told the court, about 200 of Weaver's 1,400 students failed to show up for school. Of 500 freshman, about 300 graduated four years later, only about a third of them boys. For the 1,400 students at Weaver—most poor and from single-parent families and 10 percent either pregnant or already parents—there was one social worker. The school's valedictorian went off to college—where she was told to take remedial English. Thirty-five percent of the prior year's graduates hadn't even taken algebra, a basic for college admission.

THE COURT OFFICER swore in Don Carso, the principal of Hartford's McDonough Elementary. He'd long been an articulate advocate for kids, and he testified with a jolly sort of grit.

Ninety percent of his students were poor, he said, either African American or Latino. Each winter, many came into school shivering, without coats. Every year, Carso and the teachers scrounged up winter wear, piled it in Carso's truck, and handed it out.

The parents wanted the best for their children, same as everywhere, he said. Considering the environment, Carso asked, even if parents did play their parts perfectly, would that make much difference?

"I don't believe that youngsters can aspire to something that they don't have any knowledge of," Carso testified. "They can't really conceive of a different kind of life than what they see all around them."

And he too had to report "several cases of youngsters who have attempted or threatened suicide."

By now, the plaintiff's testimony had established that suicidal eight-year-olds went hand in hand with an immersion in poverty and isolation. It was routine news.

It's "taken for granted," Carso testified, that the school cafeteria would flood when it rained. "And in between the lunch wave, the custodians will go in with a vacuum cleaner and they would vacuum up the water . . ." Eventually they dug a trench, put in drainage. Then, the building started losing its bricks, which routinely cracked and fell to the ground. After two years, a crew came in and patched up, but so heedlessly, Carso said, that workers trapped hundreds of pigeons in the attic.

"One day it rained and the roof leaked and the ceiling got wet and under the weight of all those pigeon carcasses, just collapsed and we had . . ." Carso seemed to search for a word.

Phil Tegeler helped his witness. "A mess?"

"Pigeon carcasses, decayed pigeon carcasses . . . we've had ceilings collapse four times," Carso said. "We even had, you know, we have the hanging lights, fluorescent lights, and one day . . . five minutes before the first grade class went into that room, it just collapsed. It just let go . . . I can go on and on."

He didn't have to. The next day the *Hartford Courant*'s headline read, COLLAPSED CEILINGS AND DEAD PIGEONS. CRUMBLING SCHOOL DESCRIBED.

THE NEWSPAPER, RADIO, and television reporters who'd filled the uncomfortable court benches on opening day drifted away. A week in, most Connecticut newspapers relied on the lone Associated Press stringer who stayed. But high school students from across the state started showing up. Some teachers, mostly from the suburbs, led field trips to the courthouse. The trial triggered classroom debates about American democracy and the function of education. The high schoolers who sat there on Monday, December 21, had lucked out. It was a good day to have come.

Gladys Hernandez, a former teacher at Barnard-Brown Elementary, at the gateway to the North End, climbed to the witness stand to testify. In direct examination, she briefly recited her résumé—teacher, administrator, teacher again. She'd served the City of Hartford for 23 years. And yes, the kids she'd taught were generally very poor. Half her students were black; the other half, Puerto Rican.

Martha Stone asked a new sort of question.

"Did these children have opportunities to go outside of Hartford?"

"Very, very seldom," Hernandez answered. "The most they ever did with their mothers was to go shopping." She added, "The parents have very little transportation."

Barnard-Brown School, Hernandez explained, could budget for only one field trip a year. "And so we took these children either to the zoo at Springfield or the zoo at Bridgeport . . . And it was like they had never seen a bridge. The road was so fascinating. But the most extraordinary thing happened when they came to the river. They all stood up in a group and applauded and cheered, and I was aware they were giving the river a standing ovation. And they were so happy to see the beauty of the river, something that most of us go back and forth over and never take time to look at."

Martha Stone asked Gladys Hernandez what her compelling scene meant.

"It tells me that they're like all other children; it tells me that they are sensitive to beauty and to their environment and to the richness of the world, but so seldom do they have the opportunity to be a part of the world or to encounter the world."

This veteran teacher made isolation manifest in the event, bringing reality to the statistics. Segregation and isolation from the mainstream might be manifest in her students' low test scores—she didn't contest that—but segregation, she said, also constricts their lives and misshapes their sense of the world.

"I think that children can overcome the stigma of poverty . . . But, what they cannot overcome is the stigma of separation. That is like a damned spot on their being . . . a spot that, no matter what success you have, you can't wipe it out. And that's what segregation does to children; they see themselves as apart and separate because of the language they speak, because of the color of their skin."

John Whelan's legal team ended up in a tough spot. The plaintiffs' witnesses described actual children, told real stories connecting the abstract ideal of "integration" and the abstract reality of "isolation" to specific kids and events. John Whelan's job was to cancel out the good heart and clear picture that Gladys Hernandez had rendered. He couldn't help coming off like a spoiler.

Whelan spent little time questioning Hernandez. He got her to admit that yes, Hartford teachers are devoted and talented, most of them. And yes, they have specialized experience, and yes, usually they're committed to working with black and Puerto Rican youngsters. Whelan's questions implied that taking black and Puerto Rican children out of Hartford might damage the kids. He raised a persuasive question: Would suburban teachers know how to deal with these kids? Hartford schools, Whelan suggested, are tailored to poor kids. Suburban schools are geared to the middle class. Perhaps it's best, the state's argument seemed to imply, for each group to stay where it belongs.

• • •

FREDDIE MORRIS, THE PRINCIPAL of Wish School, in the North End, testified next about anxious, distracted pupils who'd seen too much crime. Having such high percentages of these children in the same school put enormous pressure on educators, he said. The concentration of such students inevitably created a climate in which education was pushed aside while teachers concentrated on securing students' mental health and basic safety. For example, Morris told the court, a boy named Hiram had recently gone home after school and discovered his overdosed father. A boy named William had cried in Morris's office, scared about losing his father, who'd gotten mixed up in a drug-related shooting. Poverty stressed his school's families, Morris said, and many broke apart as a result. Foster families took over, in insecure arrangements that redoubled stress on kids whose unstable emotional states had already subordinated learning.

Eddie Davis, principal at Weaver, testified that his school couldn't afford to offer laboratory biology, chemistry, or physics. In 1992, Weaver had had to cancel advanced placement biology, in part because of a lack of funds and in part because too few students had the preparation to take the course—a standard for higher-level college-bound kids in suburbia. One teacher, Yvonne Griffin, testified that Hartford Public High School offered no advanced placement courses in chemistry, biology, or human physiology.

Others followed, including some who'd quit Hartford for jobs elsewhere. The comparisons were revealing.

"I knew that when I was in Hartford, things weren't right; and now I know how wrong things are," Robert Pittoco testified. He'd been a vice-principal at Weaver in the mid- to late '80s. He'd then become vice-principal in suburban Newington, then principal of suburban Suffield High School.

Pittoco had liked Weaver and its kids. It irked him that suburbanites assumed Weaver was an all-around nightmare.

"It's not an awful place," he told the court at the start of his testimony. "I just want to emphasize that."

Day to day, Pittoco testified, he'd enjoyed Weaver students and found most of them bright, able, and wise. He judged the teaching staff as skilled as any in suburbia, "but in the same breath," he said, "it was also a very frustrating experience because, as you've heard before, I found that what we had to deal with on a daily basis, there were obstacles that I think are insurmountable . . . The attendant problems just overwhelmed all of us."

Pittoco told the court that after his move to Newington, he'd felt back in control.

"The problems were the same; kids still have problems with drugs; they'll come from dysfunctional families; kids still have problems succeeding in school; kids still come to school late; kids still have discipline problems," he said, "but the difference was that there just weren't as many of any of the above."

In Hartford, Pittoco had spent more than half his time on discipline. In Newington, discipline time dropped to 10 to 20 percent.

"If we were having a conference with a parent or a conference with a student or a teacher, or whatever the issue was, or an observation, it was more apt at Newington to occur as planned. At Weaver, more often than not, there could be an interruption or a crisis."

Start-of-the-year scheduling—the simple logistics of getting kids into classrooms with teachers—took two or three weeks at Weaver. Kids kept moving into the city, out of the city, in from other schools, across town, out of juvenile detention. The guidance office got jammed and classrooms got disrupted by students' comings and goings. In Newington, he said, "I was shocked you know, about an hour and a half after the first day of school, there weren't any kids in the guidance office . . . Everybody was in the classroom, learning."

Pittoco seemed saddened that his students at Weaver often had accurate senses of how they were perceived beyond Hartford. To suburban kids, Weaver was a joke.

"I look around the region of Hartford—we used to think about this as we talked about goals and objectives for the school," Pittoco said. "What's going to happen when, whether it's the Weaver student or the Newington High School student, when they get out into the world of work?"

Significance

ROBERT PITTOCO'S QUESTION wasn't the sort a public school administrator could have answered. Public school systems rarely track their graduates. School districts sometimes do survey seniors about their plans. The responses often reflect stubborn optimism, not manifest opportunity. On the basis of such surveys, some urban systems go so far as to claim that large majorities of graduates go on to four-year colleges. But without costly tracking programs, administrators in fact have no way to ascertain their kids' fates after graduation.

Robert Pittoco had asked a straightforward question: What *did* happen when Hartford seniors and dropouts left Weaver? Jomills Braddock, a soft-spoken, middle-aged black sociologist from the University of Miami, took the stand and mapped some ideas.

"Segregation creates this social inertia and this avoidance tendency among individuals and among subgroups to maintain their isolation and separation . . . They anticipate hostilities that may or may not be real. They develop an aversion or a fear of mixed group interactions because they have not had prior experience with those kinds of contacts to develop a comfort level."

Braddock's many studies over the years showed that people long segregated tended to remain so. And people who'd experienced desegregated schools were much more likely to head for desegregated settings.

Racial minority groups who settled for segregation in our unequal society, Braddock's work showed, faced dire consequences. Opportunities for social mobility, good jobs, the best colleges and graduate schools, the safest neighborhoods, unfortunately lay mainly within heavily white institutions. Opting to stay clear of desegregated environments constricted what minorities could do and could be.

"The theory is that desegregation can break down barriers to access to fair career opportunities in two ways," Braddock said. First, integrated settings afford minorities the personal contacts and information networks that connect anyone to opportunities.

Second, "desegregation can break down those barriers . . . by overcoming the stigma in our society that's associated with black institutions. There are stereotypes that exist with regard to institutions of various race and ethnic compositions, that influence employers as well as admissions officials."

So the school principal Robert Pittoco's fears had been accurate, according to Braddock. Even the 30 percent of Weaver kids who finished school very likely walked off the graduation stage with skimpy connections to opportunity. And gatekeepers—job interviewers, admissions officers—likely did think less of kids who'd gone to places like Weaver.

Braddock's research revealed that employers greatly preferred minority students who'd gone to suburban, rather than segregated urban, high schools. Sampling more than 4,000 employers, he'd found far greater chances that even for jobs requiring a college degree, whites would fill open slots when "social networks" were a recruiting method. And blacks who'd used racially integrated social networks to find their jobs were in higher-paying positions than those who'd used segregated black social networks—which in fact led to the lowest-paying jobs.

IF THE STATE'S ATTORNEYS were planning to get aggressive or even exacting, the time had come. Connecticut attorney general Richard

Blumenthal had imported just the right guy to impugn the plaintiffs' expert witnesses: Al Lindseth, a white lawyer from a private firm in Atlanta. Lindseth had often done well in court, defending school districts seeking to shed post-*Brown* court orders mandating desegregation. His was an intricate specialization. He had a solid reputation.

Lindseth set up poster-size charts of scholars' work and riffled pages of reports loudly. He popped quickly from the courtroom table, stood ramrod straight. He was a hopper and a pointer. Lindseth seemed pumped for battle—and still he came off as rather likable.

"Dr. Braddock, let me start with just a few general questions," Al Lindseth began his cross-examination. "As I understand . . . you have done no studies . . . specific to Hartford or its suburban areas. Is that right?"

Lindseth was correct.

"Until yesterday, had you ever been to Hartford?"

"I arrived Sunday, but . . ."

"Okay. Until Sunday, then, had you ever been to Hartford?"

"No, I had not."

Braddock had used big national databases. Subjects in the sample had been coded by race, type of high school attended, region of residence, and often family income. The data represented the country as a whole, including Connecticut, though it didn't analyze Hartford in particular. The validity of Jomills Braddock's survey methodology hardly depended upon his having specifically visited Hartford's schools. Still, Lindseth's questioning painted Braddock as an ivory-tower interloper.

Under Lindseth's cross-examination, Braddock conceded that despite his findings about the potential benefits of desegregated schools, he wouldn't argue that merely getting racial minority and white kids together triggered such benefits. It was a starting point. School principals, teachers, probably parents too, and kids themselves had to harness the potential.

• • •

WILLIAM TRENT PLEDGED to tell the whole truth next. A professor at the University of Illinois, Trent, black, with a booming voice and confident air, was a prolific scholar and a statistical whiz. Unlike many others in the field, Trent had also fluently articulated his work's real-world relevance through the years. His research questions touched the heart of *Sheff.*

Scholars such as Trent tried to solve three puzzles: (1) How did matters between racial groups get so unequal? Was it discrimination? Self-defeating behaviors? A combination? (2) What were the daily implications of such arrangements? Who got the good jobs? Who got into college? Who stayed in? Who won the power to hire and fire? (3) What might make a more equal society?

Going to a disadvantaged school, Trent said, computes negatively with whether Latino and black students achieve higher-status jobs. Likewise, for Latinos, blacks, and white students, attending such a school was related to a lower educational attainment (fewer years of higher education). For Latino and black students, attending a racially diverse school, one with a large share of white students, appeared to greatly increase the chances that students would later work in a diverse setting.

Trent made no moral plea. He didn't advocate a particular policy change. He just reported his numbers. But social science statistics are full of ifs and conditional hedging. It's an inexact science and has limitations. For example, Trent had to rely on databases that couldn't possibly take into account every plausible variable known to humankind that could affect an outcome. Among social scientists who study the mechanics and behavior of statistics, microdisputes of all sorts are normal.

Al Lindseth put those ifs and qualifiers to work.

"We still don't know whether, or if, we integrated the student bodies so there were less poor concentrated in one school, we don't know the size of the difference that would make," Lindseth stated. "All we know," he said, "is that, at some instances for some racial groups, it might make a difference . . . Right?"

Technically and literally, Lindseth was absolutely right, although his conclusion was at odds with the weight of vast evidence. Bill Trent wouldn't give anything away.

"You could argue that we don't know how much difference, but I think knowing that they would make a difference in a beneficial way is very instructive," he answered.

Judge Harry Hammer, though, didn't get it.

"Dr. Trent, I have a few questions that I've made notes of," he said. "I should preface my questions by stating that statistical analysis in the field of sociology is foreign to me . . . I'll make that confession."

"Okay," Trent answered, nodding.

"I haven't been exposed to it," Hammer reiterated.

Wes Horton had worried about exactly this, which was why he'd urged the team to take the less complicated legal route in the first place. This stuff was intricate. How on earth would this judge parse it all? Hammer had now admitted his confusion. But which side might benefit from the complexity?

Al Lindseth was good. He examined every corner. He bogged down the statistical engine that the lawyers needed. Lindseth colored areas gray that trained social scientists would fine quite clear. There was no way, short of the judge's cramming for a PhD in statistics, that Judge Hammer would be sure-handed with the material. Al Lindseth had demonstrated every last "Yes, but . . ."

THE NEXT EXPERT, Gary Natriello, was a white sociology professor at Columbia. Perky and genial, with a mop of brown hair, he remained reliably good-natured after hours of careful questioning.

Natriello's analysis showed that in 1991, high percentages of Hartford children not only failed to meet the state's goal in reading, writing, and math but hadn't even met basic "remedial" standards. In math, 41 percent of fourth graders hadn't met this low standard. In reading, 64 percent of fourth graders and 62 percent of sixth graders had failed to reach it.

"This is a tragic situation," Natriello told the court, his eyes turning briefly to Harry Hammer. "I mean, there is no other way to characterize that."

Hartford, he testified, was getting shortchanged. The city spent $78 per student on textbooks and supplies; surrounding districts averaged $159. Hartford spent $5 per pupil over three years on library books. Surrounding districts averaged more than three times that. Only 2 percent of Hartford kids earned college credits during high school; 44 percent of kids in the top suburban district did.

"So," Natriello testified, "the thing about the Hartford situation, there are several dimensions . . . which I think are particularly depressing." He appeared incongruously bright-eyed while delivering his somber news: "One is how severe the deficiencies are; two is how consistent the deficiencies are . . . and three is how stable they are . . . So the overall conclusion is one which, given current circumstances, does not give one much room for hope for improvement in the future."

Hope

ON JANUARY 6, 1993, two weeks into the trial, hope materialized from an unexpected place.

"The racial and economic isolation of Connecticut's school system is indisputable," Connecticut's governor, Lowell Weicker Jr., intoned from the floor of the legislature.

It was his annual State of the State address, and Weicker turned to the same questions about the consequences of segregation that the court had taken up.

"Whether this segregation came about through the chance of historical boundaries or economic forces beyond the control of the state, or whether it came about through private decision, or in spite of the best educational efforts of the state, what matters is that it is here and must be dealt with."

Weicker was not your average governor. He was a moralistic, outspoken thinker. His 1995 memoir, *Maverick*, is a boastful, wistful recounting of his longstanding independence. As a U.S. senator in the 1970s, he'd interrogated fellow Republicans about Watergate, and he also went against party line in opposing a Nixon bill that would have circumvented federal school desegregation orders.

"It was a moral issue for me," Weicker said of *Sheff*, years later. "Connecticut should not have separate and unequal schools. Period. I was the governor of the state. I was technically the one being sued. But I agreed with the plaintiffs. The plaintiffs were right."

Weicker proposed, as Gerry Tirozzi had, that the state be divided into regions and that citizens in each region submit plans for reducing racial isolation. The legislature eventually watered down Weicker's proposal, and none of the plans came to action.

THE DAY OF WEICKER'S announcement, Elizabeth Sheff testified in the courtroom.

She'd had a busy three years, keeping up her ministry work and traveling to meeting halls, suburban and urban high schools, and churches, spreading the gospel of her very own legal case.

Elizabeth, bold as she is, had a fit of nerves before testifying. She'd overprepared. She walked, head high, shoulders back, ignoring her butterflies, to the witness chair.

Questioning her, Wes Horton was spare.

"How old is Milo?"

"Thirteen."

"And where is he now attending school?"

"Quirk Middle School."

"And what grade is he in?"

"Eighth."

"Where did he go to school since kindergarten?"

"Annie Fisher School."

"Until what grade?"

"From K through 6."

"From kindergarten through eighth grade . . . how many students have there been in each of his classes?"

"Around 26, 28."

"Now in kindergarten, how many of his classmates . . . were white?"

"None."

"And in first grade, how many of his classmates were white?"

"None."

"And second grade, how many of his classmates were white?"

"None."

"In third grade?"

"None."

"Fourth grade?"

"None."

"Fifth grade?"

"None."

"Sixth grade?"

"None."

"And when he moved to Quirk Middle School, how many of his classmates in seventh grade were white?"

"One."

"And in eighth grade, how many of his classmates are white?"

"None."

"Now, Ms. Sheff, does it make any difference to you that almost none of Milo's classmates have been white over the years?"

"Yes, it does."

"Why does it make a difference?"

"Well, I grew up in Charter Oak Terrace, which is a public housing development in the Southwest side of the city . . . Ms. Basevich used to make spaghetti for us. Mrs. Caron used to make hot pepper sandwiches. The Baileys who are African-American, lived next to the Meyers, who were white. We all went to school with Alice, who was of Asian descent. And so I was able to learn and grow with people of different perspectives. And it afforded me the opportunity to be able to look at people as people. I hold no shadows in my heart based on the color of people's skin or the angle of their eyes or their material possessions . . . My son is not being afforded that opportunity and I think that that is not good."

It was John Whelan's turn to question Elizabeth Sheff. In the newspapers she was the case's compelling public face. John Brittain had figured John Whelan would mount a tough cross-examination, the way other opposing lawyers had worked over past plaintiffs of his cases down south in the late '60s and early '70s.

John Whelan just barely stood.

"No questions, Your Honor."

Elizabeth Sheff looked astonished as Judge Harry Hammer said to her, "All right, you may step down."

She stepped down, looked over at Wes Horton, as if waiting for something more. But he only shrugged and smiled.

"I had so much to say. I wanted the world to hear it," Elizabeth told me years later. "I prayed for strength that morning. I was so nervous. But by the time it came, I was ready, oh so ready. Humph! Turned out, they all wanted nothing from me."

"CONNECTICUT HAS BEEN a leader in studying the problem of segregation, but has not been a leader in taking constructive action," William Gordon, a professor at Wright State University in Ohio, told the court. He'd studied and designed school desegregation plans across the country during the 1970s and '80s in his capacity as a consultant. He testified over two long days.

Gordon had brushed the cobwebs from the old reports and recommendations of commissions, boards, and consultants that John Brittain and Marianne Lado had collected and filed away years back. Time and time again, official report after report had taken measure of the rapidly worsening racial segregation. After two and a half decades of urgent recommendations, racial isolation in schools was still worsening, Gordon said. Little or nothing had been accomplished, though many university consultants and respected educators had offered "feasible" plans over the years.

For example, Gordon testified, in 1969, Hartford's school superintendent called for expanding Project Concern, the voluntary school-choice program that had bused several hundred black and Hispanic children from Hartford to suburbia. The superintendent had argued that unless it built up a program involving some 5,000 students—a quarter of Hartford's minority student population then—the city could neither stop whites from moving to the suburbs nor provide quality education for remaining students. But the legislature had never expanded the program beyond some 1,500 students. Funding was cut. Enrollment declined. In 1988–89, only 747 kids were enrolled in Project Concern—less than 3 percent of Hartford's total enrollment.

Moreover, Gordon testified, the state didn't merely oversee a segregated system but in fact reinforced it by continuing to build its new schools in segregated (white) suburbs and segregated (black and Hispanic) city areas. Between 1950 and 1980, the state approved and helped to pay for the construction of more than 100 schools in "virtually" all-white suburban communities. In many cases, these suburbs sat less than 15 miles from Hartford.

Given the state's long and passive record, Gordon concluded, the state was unlikely to embark on a self-guided mission to desegregate the schools. After 25 patient years, he suggested, it was time for the court to step in.

LATER THAT AFTERNOON, back on the spectators' benches, high school kids from nearby Ellington napped, examined their split ends, chewed gum, and shifted in their seats.

Elizabeth Sheff, in a gray business suit, her back straight, hair pulled off her face into a neat bun, sat in the front row.

Mary Kennedy, an education professor from Michigan State, testified. Kennedy, with face expressionless and demeanor serious, reported findings from a huge statistical study she'd supervised.

Elizabeth Sheff understood that Mary Kennedy's findings were vitally important, so she took notes during testimony. In Kennedy's analyses of the government program to aid schools with a lot of poor students (it's called Chapter 1), she'd confirmed that family poverty was closely associated with low student achievement and with kids' falling behind in school over time. No surprises there.

Another finding was especially useful for the plaintiffs. Poor children in high-poverty schools, the study found, performed far worse than similar poor children who attended schools *without* a high poverty rate. And the mirror image was also true: Children who *weren't* poor did less well in schools of concentrated poverty than similar kids in schools without a high poverty rate. In the real world, it meant that having a poor family worked against a child in school. But it hurt more when most of the other kids in the school the poor child attended were also poor.

The analysis was strong. But Al Lindseth stood up and asked a sensible question: Chapter 1 is a program intended to aid schools with high numbers of poor children, right?

Yes, Kennedy replied. And at the time, schools could use the money for a variety of programs — preschool, reading support, dropout prevention. So, Lindseth asked, wouldn't a Hartford child lose out on such programs, were he to leave a poor school for one with fewer poor kids?

"Based on what I know," Mary Kennedy answered, unfazed, "the children would benefit more by a change of school than by going to a high concentrated poverty school with Chapter 1."

SOON IT WAS Milo Sheff's turn to amble up to the witness box. He wore red pants and a silk shirt covered with boldly colored blocks. The microphones nearly hit his eyebrows. He was 13, in transition between cute and handsome. The lawyers hoped he'd provide a snappy end to the long day.

Milo plopped down to testify. He hadn't a trace of that timid look that comes over some kids when merely told to answer a question in class. He looked Wes Horton straight in the eye. He confirmed that his mother's previous testimony had been true. He'd had only one white classmate in eight years.

"Now, does it make any difference to you," Wes Horton asked, "that you've had only one classmate who was white?"

Of course, the content of his response had been well rehearsed. He'd gone over it with Wes Horton, with Elizabeth. Even so, Milo came out sounding exactly 13. "No words had to be put in this boy's mouth," John Brittain said a decade later. "His own worked fine."

"Umm. It makes a lot of difference . . . we need to put more of everybody in the class. It's really hard to know about somebody if you haven't talked to them," he said. "It bothers me because there was only one. And I have had experiences, other experiences. But what about the other people in the class?"

"Now, Milo, have you ever had the experience in which you've been with a lot of white kids?" Horton continued.

For three summers, Milo told the court, he'd been attending a United Church of Christ summer camp. There, of course, he went to church. He also acted in plays, shot hoops, swam. The first year, he was the only black person there.

"When you first went there, did you have some trouble?" Horton asked.

"Yes. It was hard to relate to other people because I didn't know what to talk about . . . I dressed different. I talked different. We didn't have the same interests."

After a while, things had changed. "We got to know each other and it's not so hard to talk anymore," Milo testified. And in the past two years, the camp had "become more racially mixed."

"And what difference does that make to you?"

"It makes a difference . . . so that they can get and I can get the social education that I need."

"Do you have friends in the Camp?" Horton asked in a suddenly slow, soft, sweet voice. He sounded then more like an empathic child psychiatrist than a shrewd lawyer.

"Yes. Yes," Milo answered. "It's good for the whole so that no one will be confused the way I was." There were smiles all around.

John Whelan again had no questions. He grinned and nodded to Milo as the boy walked past. Milo waved back. Elizabeth, in the front row, started beaming. As Milo passed, John Brittain leaned back in his chair and shook the boy's hand, nodded, winked. Milo slid toward his mother on the bench. She draped an arm around his shoulder, pulled him close, patted him on the back.

Milo's testimony would have provided a poignant end. But the plaintiffs had still more grown-ups to offer.

Rest

To SOME IN THE GALLERY, Christopher Collier, Connecticut's official state historian, may have sounded like a traitor. "The towns are not now, and never have been since the founding of this state, autonomous in any respect," Collier, a white-haired professor at the University of Connecticut, testified. In other words, separate school districts that matched town and city borders were, for all intents and purposes, mere creations, "social constructions" that could be legally and quite easily altered by the state. For his scholarly article "New England Specter: Town and State in Connecticut History, Law, and Myth," Collier had dug deep. For two years, he'd sifted through old documents, charters, transcripts of Constitutional Conventions, and official *Records of the Colony of Connecticut*.

There was a centuries-long history, Collier said, of state action to enlarge, reduce, and redraw school district boundaries. Very much to the point in *Sheff*, Collier said that in the 19th century, the state had routinely established school districts *across* town lines, bringing in kids from one, two, three, or more communities.

But to many in New England, local control, expressed in small school districts coterminous with municipal borders, seemed close to a religious tenet—the way things were and ought to be. But as Collier's work revealed, the myth of local control engendered a convenient, distracting detour around central matters in equal education—place, race, and class. "Local control" rarely surfaced in debates over what to do with suburban trash or how to provide everybody enough water or suitable transportation routes. Politicians and citizens played the local-control card most vigorously when "regionalism" translated into letting more poor people slip across the lines. Most other Northern and Midwestern states clung to similar myths. It was a myth the U.S. Supreme Court had perpetuated in its 1974 decision in *Milliken v. Bradley.* And it was this beloved myth that *Sheff v. O'Neill* threatened.

BADI FOSTER WAS an expert of a different sort. Neither professor nor teacher, Foster was vice president for the insurance giant Aetna, one of the region's largest employers. The company had hired Foster to find, attract, and retain talented employees.

In the early '90s, he'd traveled with other black business and government leaders to study apprenticeship programs in Germany and Denmark. He'd served on several state commissions, including the one headed by the first witness, David Carter, the Governor's Commission for Quality and Integrated Education.

"I'm somewhat embarrassed," Foster said under direct examination by John Brittain. "I've been on so many commissions, and we seem to get so little done that they appoint another commission."

Foster had raised a few eyebrows on the Quality and Integrated Education Commission. He'd stepped away from the pack, recommending that if voluntary measures didn't integrate schools, the state should use mandatory measures.

"I do not believe you can have a quality education today unless it is an integrated education," Foster testified.

In part he based his opinion on his own experience. For the past seven years, he'd gone to Aetna's Saturday Academy, which he'd help set up. It brought in a handful of selected middle schoolers from Hartford to Aetna's offices. Sometimes the students went on field trips. Sometimes Aetna executives taught workshops on computers or on public speaking. Foster had also started a small internship program for Hartford's high school kids.

"But quite frankly," he said, his face tightening, "we do not hire them."

"And why don't you hire them?" Brittain asked from the podium.

"Because they don't have the skill level necessary to do the jobs that have to be done."

"Does the racial or the economic percentages within the district of Hartford have any effect upon their employment opportunity?" Brittain asked.

"Yes," Foster replied. "Aetna is a predominantly white environment. The majority of these students have never even been in a building like Aetna . . . it really was a world of enormous difference."

Brittain asked Foster whether he'd "observed" minority students who'd had racially diverse backgrounds come to work at Aetna.

"Yes. Yes," Foster answered, perking up, leaning forward.

"And what observations have you made about them?"

"They have—well, it's interesting. They seem to have a better understanding of the context of work, kinds of norms, sort of rules, rules of the road, ways of handling conflict that are more appropriate in the corporate setting than elsewhere."

The white kids from Connecticut's suburbs, meanwhile, did well at Foster's jobs. But, Foster testified, they too were missing something: "In the case of white students, they come across with a false sense of arrogance."

John Brittain had known Foster would be a good witness. His front-line, real-world experience dovetailed with what Braddock's and Trent's studies had suggested. Foster talked in frank—even brutal—terms: "The more racially segregated and economically poor, the less opportunity you have to work for a company like Aetna," he told the court.

Under cross-examination by John Whelan, Badi Foster easily admitted he had little idea how to integrate the state's schools. He did believe, however, that the legislature should redraw school district lines so that children didn't have to go to school where they lived. Whether parents might be able to choose from many options, or whether schools in the city would have to be shut down, or whether or not new schools should be built, Foster just could not say.

"I don't have a magic solution, but the solutions are there," he said.

FOSTER WAS RIGHT—more or less. Solutions were indeed there, including some that had worked elsewhere.

Connecticut, testimony suggested, was being provincial about its school district organization. Witnesses named several places that had organized schools by county and by region, resulting in more stability and racial integration over time. In 1975, for example, officials had merged schools in Louisville, Kentucky, with suburban schools. And in that same decade, Wilmington, Delaware, had too. In Louisville, plaintiff exhibits showed, integration levels had been steady in the last decade. In Delaware, initial protests soon calmed. Delaware's State Department of Education had even thrown a "tenth year celebration" a few years back.

But remedy, the plaintiffs had agreed, would be left for later. That was a strategy. If plaintiffs had offered a concrete plan, John Brittain worried, the plan would "be the center of attack, and the focus would shift away from the problem that needs fixing."

The combined testimony of experts suggested the elements of a comprehensive plan. A useful plan needed the suburbs and needed "mandatory" and "voluntary" components. This meant that school districts—all school districts—needed to be compelled to participate. But within that structure, parents might retain options for choosing schools, perhaps even for staying in a neighborhood school. "Educational enhancements"—a wider range of course offerings, teacher training—fit with any desegregation order. So did affordable suburban housing programs.

After presenting these possibilities, the plaintiffs rested their case. It was the defense's turn now.

Defense

THE DEFENSE'S CASE PROMISED to be far shorter than the plaintiffs'. To counter the parade of teachers, counselors, and principals, the attorney general's office had, at $280 a day, hired West Hartford's retired school superintendent Lloyd Calvert to come up with his own assessment of the city schools. Calvert had gone through annual reports of the State Board of Education, noting the rising number of statements of concern regarding the needs of poor children and their families. He had visited 6 of Hartford's 33 schools. He'd interviewed principals, taken their guided tours.

And he'd concluded that all was well with the Hartford schools. They were clean, for one thing. Teachers seemed well qualified. The principals were proud of their accomplishments. The curriculum, up-to-date in his eyes, was appropriate. It was Calvert's informed opinion that, besides the imperfections you'd expect to find in any public school — cramped space, budget uncertainties — Hartford offered children good educations. The problem was not the schools, Calvert testified, but the children's poverty, which kept them from using all the opportunities.

Hartford students, Calvert testified, "arrive with all kinds of strengths and weaknesses." These include physical, mental, and emotional handicaps. "And then," Calvert added, "there are socioeconomic problems that children bear."

Where a person stands on the seemingly academic question of whether school can be the key difference in the lives of poor children determined that person's sense of how much more should be done to improve schools and whether the very structure of schools—of opportunity in American society—should be rearranged. A witness seeing the central problem as a child's poverty, as Calvert and the state did, differed fundamentally from John Brittain and the other plaintiffs. Yes, the challenges of poverty were considerable, John Brittain admitted. But he maintained that going to a school with concentrated poverty compounded those problems. Kids in Hartford, as teachers and administrators had said, were not only poor but experientially impoverished, immersed in poverty, so surrounded by poverty that it shut out the rest of American life and defined, shaped, and marred their social institutions.

John Brittain cross-examined Calvert, getting him to admit he'd not visited any middle schools or high schools. He'd visited slightly more than half of the city's elementary schools but hadn't taken notes. Many of his impressions of what schools offered derived from documents and brochures he'd been handed by central-office administrators.

G. Donald Ferree, who helped run the Institute for Social Inquiry at the University of Connecticut down the highway, took the stand for the defense.

Ferree's polling showed that generally, people in Connecticut—black and white—valued "integration." A vast majority, he said, even agreed that more should be done to achieve it. On the other hand, Ferree said, people's other values might conflict with their desire for integration, including the desire to educate kids close to home. And nonwhites, Ferree's survey found, cared more about quality of education than about integration.

Picked apart, the surveys the institute had conducted revealed intricacy more than anything else. Nothing broke down simply. The data invited no safe predictions about how a parent might respond to school assignment changes or new schooling options. One thing was clear. The findings debunked a notion that by the late 1980s had taken hold in the press: that racial minorities, African Americans in particular, had found integration a failure, a negative, or at least something not worth fighting for anymore.

Years after *Sheff,* a Connecticut political scientist from the University of Hartford, Darryl L. McMiller, would sort through every question in every poll ever conducted on *Sheff*-related matters in the state. There had been four major ones. He'd find the attitude toward integration in Connecticut favorable. A growing portion of residents, he said, believed that "more, rather than less, should be done to integrate local schools." By 1990, 84 percent of residents agreed with that statement. And, McMiller would observe, "people of color" were "substantially more eager" than whites to see schools integrated.

In the early 1990s, the *Hartford Courant* had commissioned Ferree's Institute for Social Inquiry to conduct a poll. Ninety percent of "people of color" answered yes to the question, "If there is racial imbalance in the schools in part of the state, should the towns in the area cooperate to solve the problem?" Among whites, 72 percent answered yes.

John Brittain, in his cross-examination of Ferree, set the data's complexities to work against Ferree. He homed in on responses to question number 40. Eighty-five percent of a racially mixed group of respondents felt that more should be done to integrate the state's schools. About 46 percent said such efforts should be voluntary, and 39 percent said they should be required.

Ferree had concluded, "School parents throughout the state, believe that all things being equal, a more integrated education is a positive thing for their children's education and for society. But how they would react to any particular effort, whether it was done at the instance of this Court or any other way, would have much to do with how it played out against the other values they hold."

So even the state's expert on public approval of desegregation had to admit to something of a toss-up.

The center of the state's case lay with two other expert witnesses — Professors Christine Rossell and David Armor.

Christine Rossell, chairperson of the Political Science Department at Boston University, had already recounted her appealing personal narrative before many other judges. By 1993, Rossell, middle-aged, her face nearly always expressionless, had become a sought-after witness for states and school districts hoping to dismantle their court-ordered desegregation plans. Calmly, without inflection, Christine Rossell repeated her life story again for Judge Harry Hammer.

She'd started out an idealistic, unsophisticated liberal who'd believed in mandatory desegregation, she told him. Then she'd seen the light. She'd grown into "pragmatism." She applied science purely.

"So your views about the effectiveness of mandatory plans have changed?" the state's attorney, Martha Watts, asked Rossell in direct examination.

"Yes. As I, as I do—I like to call myself a crass empiricist," Rossell answered, nodding.

Mandatory plans (which reassign kids to schools, without parental choice) didn't work, Rossell had decided after several statistical studies. As many as half the whites don't show up, she said. Meanwhile, white people trickle out of the public system as the years go on, never to return, unless the school district dismantles its desegregation plan. And thus, Rossell concluded, many "desegregation" plans had turned out to be counterproductive. Desegregation efforts, she said, cause further segregation.

Ron Ellis suggested that Rossell's data didn't support her findings. But more important, he noted, none of it seemed applicable to Hartford, as the city was so close to its suburban communities.

"Have you conducted any studies about the existing suburban bus routes, to know whether or not it would be easy to change them or to adapt them to a plan?" Ellis asked.

"No, I haven't."

"Okay. Do you know how far or how long students in the suburbs are now bused?"

"No. I don't."

Hartford had never had a court-ordered desegregation plan, even within the city. And its whites, and later its middle-class blacks, had fled anyway. Same for New Haven, down the highway, and Bridgeport, the next big city after that, farther down the coast. Whites had been abandoning urban cores since World War II. In many cities, especially those in the North, white exodus from the city school systems was as high in cities that had never even flirted with mandatory desegregation as in those that had, if not higher. But mandatory desegregation or even semimandatory desegregation did appear to exacerbate that process. In Hartford, however, the white flight process was over. This was the reason for bringing the case in the first place. And, Ellis established, *Sheff* plaintiffs had never asked for, nor even considered, a strict mandatory busing plan of the sort that troubled Christine Rossell.

Rossell went on to suggest that "dismantling" a desegregation plan would result in whites returning to a city. But that didn't apply to Hartford either, Ron Ellis again pointed out, as there had never been a mandatory plan to dismantle.

THE STATE'S NEXT ARTILLERY came from a George Mason University professor, David Armor. By 1993, Armor, like Rossell, had become a familiar face, a frequent expert at desegregation trials. Four years earlier, Armor had been the Norfolk, Virginia, school board's key witness. He'd testified in federal court that a return to segregated schools in Norfolk would probably bring whites back to city schools, resulting in a more integrated system overall. The judge, citing Armor's predictions, had allowed Norfolk's school board to reestablish ten all-black, high-poverty schools. Armor's predictions never came true, but the ten resegregated schools remained so. That 1986 case, *Riddick v. School Board of the City of Norfolk*, had been the first of a series of conservative federal court decisions that had struck down *Brown*-inspired desegregation plans and invited a deliberate return to segregated schools. In coming years, scores more followed.

"There's no, at least surface reason, to say that their scores indicate that that system is failing as a matter of fact," Armor testified. He went further: "I think you could, you could make just about the opposite conclusion," he said, adding that "given these very different kinds of students, Hartford is doing quite a good job."

Armor testified that generally higher test scores among suburban black children probably stemmed not from their desegregated school settings per se but from their wealthier family situations. Ron Ellis jumped upon this curious conclusion. The problem, Ellis noted, was that Armor's analysis assumed that the black children in Vernon or West Hartford had the same socioeconomic status as the overall community. In some cases, his analysis included as few as 10 suburban black children. Were they sons and daughters of surgeons and professors, or did they live in subsidized housing? Did they come from two-parent homes or single-parent homes? David Armor could not say. Perhaps these children were actually poor kids who'd moved from Hartford, and their change to less burdened schools indeed had accounted for their academic success. How could one consider the source of the differences without knowing the economic levels of the children? Ellis wanted to ask. Judge Harry Hammer didn't allow the question.

THE TRIAL WAS NEARLY OVER. Almost seven weeks had passed since the trial's opening day. Everybody, even John Brittain, but especially Judge Hammer, with increasingly messy, flyaway hair, looked worn. John Brittain found it telling that John Whelan and Martha Watts hadn't called the principal defendants in the case, the people in the best position to defend the state. It was the plaintiffs, in fact, who had deposed Gerry Tirozzi and filed the comments he'd made during that questioning—the much-cited exhibit 494—to support *their* case. Neither had the state called on the current governor, Lowell Weicker. Weicker later said he'd felt he *had* testified—delivering his State of the State address in January 1993. A decade later, Weicker remained proud of that speech.

"My feeling is you use your power to do good, to do the right thing," he told me. "You don't spend all your time working to hang on to your power . . . And this was something worth using my power for. The thing I still believe about *Sheff*? *Sheff* told the goddamn truth."

Closing

O N April 28, 1994, a few weeks before scheduled closing arguments, the lead attorney for the defense, John
Whelan, committed suicide at home. He was 41 years old. He left a
wife and two young sons. A small notice in the *Hartford Courant* reported a self-inflicted gunshot wound and offered few other answers
about his private act. It did mention Whelan's current public role—
defending the state in *Sheff v. O'Neill.*

Whelan's death delayed closing arguments for six months while another assistant attorney general, Bernard McGovern, read through
transcripts. The trial that had begun in late 1992 concluded in November 1994. The two sides—John Brittain and Wes Horton on one
and the attorney general, Richard Blumenthal, and his new assistant,
McGovern, on the other—stood in the suburban courtroom before
Judge Harry Hammer for the last time.

John Brittain closed things up as he'd opened them—with poetry
by Langston Hughes.

"What happens to a dream deferred? Does it dry up like a raisin in
the sun . . . or does it explode?" The black poet laureate had published
the poem in 1967.

"This poem captures the experience of children without an equal educational opportunity," Brittain said. The plaintiffs' case had shown "racial
segregation and poverty" to be "two evils with a malignant kinship."

The plaintiffs had assembled a graphic time line summarizing the state's nonaction over the years. They stood it up on an easel. In the rectangular white graph space above the time line, a bold red hill slanted upward, representing increasing segregation levels in the Hartford Public Schools. John Brittain pointed often to that rising line.

"Many believe the *Sheff versus O'Neill* case is to Connecticut what *Brown versus Board of Education* was to the South and later the nation," Brittain said. "What Connecticut has said, though, for nearly thirty years, throughout this long time line, is 'Wait.'"

"This wait," he said, pausing, "almost always means never."

THERE WERE PLENTY of facts in this trial, Wes Horton told Harry Hammer. And considered together, they added up to an "overwhelming" case of unequal educational opportunity. But, he continued, good as the facts were, the plaintiffs' case didn't need them.

Segregation, Horton reasoned, harking back now to the original complaint and the posttrial brief, is simply a violation of the state's constitution. The constitution says, "No person shall be denied the equal protection of the law nor be subjected to segregation or discrimination." Simple as that.

Finally, Horton stressed, "We're here because we say the law requires that all students receive an equal educational opportunity, and they're not receiving it."

RICHARD BLUMENTHAL, the state's attorney general, now stood in court for the first time during the case. Blumenthal had a disarming ear-to-ear grin, a ruddy complexion, and a wiry build. He made brief but deep and effective eye contact. He looked especially good on television. At conferences and public meetings, he was always even-tempered, unflaggingly pleasant.

John Brittain respected but deeply disagreed with Blumenthal. They also shared a personal connection. Brittain's mother, Ardessa, had briefly been a nanny to Blumenthal's significantly younger wife in the 1970s. The nanny's son was in court advocating a reordering of social privilege and the cared-for child's husband was trying to hold the status quo.

There is no "legal basis," Blumenthal told Judge Hammer solemnly, for a court's "taking over the running of school systems . . . eviscerating local boards of education in setting educational policy, eliminating school districts based on the boundaries of town and city line—in effect, ordering massive interdistrict transportation of students, eliminating the system of governance of education as we know it in this state." He added, "The kind of solution and process for which plaintiffs are advocating—they are not only futile . . . but they are antidemocratic."

And anyway, he stressed, demographic change was already "occurring," alluding to an increase of minorities in some suburbs.

If the plaintiffs were to prevail, Blumenthal continued, "this Court will be sitting as a super legislature, assessing every single legislative and executive branch decision, eviscerating local control, eliminating local school districts." He went on, "It will be literally, a cataclysmic upheaval in the educational structure of the State of Connecticut."

THIS "PARADE OF HORRIBLES" that Blumenthal had just marched past Judge Hammer was not, Wes Horton said, "supported by the record." The plaintiffs never asked for a court takeover of schools. Wes Horton waved a dismissive hand at the very notion. "To a large extent, remarks you've heard remind me of this . . . judicial opinion that I will give the name of very shortly."

He read, "In the nature of things, the statute [read: the 14th Amendment] could not have been intended to abolish distinctions based upon color, or to enforce social, as distinguished from political, equality, or a co-mingling of the two races upon terms unsatisfactory to either."

"Your Honor," Horton said, shuffling through his papers on the podium, "that's very similar to what Mr. Blumenthal has just said, and

that's a direct quote from the majority opinion in *Plessy v. Ferguson.*"
Horton meant this: In *Plessy,* in 1896, the Supreme Court had mis-
read or at least misstated the intentions of the 14th Amendment to
the U.S. Constitution, which, historians agree, was in there to establish the equal citizenship of blacks and protect them from legislative
harms. Similarly, Horton implied, Richard Blumenthal was either ignoring or misreading the Connecticut Constitution. By guaranteeing
an equal educational opportunity to all, the state constitution ensured
equal treatment under the law. Indeed, the Connecticut Constitution's
clauses were, Horton argued, very much intended to enforce equality
and to protect absolutely the more vulnerable members of society from
inequality that might arise from unfair laws, the law in this case being
the statute forcing students to attend neighborhood schools.

Plessy is universally seen, 50 years after its reversal by *Brown v.
Board of Education,* as a hideous, mortifying, and too-lengthy chapter
in American law. It condoned "separate but equal," and that sounds
downright barbaric today. But *Plessy,* which was written not by a South-
erner but by Justice Henry Billings Brown, a native of Massachusetts,
endured as good law from 1896 until *Brown* in 1954. Fifty-eight years.

Wes Horton's comparison to *Plessy* was a strong accusation. Perhaps sensing that Horton had thrown a mighty punch, Judge Hammer
looked immediately toward the attorney general. "Do you want the last
word, Mr. Blumenthal?" he asked.

"When I feel I'm right, your Honor, I never insist on the last word."

It was a charming, principled response. And one Blumenthal didn't
quite stick to. The hearing drew to a close. Lawyers gathered up papers.
Hammer straightened piles. This was it. In less than a minute, the long,
historic trial would be over.

"Just for the record, your Honor," Blumenthal said, smiling, voice
deadpan. "I wasn't around at the time of *Plessy.*" Even a few of the plaintiff lawyers chuckled at that.

Blumenthal's quip would not have surprised Jack Boger, who'd helped set *Sheff* in motion but had left the case years before for the classrooms and courtrooms of North Carolina.

"There is this kind of 'Look, Ma, no hands!' quality to segregation in the North," Jack Boger reflected, some ten years after the *Sheff* trial ended. "Everyone is utterly blameless. That's what always struck me most about this case and about the state's logic. Everyone, always, was so innocent. No one was ever responsible."

Decision
1995

NEARLY SIX YEARS AFTER plaintiffs had filed their complaint, a clerk phoned Wes Horton. Horton drove to West Harford and picked up Judge Harry Hammer's decision.

The lawyers filed into Horton's office one by one. A secretary's mournful glance provided an abbreviated version of the disaster. Wes Horton soon told his colleagues the full story.

To John Brittain, it felt a little like hearing of a loved one's death. In a daze, "shell-shocked," he "only half heard the details."

Horton told his colleagues the decision was "bizarre"—no other way to characterize it—"just bizarre."

John Brittain glanced through the 72-page document. "I couldn't believe," he said. "I could not believe what I was reading."

It wasn't so much that they'd lost. For John Brittain, what shocked him was the manner in which they'd lost, how completely they'd been dismissed.

HARRY HAMMER ADMITTED he'd decided not to decide a lot of issues.

"The divergent and apparently irreconcilable opinions of the expert witnesses," Hammer wrote, reflected the disagreements between the two sides in the case.

Wes Horton's instinct had been right. Hammer hadn't been able to parse it—any of it. On the facts, he found neither side right and neither side inherently wrong. To Hammer, it was irreconcilable. So the plaintiffs' narrative of the case, told from various vantage points by Gladys Hernandez, Mary Kennedy, Bill Trent, Edna Negron—all of it Hammer had simply declined to touch. He decided not to be the judge.

Judge Hammer later supplied the requisite "findings of facts," which asserted the official "truth" undergirding his decision. He appeared to have bought a point put forth by the defendant's witness David Armor—that a student's poverty (not segregation and not concentration of poverty) lay at the root of poor performance. But his decision rested upon neither Armor's logic nor any opposing analysis. It turned on the law.

The plaintiffs had relied heavily on the legal rights established in *Horton v. Meskill*—that the state constitution guarantees students an equal educational opportunity. But there was a key difference here, and the difference, Judge Hammer ruled, was that *Horton* took issue with actual statutes, actual laws that had been passed—laws that formed the basis for the school-financing system. But *Sheff*? *Sheff* was mostly about a *lack* of action, a lack that had maintained the only plausibly harmful social condition of segregation. In other words, the state couldn't be faulted here, Judge Hammer said, because there was no specific law or set of laws that could be named as the instrument or cause of the inequity, such as it was.

But then, things became more confusing.

Hammer rested his decision upon opinions written by former U.S. Supreme Court justice William Douglas. Often these were dissenting opinions. Hammer centered his analysis not even upon federal law but upon the nonbinding writings of a U.S. Supreme Court justice. From the plaintiffs' view, of course, Hammer had just plumb missed the point. The plaintiffs had brought their case in state court precisely *because* the state constitution afforded citizens fuller protection in the field of education than the U.S. Constitution did.

Hammer's reasoning went like this: First, Connecticut's government had a long history of general decency to racial minorities. There was no evidence that Connecticut had ever purposely required black and white schoolchildren to attend separate schools. Second, Justice Douglas had devised his own personal standard for what might constitute "subtle" forms of intent. This might include, for example, a demonstration that "the construction of a freeway effectively isolated blacks in the area" or a showing that state-licensed real estate agents or state-chartered banks had contributed to segregation. The plaintiffs' case, Hammer said, failed to meet those standards.

John Brittain recalls angrily thinking that "we weren't trying to meet that standard." If Judge Hammer had wanted them to come up with evidence that real estate agents, banks, and highway construction, overseen and regulated by the state, had contributed to segregation, there would have been many examples.

Hammer wrote, "The court finds that the plaintiffs have failed to prove that state action is a direct and sufficient cause of the conditions and that accordingly the constitutional claims asserted by the plaintiffs need not be addressed." Following from Judge Hammer's analysis, every other piece of evidence from every other plaintiff witness was irrelevant. Because there wasn't a law with which the plaintiffs took issue, there was, in Hammer's mind, no issue at all.

Brittain and his team hadn't felt sure they'd win. But none of them had predicted this.

Up on the bench, Judge Hammer had been unflaggingly attentive—squinting, leaning forward to hear better, inquiring about footnotes and chapter titles. He'd stacked big piles of papers festooned with Post-it notes. He'd scribbled comments in margins. He had been businesslike, respectful, and—at least it appeared to everyone—completely open to both sides.

The ruling puzzled, angered, and pained John Brittain. For years afterward, he would privately try to contact Harry Hammer. He wanted to hear the judge explain his process in making the decision. Did he go into chambers with his mind made up? Through a clerk, Harry Hammer would refuse John Brittain's requests.

Elizabeth Sheff came away with her own questions. "Harry"—unlike the lawyers, she never referred to him as Judge Hammer—"was smarter than this," she said. "He wasn't acting like some person who was going to blow everything off."

Elizabeth had an especially hard time explaining things to Milo, who'd felt all along that the evidence clearly stacked up in his favor. He knew this case wasn't being fought only on his behalf and he understood his role as a symbol and spokesman. He believed in the case and its cause. He'd grown up watching Judge Wapner on *The People's Court,* where regular people like him and his mother stood up and complained and their problems got fixed.

"He did always think it would be like that, like Judge Wapner," Elizabeth said. "I try to explain that this is one part of a long, long struggle. He does understand that in the abstract. But he was a child. To him things were wrong and they should be made right."

Elizabeth cried. Briefly.

"Okay," she thought to herself. "Okay. The first step is done. We took the first step. They pushed us down. Now we just get ourselves up. We take the second one."

The team didn't even have to get together and discuss it. Tomorrow, all of them would sit again, study the papers, look for a fresh start, a new square one.

JUST AROUND THE corner from the somber scene in Wes Horton's cozy law office, Governor John Rowland convened a festive press conference in the posh Legislative Office Building. Rowland handed Dick Blumenthal a celebratory bottle of champagne.

"We take great pride in what we've done in all our schools—urban and suburban," Rowland told reporters. "This decision reiterates what we've done on behalf of our schoolchildren." Rowland continued, "The state did not force whatever racial balance or imbalance exists . . . It's a natural occurrence. It's a result of human nature, people's decision to live where they want to live."

Back in the North End, Jeremy Otero and his classmates might have quibbled with that. Perhaps luckily for Rowland, the press didn't check out his sociological observations by wandering the North End and asking people where they "want to live." The governor's champagne bottle, the party scene at the press conference—those didn't go over well in black and Latino activist circles, in urban high school classrooms, nor in the many black churches in the North End.

Churches sponsored rallies and vigils opposing the decision and Governor Rowland's giddy celebration. Some 200 high school students walked out of class and marched on the Capitol lawn. About 150 students protested at the University of Hartford. Elizabeth Sheff gave the keynote talk at their rally. City leaders and school officials spoke out and marched too. More than 100 people crammed a Hartford Board of Education meeting, protesting the ruling.

"Both the judge's decision and the Governor's arrogance have motivated the community like nothing I have ever seen before, and reminds me of how people worked together to fight for civil rights 30 years ago," a Hartford pastor, Rev. Michael Williams, told the *New York Times*. "People are appalled not only at the court's ruling, which will be reversed on appeal, but by the very callous attitude by the state in publicly celebrating a decision that keeps our children in inferior schools where they continue to have their constitutional rights violated."

After the champagne controversy, Richard Blumenthal told the people of Connecticut that he, for one, didn't drink any of it. As far as he knew, the cork had never been popped. He quickly issued a formal apology.

To Brittain, who'd drunk and who hadn't was irrelevant.

"What's to celebrate? We still have segregated schools? You want to go on record celebrating that?" he said years afterward. "You'd think it was a sports victory. It was disgusting."

The plaintiffs soon convened their own press conference, at a church in Blue Hills where they announced their intention to appeal the decision.

Elizabeth Sheff told a *Hartford Courant* reporter, "We will continue here . . . Truly, truly I feel we have proved over and over again in court the unequal educational opportunities of children in the city of Hartford. I am truly disappointed, but undaunted because the first rule of struggle is perseverance."

Lawyers are careful about what they say, even privately, about judges, before whom they may well appear again some day. When disagreeing with a decision, conventional wisdom dictates that an attorney never dis a judge. John Brittain didn't want any part of that etiquette.

"Harry Hammer," he told a *Courant* reporter, "swept the case under the rug."

Appeal
1995

SIX MONTHS LATER, in September, as Ms. Luddy welcomed her 20th consecutive class of black and Latino children in a nearly all-black-and-Latino elementary school, the plaintiffs delivered a brief to the state supreme court that challenged many of Harry Hammer's "findings of fact" and all his findings of law. Hammer, the lawyers argued, had mistakenly applied the writings of a federal judge to a state case. And besides, the lawyers wrote, the judge's implication that there was not sufficient "state action" to implicate Connecticut as a responsible agency of school segregation was wrong. The state oversaw the schools. The state had in fact applied a districting statute that officials had long known resulted in segregated schools. And the state built schools on top of segregated housing patterns.

Briefs wage battle on paper, not on the court floor. An appellate lawyer—in this case, Wes Horton—is akin to the trial lawyer, employing similar skills of logic, but with rarefied methods and fewer raw materials to work from. For the *Sheff* appeal, Judge Hammer hadn't given plaintiffs a whole lot to sculpt with. But the day after the decision, Wes Horton sat down in his office with the documents and focused on Hammer's 22nd finding of fact. He saw a kernel of hope in it. Hammer conceded, "The single most important factor that contributed to the present concentration of racial and ethnic minorities in Hartford was the town-school district system which has existed since 1909, when the legislature consolidated most of the school districts in the state so that thereafter town boundaries became the dividing lines between all school districts in the state." So, the lawyers decided, they could indeed point to a law that was causing all the problems.

THE SUPREME COURT'S hearing room was elegant compared to Harry Hammer's plain, chilly West Hartford courtroom. The lamps there had wide shades and intricate, wine-colored designs. The justices' chairs bore carved heraldic shields. A plush carpet ran under long adjacent lawyers' tables.

At the plaintiffs' table sat Wes Horton, John Brittain, Phil Tegeler, Martha Stone. A newer face, Dennis Parker, a seasoned NAACP Legal Defense team lawyer who had taken over from Ron Ellis a year earlier, sat near the end. Parker had litigated school desegregation cases across the nation, mainly in the South, for more than a dozen years. During his first visit to Hartford, he'd been struck, as John Brittain had, by the "depth of racial segregation," he said, and later too "by the lengths people will go to avoid talking about it." "They are very polite in Connecticut," he observed. "They don't talk about sex and they don't talk about race."

At the next table sat the attorney general, Richard Blumenthal, and his few assistants.

The seven supreme court justices emerged through a door from their separate chambers. The lawyers stood. The justices—five men and two women, in long black robes—remained standing as a sheriff called the court open. They eased into their high-backed chairs and sat on a podium several feet above the lawyers. The U.S. flag and the bright blue and white Connecticut flag hung behind them.

THE JUSTICES HAD READ through the brief from the plaintiffs and one from the state. But as was customary, lawyers from neither side could speak for long without interruption.

The chief justice, Ellen Peters, sat at the center. She was in her mid-60s and she'd occupied her position for six years. Chin-length chestnut hair framed a pensive expression. *Sheff* was the most important, most closely watched case to come before Ellen Peters's supreme court in a century. She began softly but clearly.

"Now, I know that every person here today is interested in seeing that justice is done," Peters said. Horton stood at the lectern, between the two lawyers' tables.

"You may proceed," Peters said, nodding.

"My name is Wesley Horton, and I represent the plaintiffs in this case," he began, gripping the sides of the lectern tightly. "Your Honor, I think we need to start in this case . . ."

"Could I ask you a question before you start?" Justice Callahan interrupted. "Tell me what it is . . . what exactly are you claiming is unconstitutional? Is it the districting statute?"

"We claim it is a system," Horton answered, his hands lifting from his sides, palms outstretched. The system *as represented* by the districting statute, he said. He took a few steps back. "It is an overall system."

Wes Horton made an unlikely champion of the poor in his fine dark suit, a folded silk handkerchief sprouting from his breast pocket, that cheery smile on his face. He was the picture of Old Yankee Connecticut. He was in fact a member in good standing of one of Hartford's last bastions of elitism—the downtown Hartford Club, where waiters served elegant lunches beneath pictures of yachts.

But Wes Horton meant to do just what he was doing, thrusting his hands heavenward, locked in battle over the wrongs perpetrated by the "system." He'd sought this role on his own time and his own dime.

Ellen Peters often closed her eyes before speaking, perhaps to envision her every crafted sentence before uttering it. Her expression revealed the strain of grappling, of trying to understand deeply. Most of the other justices kept alert poker faces. Ellen Peters looked to the ceiling, brow furrowed.

"I would like your help," she pleaded, "as to why the redistricting statute, which everybody agrees was neutral at the time it was enacted, why it is now unconstitutional."

"Oh, because as it operates, it denies students an equal educational opportunity," Horton answered without pause.

Justice Callahan headed somewhere else: "Suppose the students in Hartford were doing swimmingly? They were doing well on the mastery tests?" he asked, stone-faced. "Would you still have a claim?"

"Yes, Your Honor," Horton answered.

Even were it so, the long-term chances for kids from segregated schools were inferior and fewer than the opportunities suburban kids have, Wes Horton said. "But," Horton began a next thought.

Callahan interjected: "So, then, it's not a question of race? It's a question of adequate schools?"

"Well," Horton started to explain, "it's both."

But just as might happen in a barroom debate on such questions, causes and cures spun and tangled. "Wait," the justices seemed to be wondering, "is it race? Is it poverty? Is it family poverty? Is it adequacy? Is it school poverty? Is this a funding-equalization case or isn't it?"

Ellen Peters put her thumb and fingers to her temples. Justice Callahan gnawed on the stems of his eyeglasses and took a turn looking at the ceiling. Justice Borden squinted. Justice Katz plopped her chin into her cupped hand.

Wes Horton marked the way down a treacherous trail. Segregation and concentrated poverty made schools inadequate—made them unequal with regard to opportunity, Horton explained. That was the first thing.

But there was another matter—the question of whether students in Hartford were receiving a minimally adequate education. They weren't, Horton said. They just plain weren't. Sure, that might require more money for the city schools. But that was not the case's major focus.

"I think you have to look at all . . ."

Ellen Peters stopped him cold. She'd scampered up the intellectual ladder to the top. She threw down a challenge.

"Okay. Let me ask you this now. Suppose that someone who grew up in the city of Hartford and has now had the fortune, the good fortune to strike it rich?" Someone like Bill Gates, the founder of Microsoft, she suggested.

"He says, 'I will provide the money to fix up the schools and to provide enough money for breakfasts, lunches, pre-school, after-school programs, computers, all the equipment and supplies and personnel that are required to run a first-rate school system,' and he, in fact, endows the city with monies to accomplish that."

She paused, looked at Horton, tilted her head.

"If I understand what you are saying to Justice Callahan," she asked, "you would still be here?"

That was an easy one.

"Absolutely," Wes Horton answered. "Yes."

ELLEN PETERS HAD ASKED the central question—the one forever resurfacing in a society in which inequality and high principle were still at war. Essentially she wanted to understand: Can separate be equal? And if it can't, well, then why? Wes Horton invoked the history of the country, the fact that most of the power in the nation, the state, lies with white people. There was no time, however, for a course on the sociology of discrimination. Wes Horton had little choice but to use conceptual shorthand—"history of discrimination," "mainstream," "interaction," "exposure." He threw the words into the fray.

"I gather your focus is really segregation?" Justice Berdon asked.

"Yes. Segregation in terms of poverty concentration and in terms of racial and ethnic isolation. That's correct," Wes Horton answered.

Justice Borden (not to be confused with Justice Berdon) pushed on. Did that mean that a school district that was all Jewish would be unconstitutional?

Probably not, Horton said. "I think that it makes a difference, just as I was saying earlier about the society we live in. I think it may make a difference that we are talking about race and ethnicity." Race was "different," Horton said, from religion.

Justice Norcott, the only African American on the panel, helped crystallize this with a question of his own: "Doesn't part of your answer have to be that it makes a difference because of the negative racial history in this country?"

"That's exactly what I was getting at," Horton said.

"So, isn't part of your answer that the negative baggage of the racial history in this country, that it affects the fundamental right of education quite differently than religion," Justice Norcott suggested.

"I agree with that, Justice Norcott," Wes Horton answered. "That's exactly my point." Horton added, "I mean, we've gone through a Civil War." He sounded mildly exasperated, perhaps from the challenge of making the obvious apparent. The special nature of race in America, its enduring consequence and import, wasn't something you could glance over and see, at least not in a few seconds of judicial repartee. In the academy, it had even become fashionable to call race "socially constructed"—that is, based not on fact or science but on judgments, categories that we, together, concocted as part of a social process. But if "race" were a social construction, it's one that is applied to real, live, nonconstructed minority individuals, who experience real consequences at real institutions, in real places, right now.

EVERY 10 MINUTES OR SO, Wes Horton heartily belted back water from a paper cup, like a frat boy swigging a shot. He took an especially quick gulp as the justices turned to the specific language contained in Connecticut's state constitution. The subject was the 1965 amendment, in Article 1, Section 20. It read, "No person shall be denied the equal protection of the law nor be subjected to segregation or discrimination in the exercise or enjoyment of his or her civil or political rights because of religion, race, color, ancestry, national origin, sex or physical or mental disability."

In sum, it meant that de facto segregation was prohibited, Horton repeated. Otherwise, as the plaintiffs had told Judge Hammer during the trial, why would the constitution specifically include both the words *segregation* and *discrimination?* Since the words weren't used interchangeably, it implied that the writers saw them as separate evils, Horton argued.

Then the focus shifted: "Aren't you saying intent is not part of this equation?" Justice Norcott asked, pointing a pencil. Aha! He'd zeroed in on Hammer's logic — that there was no explicit law mandating segregation — and was questioning it outright.

"There's a cause," Horton answered, "because of the districting statutes and if it weren't for that, then this would not be happening. The segregation because of race is caused by the state forcing people to go to school" in the towns where they live, Horton said.

Justice Norcott nodded.

Ellen Peters backtracked.

"Just bear with me and I'm sorry to be dense on this point. It cannot be the case that the school statutes compel attendance at a school within the district if there are underfunded and inadequate and nonetheless-in-existence interdistrict programs . . . Why isn't that inconsistent?"

These programs — she was referring to Project Choice and to the state's interdistrict magnet schools — only took care of several hundred kids out of 24,000 in Hartford, Horton said. If the programs were bigger, maybe that would be different, he suggested.

Justice Berdon asked, sensibly, "Are there students waiting in line to get into those [interdistrict] schools?"

"Yes," Horton said. "Oh, yes!"

The justices kept firing questions. What if this wasn't about African Americans, against whom there'd been racist laws and a history of slavery? What if it were just Puerto Rican kids? What constitutes a segregated school?

"Being an appellate judge is line drawing," Horton finally responded. "I don't know where the line is . . . All I know, in this case, you are far beyond the line. And it's getting worse every year."

Justice Norcott seemed to want to drag Harry Hammer's questionable logic right into the open. Norcott reminded everyone that education was an "affirmative obligation" under the state constitution—the state was compelled to provide it, and if it did not, that failure was a constitutional violation. Justice Norcott said that *Horton v. Meskill* indeed established that the state had to provide a "substantially equal educational opportunity." Thus, Justice Norcott asked Wes Horton, under the law, wasn't "non-action . . . tantamount to action"? If you didn't do what you were obligated to do, he was saying, then, right there—that was a violation. Wasn't it?

"That's right. That's right," Horton said, smiling. Again, he pointed to Justice Norcott, the way a seminar leader bestows brief honor upon the insightful scholar. Wes Horton glanced at his watch. It was one minute before 11 a.m. His allotted hour was gone. So often he'd been unable to articulate an argument, even finish a sentence, before a justice's interruption moved him down a new path. At the first syllable of a justice's interjecting voice, Horton had always obediently stopped speaking. He'd straightened up, met the justice's eyes. He'd had to leave half-articulated chains of ideas hanging. He'd managed to answer some questions fully, veering around the state constitutional terrain at dangerously high speed. He'd stayed mindful of the precious minutes ticking away, had kept seeking openings that might bring him back to half-made points.

Horton looked at Ellen Peters. "Well, it's almost 11 o'clock," he suggested. Ellen Peters asked him to please finish up.

"I would simply say . . . seeing what exists and looking at the history

of our country and our state, you cannot say these students are receiving an equal educational opportunity, under whatever legal theory." He
added that education is "the most important function under our Constitution and I don't know how any one could look at the Hartford
Public Schools today, or any big city within a metropolitan area in
this state, and say that these students are receiving an equal educational opportunity or that it is ever going to happen without this Court's
intervention."

THROUGHOUT HORTON'S PRESENTATION, Richard Blumenthal
had sat expressionless at the table to his adversary's right, flanked by
his assistants. His long fingers formed a steeple in front of his face.

Standing before the podium, starting his allotted hour, Blumenthal
piloted a smooth return to Justice Ellen Peters's first hypothetical
query.

"I would gratefully accept the Chief Justice's suggestion that we invite Mr. Gates here," he said. "Because what the plaintiffs are asking
is that we create an affirmative obligation to cure poverty." The fact
that the city kids were poor, he said, was the underlying cause of un-
derachievement and inequality. Segregation was bad, yes, Blumenthal
said. But segregation, as a condition, was not causing educational
inequality.

"But we do have separation here, as a matter of fact, here, don't we?"
Justice Berdon asked, squinting.

"Yes, there are imbalances in Hartford," Blumenthal answered,
nodding.

"Because of the lines that have been drawn by the state itself,"
Berdon continued. It was a statement, not a question.

"But not *caused* by those lines, Justice Berdon," Blumenthal said, his
index finger jabbing the air, conducting.

"Now, are you saying now that if a child in Hartford wants to go to a West Hartford school, that child can just walk over to West Hartford and attend that school?" Berdon asked, peering back skeptically.

"I don't know if there's anything in the record," Blumenthal said, seeming undaunted. "But there's no statutory bar for it to happen," he continued—that is, no law *against* it.

"So, though, West Hartford has no obligation to educate a child from Hartford or educate a child from Glastonbury?" Justice Berdon pushed.

"That is absolutely right, Justice Berdon."

"So, then, it *is* the lines that are causing the problem," Justice Berdon said, leaning forward, his bow tie poking out from under the black robe, his sandy hair mussed. "Not intentionally . . . but that has caused this separation."

There weren't any out-and-out enemies in the courtroom. Richard Blumenthal wasn't against racial integration per se. In fact, eight years later, he'd write a strong, eloquent "friend of the court" brief for a controversial U.S. Supreme Court case, supporting affirmative action in higher education. In his role as the state's top lawyer, however, the best Blumenthal could do was to show himself to be just as fair-minded as this squad of well-intentioned but wrongheaded idealists, only more practical.

"As a citizen of Connecticut, and perhaps everyone in this courtroom would agree with me, more should be done. That's an obligation for the folks across the street," he said, in reference to the legislators at the State Capitol.

Ellen Peters changed direction.

"Let me put the discussion to you specifically. The buildings are fine and the school day is terrific . . . and it is still the case that 90 percent of the children who go to school in Hartford are not having the opportunity to be part of a diverse educational experience," Peters said. "How can we say that it is a minimally adequate education?"

Racial balance should be a social goal, Blumenthal repeated. But it just wasn't part of a minimally adequate education. Judge Hammer had even said so.

"Why isn't that part of a minimally adequate education in a society in which people are going to have to live and work in the foreseeable future?" she asked again.

Justice Norcott jumped in.

"Okay, if I could make an analogy, that if education were to be seen as the key, the opportunity to open the next door, to open the next phase of life, you are saying that the children of the suburbs and the students in the city of Hartford would have that same key to open up that same door?"

"There are children who don't have the same kind of access, who are disadvantaged coming to school because they bring with them in the Hartford schools, the problems of whether it's poverty or drug abuse or the failure to do homework at home . . . but they have available to them resources of comparable type and magnitude," Blumenthal answered.

Were the court to order a remedy to segregation, Blumenthal said, "it would be striking down district lines," and "massive reassignment and redistribution of students would have to occur across town boundaries."

This was the first time Blumenthal played the busing-fear card.

"Well, [segregation] affects the educational opportunities of everyone in this state," Justice Berdon retorted. "Why shouldn't the state have to do something to avoid this segregated pattern that we have?"

JUSTICE KATZ JUMPED into the game after her colleagues had returned to the question of whether the state's knowing inaction amounted to "state action" and whether even proving "action" was required in this case. That circled back to Justice Norcott's seeming conclusion that "action" need not be proven and that "inaction" in not preventing the inequality was enough in this case.

Katz pointed to Hammer's finding of fact, right there, number 22, the very one Wes Horton had felt hopeful about the day after the loss in trial court. She read aloud at double speed: "The single most important factor that contributed to the present concentration of racial and ethnic minorities in Hartford was the town-school district system." She pushed her outstretched palms out toward Blumenthal in a gesture that substituted for a question.

Yes, Blumenthal, said. But the passage needed to be considered in context. The real causes of segregation, he asserted, were demographic patterns. The school boundary lines lay atop these demographics, just sitting there, neutral and benign, innocent, innocuous. They didn't *do* anything.

Blumenthal warned again that a decision for the plaintiffs "might well be making schools worse rather than better."

Justice Berdon smirked. Especially with that bow tie, he looked like a disappointed dad whose son had gone too far.

"Why do you go to an extreme? . . . You suggest extreme things. Oh—that we must eliminate local education," Justice Berdon said in a chiding tone, sweeping a hand in front of his chest. "Those are extreme remedies."

As the plaintiff, Horton had the advantage of final rebuttal. He said that his adversary, Blumenthal, had cast "racial integration" as a "moral" goal—an admirable one, but possibly unreachable.

However, Horton pointed out, "law and morality many times intersect." And a child who's been compelled to attend segregated schools probably can't later enter mainstream society successfully.

"That's the sort of thing that the U.S. Supreme Court said in *Brown v. Board of Education* in 1954. So, to a large extent, this was a felt necessity of the times," he observed. "It's the law that needs to take those aspirations up to date."

There. He'd assigned them all a noble duty.

Finding
1996

IT TOOK THE JUSTICES a reasonable 10 months to decide on the appeal. In July 1996, three years after the opening of the trial and eight years after *Sheff* had been filed, another phone call brought news of another verdict to the plaintiffs. A supreme court clerk called Wes Horton at his office. The court had made its decision, the clerk said. The decision hadn't yet been filed. At the supreme court building, she told him, at 10 a.m. the next day, they'd get copies of the decision to read in a locked room.

Wes Horton, in a round of phone calls, summoned his colleagues from their daily lives. They met the following morning. A clerk ushered the group into a small conference room. Blumenthal and his assistants came too. If anyone needed to use the bathroom, she explained, he or she would need to call for an escort. Dennis Parker, the LDF lawyer who'd litigated civil rights cases all over the country, already saw Connecticut folk as extreme in their discretion. He felt this lockdown procedure was excessive.

The clerk lugged in a tall pile of stapled documents. She passed one out to each lawyer, facedown. She instructed the lawyers not to begin reading until she gave the order. Everyone obeyed. The clerk gave the sign and left the room.

Marianne Lado looked up now and again to search her colleagues' faces. Wes Horton was smiling, but she knew him to smile a lot.

Blumenthal's face was contemplative, all serious business, Lado remembered. The sound of flipping pages whispered in the awkward silence. Some of the lawyers wondered if it would be rude, in the presence of opposing counsel, to turn to the end, get to the bottom line. Phil Tegeler scanned the room. Everyone else had started at the beginning. He began there too.

Wes Horton broke the silence.

"We won," he said.

At that cue, Blumenthal stood. He extended his right hand. Wes Horton took it.

"Congratulations," Blumenthal said.

But to Brittain it felt anticlimactic. They had to go right on sitting there for the rest of their hour, stifling their glee, until the clerk released them from the room. The two teams of lawyers had little more to say to each other.

"A moment like this, you want to hug your colleagues," Brittain recalled. "But it didn't seem appropriate."

Later that afternoon, they did commence a celebration and press conference at a church in the North End. A *Hartford Courant* photographer snapped the day's defining shot — 16-year-old Milo and his mother. A glowing Elizabeth Sheff had wrapped her arms tightly around her son. In her right hand she clasped the court papers.

"Oh man, did I hug my son that day!" Sheff remembered. "I had that decision in my hot little hands. And I had my son there, hugging me. That was something good."

CHIEF JUSTICE ELLEN PETERS spelled out the court's thinking: "Students in Hartford suffer daily from the devastating effects that racial and ethnic isolation, as well as poverty, have had on their education," Peters wrote. "Federal constitutional law provides no remedy for their plight. The principal issue in this appeal is whether . . . the state, which already plays an active role in managing public schools, must take further measures to relieve the severe handicaps that burden these children's education. The issue is as controversial as the stakes are high. We hold today that the needy schoolchildren of Hartford have waited long enough . . . The judgment of the trial court, must, accordingly, be reversed."

But her eloquence could not hide the fact that the final score was just 4 to 3. Newspaper reporters termed *Sheff* "closely divided." The plaintiffs had prevailed by one measly vote. In addition to Peters, the bow-tied Berdon, Norcott, the crystallizer, and Justice Katz sided with the *Sheff* team. Justice Borden penned a vituperative, compellingly written dissent. Justice Callahan and the third vote, Justice Palmer, joined him.

Ellen Peters's reasoning relied on the obligation *Horton I* had established: to provide all children in public schools with a "substantially equal education." She went on to read, conjointly, two important constitutional provisions: Article 8, Section 1, which embodies that obligation, and Article 1, Section 20, the amendment that prohibits "segregation." Considered in tandem, Peters concluded "that the existence of extreme racial and ethnic isolation in the public school system deprives schoolchildren of a substantially equal educational opportunity and requires the state to take further remedial measures." Such remedial measures are required, she said, regardless of whether that segregation was the result of intentional state action. She put an end to the splitting of hairs over the relative importance of misfortunes.

"The fact that, as pleaded, the plaintiffs' complaint does not provide them a constitutional remedy for one of their afflictions, namely, their poverty, is not a ground for depriving them of a remedy for the other," Peters said. And later: "The trial court's findings simply demonstrate that Hartford's schoolchildren labor under a dual burden: their poverty *and* their racial and ethnic isolation."

She continued: "Racial and ethnic segregation has a pervasive and invidious impact on schools, whether the segregation results from intentional conduct or from unorchestrated demographic factors."

Ellen Peters, though, also narrowed the case into a strict desegregation complaint. The court "need not" consider the impact inadequate resources had on the schools, she concluded. That the education was clearly unequal because of racial isolation was enough for today. So she evaded the case's third count, that plaintiffs were not receiving a minimally adequate education. In legal parlance, it was simply "not adjudicated."

In one sense, Ellen Peters's majority had gone very far. They'd boldly written, "We conclude . . . that the school districting scheme . . . as enforced with regard to these plaintiffs, is unconstitutional."

But they'd also held back. What had the court directed the state to do? Nothing very clear.

On the matter of a remedy, Peters wrote that the "separation of powers" convinced the majority that ridding the Hartford region of segregated schools should not be up to the court, but to the legislature and the governor. The majority decision raced right along with smooth, speedy, spirited language. Yet as the seasoned civil rights lawyers had suspected during their initial cloistered reading of the text, the court hit a wall near the finish line. By the end, Ellen Peters just strung together phrases that might prod, motivate, convince, the legislature and governor.

"In staying our hand," she wrote, "we do not wish to be misunderstood about the urgency of finding an appropriate remedy for the plight of Hartford's public schoolchildren. Every passing day denies these children their constitutional right to a substantially equal educational opportunity. Every passing day shortchanges these children in their ability to learn and to contribute to their own well-being and to that of this state and nation. We direct the Legislature and the Executive branch to put the search for appropriate remedial measures at the top of their respective agendas."

She quoted *Brown v. Board of Education*.

> As the United States Supreme Court has eloquently ob-
> served, a sound education is the very foundation of good
> citizenship. Today, it is a principal instrument in awakening
> the child to cultural values, in preparing him for later profes-
> sional training and in helping him to adjust normally to his
> environment. In these days, it is doubtful that any child may
> reasonably be expected to succeed in life if he is denied the
> opportunity of an education. Such an obligation, where the
> state has undertaken to provide it, is a right which must be
> made available to all on equal terms.

IN HIS DISSENT, Justice Borden carped at the invocation of
Brown. *Sheff* was different, he said. *Brown* had been based on evidence
that segregation made black children see themselves as inferior. No one
made any such claims in *Sheff*. Most important, though, Borden said,
was that the majority was really stretching things by reading conjointly
the "segregation" prohibition and the "education" provision of the Connecticut Constitution.

The problem, Borden said, was that the constitutional theory es-
poused by the majority "bears only a passing resemblance to the claims
of the plaintiffs." In other words, the plaintiffs hadn't suggested reading the two clauses as one, so why was the court ostensibly creating a
new legal argument for the plaintiffs? And putting those two clauses
together, Borden charged, was more than simply inappropriate. It was
an abuse of power.

But there was, as Ellen Peters pointed out, nothing in *Horton I*
that limited its underlying theory to school financing. The question
of whether schools were "substantially equal" thus hinged on a central
question: Were Hartford's schools as effective as, say, less segregated,
less poor schools at preparing students for life, work, and success in the
United States? Ellen Peters's majority said no.

Just as the nation had once been captivated by the moral magnificence of *Brown's* sweeping assertion, "In the field of public education the doctrine of 'separate but equal' has no place," *Sheff's* believers would, for years to come, reach for the legacy that Ellen Peters had left tiny Connecticut. The statement "Every passing day shortchanges these children in their ability to learn and to contribute to their own well-being and to that of this state and nation" endured as their rallying cry.

In 1954, *Brown v. Board of Education* had immortalized Chief Justice Earl Warren's U.S. Supreme Court. Ellen Peters, in her unexciting state court, would never win such glory. But four decades after *Brown,* her decision reflected a sense that in spite of its relative obscurity, *Sheff* was, or could be, the conscience of this generation — the new *Brown,* a considerate and definitive morality, expressed in law.

What would happen next, though, was anybody's guess.

PART FIVE

Back to School

"I should see the garden far better," said Alice to herself, "if I could get to the top of that hill: and here's a path that leads straight to it—at least, no, it doesn't do *that*—" (after going a few yards along the path, and turning several sharp corners), "but I suppose it will at last. But how curiously it twists! It's more like a corkscrew than a path! Well, *this* turn goes to the hill, I suppose—no, it doesn't! This goes straight back to the house! Well then, I'll try it the other way."

—Lewis Carroll, *Through the Looking Glass*

Best-Case Scenario

JEREMY, OUT DELIVERING the morning attendance sheet, had found me wandering Waverly's halls. It was the fall of 2000, four years after the *Sheff* decision. I told him I was searching for Ms. Luddy's classroom. He'd piloted me in for a landing.

"Up on the second floor? You step off the elevator and go right across and you see this bulletin board," he began. "Our work is on it, and okay, so you can look at the work once you get there. That's your reward. You walk twenty steps or maybe twenty-two. Walk straight. Then turn a little to the left 'cause if you don't you hit into a wall. You'll see her name: Ms. Luddy. It will be on the door. And you walk in. Well, the door's open, so maybe knock a little. She'll be in there with us. She's nice. But she's not gonna let you mess around, though. You'll have to work with us. I don't think you can just sit in Ms. Luddy's class. Just watching? No way! Not if you're not on task."

Principal James Thompson, in a recent discussion, had delivered a string of superlatives in Ms. Luddy's praise. He judged her one of the most skilled and successful teachers he'd ever worked with.

It took a while for me to understand the full scope of Ms. Luddy's skills and spirit. It was immediately obvious that Ms. Luddy was indeed the taskmaster Jeremy had warned me about. Other kids in the room would mention the same trait. But she was a taskmaster of the encouraging and gentle sort. She balanced an exacting nature and high standards with humor, warmth, and affirmation.

"I wish I could clone her," James Thompson had said. "Lois just has *it*."

Thompson had an eye for *it*. His Waverly boasted the lowest teacher turnover rate in Hartford. He'd managed to keep the most experienced staffers onboard. And Waverly had another advantage besides Thompson's management. It was one of the city's smallest elementary schools. "Right there," Thompson had said, "that makes a big difference, a huge difference in the environment." Small size, he'd told me, provides "a sense of manageability." "This is about as good as it gets in Hartford, what those kids have, right there."

In Jeremy's and Ms. Luddy's case, right there was a windowless, generic, fluorescent-lit classroom. She'd decorated it brightly, with special regard for the changing seasons: autumn leaf cutouts for fall, flowers later for spring. She'd granted social studies and science a wall apiece and some shelves for materials—though she rarely had time to touch them these days. Reading program booklets filled most of a third wall. Around the classroom, pink, blue, and yellow baskets held chapter books appropriate for 7- to 10-year-olds. Ms. Luddy had pushed the beige student-size chairs and desks into five clusters. Rows had seemed "too rigid, too cold" to her. So the students faced one another, not Ms. Luddy. The clustered tables encouraged "teamwork," "healthy socialization," and the "sense of community" she often mentioned. In fact, Ms. Luddy insisted upon remaining with her students through two grades, not the standard one.

"After two years, you'll see. We will be a community," she told me early on. "At least that's the idea. Stick around. Check it out."

ONE DESK CLUSTER away from Jeremy, Patrick, who was beginning his second trip through third grade, pushed his math worksheet away. He sighed so loudly and impatiently at his desk that other kids glanced toward him. He muttered angrily to himself. A few kids stopped working, trying to catch his words. That did it. Ms. Luddy stood by him and said, "Patrick. The hallway." She followed him out there.

"Look at me. Patrick? Look at me," Ms. Luddy scolded. "I know what you can do." Ms. Luddy nodded her head and softened her tone. "In my classroom you will be expected to do the work because you can do it." Then a little louder, "Get. In. There. Now!"

Patrick, head down, teary, sat back down at his desk, pulled the worksheet toward him, and huddled over his math facts.

At the next table, Jeremy, hands cupped around his mouth, whispered in my ear, filling me in on the situation and context. "One thing you gotta know. Patrick acts tough, but one day I had a cough and he came over and gave me these little red candies to help me. Ms. Luddy talks tough back to him I think 'cause she knows he has gifts and could learn good if he tried."

"Uh, Jeremy?" Ms. Luddy joined our whispering. She lifted a finger to her mouth. "Shh. On task, please."

"Whoops, oh," Jeremy answered, smiling. "Okay. But I'm done."

"Read a book," she told him, sounding firm but smiling back.

So she was indeed a fearsome disciplinarian, though on a few Friday afternoons she had shut the door and everyone had danced. During breaks in the day, a line of children often waited to hug Ms. Luddy, report news from the weekend, or win some of her praise. At dismissal, some of the girls blew her good-bye kisses. The kids relied on her for validation and, just as important, for clear limits.

Rashida, like Patrick, pushed the limits, especially in the first months of third grade. In clear earshot of Ms. Luddy, she'd told a classmate just an hour after Patrick's hallway conference, "Ms. Luddy can't be tellin' us what do to. She ain't our mothers." A withering look from Ms. Luddy had sent Rashida cowering. Rashida offered rushed apologies but still earned a hallway conference of her own.

Just as often, Ms. Luddy played enforcement officer for optimism.

"Oh, you've got *Patrick* this year? Oh, you poor thing. I feel for you," a colleague gossiped to Ms. Luddy by the photocopier at the end of one day.

"No. No," Ms. Luddy replied. "Let me tell *you* about Patrick. You should see him. He's having a great year."

Parents knew all about Ms. Luddy's gifts and grit. Each year, requests stacked up for children to join her class. Kayla's mother said it right out: "I like that Ms. Luddy because she don't put up with any shit. Everyone knows that."

Ms. LUDDY NEVER SAT for long while teaching and never, ever sat or stood behind her desk. She had set the metal desk off in a corner and hung photographs of former students, nephews, her grown brothers, her sister and fellow educator Eileen, other friends. A few American flags hung there too. When she wanted to sit, she pulled her white barstool with yellow painted sunflowers out to the middle of the room and perched there among the children. Usually, though, she walked around, looking over students' shoulders, or sat with them scrunched into a kid-size chair in this or that cluster, guiding them along. She taught fewer children than the average Connecticut teacher. By 2001, Jeremy's initial class of 25 or 26 kids would dwindle to 18, then end up at 20. The small class reflected the neighborhood's population drop.

"It's a depressing sign for the neighborhood," James Thompson had said. "But no doubt about it, it makes our job a little easier."

No doubt about it too that for a couple of years, because of the small class, the great teacher, and the committed principal, Jeremy Otero and his classmates received best-case-scenario segregated schooling. Simpson-Waverly was, ironically, *Plessy*'s "separate but equal" achieved—at least on paper.

• • •

But Lois Luddy didn't see things in such grand terms. She'd been teaching in "segregated" schools—she'd never thought to call them that—since 1975. Teaching had been her first real job. At 21, she'd stood near the top of Barnard-Brown Elementary School's entryway stairs in Hartford's Clay Arsenal neighborood. Brown and olive faces—her new and future students and their families from the North End—had peered up at the new white teacher. Spanish words had floated up to her. She'd panicked. She hadn't yet learned Spanish.

She was Irish Catholic, the daughter of an insurance broker and a homemaker. A few months earlier, she'd graduated from St. Joseph's, the small Catholic college in West Hartford. And just like that, she'd moved from student to teacher.

She'd "felt terrified" all that day and most of that first year. She hadn't feared her students, but her limitations. After a year or two, teaching had gotten easier. She'd learned Spanish.

"But that was the least of it," she said. "It was so good for me—being in a community very different from how I'd grown up? It helped make me who I am."

To her nieces and nephews, she was the favorite, fun aunt with the schedule crowded with friends and good works. She was chairwoman of the board for a city charity that found clothing, food, and shelter for the poor. She sang in the church choir. With friends, she regularly kayaked along the Connecticut River, which gave her the arm strength of an athlete. She also savored corny, old-fashioned New England harvest fairs. Her job wasn't her whole life.

"But it is a ministry, a calling," she said. From the start, teaching wasn't about "saving" kids and certainly wasn't about "fixing" them. It was about "contributing as best I can." She cringed when people referred to her as a teacher of "inner-city kids."

She'd read many oversentimentalized and too-optimistic newspaper features and books about these "inner-city children," distanced portrayals of saintly, romantic, noble ghetto kids, somehow purer, more resilient and adaptive (and often better writers of poetry) than coddled suburban children. She rolled her eyes at such notions. Not one of the kids in Ms. Luddy's class, I'd soon come to understand, fit this romanticized cliché. A few had wisps of poetic sensibilities. But most, even with expert instruction, penned age-appropriate simple doggerel about whatever holiday was nigh.

"It sounds sort of academic, that 'inner-city children' phrase," she said. "I never really liked the ring of those words. It's not like there aren't some big differences between a lot of these kids and kids in the more privileged areas. But my take on this is that we can't just feel sorry for these kids. Not everything that we do for them should grow from sympathy, because you get to know them and you see a lot to admire. I see traits in a lot of these kids that I wish I had—honestly."

AROUND THE TIME I began visiting Ms. Luddy "at school" (she always said she was "at school," never "at work"), administrators were pressing Simpson-Waverly's flashy test-score improvements into service. Hartford's local media had reported on Waverly's test gains for some time. (In 2001, a reporter and a photographer from the *New York Times* would wander Waverly's halls too. The paper ran a front-page story about Hartford's turnaround.) Educators in this maligned underdog city had boasted with abandon, but James Thompson had tried to keep his head down during the public fuss over "his" high test scores.

"Numbers—and what have you? I know how fragile these things are," Thompson told me. "Test scores are sensitive to a lot of factors over which we have no control. Who knows what the next year is going to bring?"

Thompson never abandoned that apolitical, cautious optimism through the half decade I reported on his turf. As time went on, he discovered that compelling stories about "beat the odds" schools served to bolster the Republican national education agenda. The glory of triumphant "miracle school" narratives became clear during George W.

Bush's 2000 presidential campaign. Bush claimed credit for improving school performance back while he was governor in Texas, dubbing the purported gains the "Texas miracle." The story cited the large urban school district of Houston. There, the tale went, dropout rates had fallen and test scores had risen. Rod Paige won his post as Bush's first education secretary largely on the basis of his record as Houston's school superintendent then. It wasn't until 2003 that independent researchers and major media investigations revealed that Houston had long underreported its dropout rate—by as much as 48 percentage points—and had manipulated testing data and college attendance rates. Independent analyses showed no reliable evidence that public education in Texas had improved markedly during Bush's tenure.

But before the miracle had fizzled, the good-looking numbers out of Texas had helped make the case for the test-heavy No Child Left Behind Act. Anecdotes about other "miracle schools" would continue to spread. A powerful proponent, the conservative Heritage Foundation, published its polemic *No Excuses* in spring 2000. The booklet offered snapshots of "successful" schools that had boosted test scores. Yes, they shared common traits: clear "standards," curriculum aligned with test objectives, behavior controls, and teachers and principals who'd consented to punishment for low student achievement. Any school, Heritage concluded, regardless of poverty rates, can maintain high test scores.

A few years later, in 2003, Abigail Thernstrom, a senior fellow at the conservative Manhattan Institute, and her husband, Stephan Thernstrom, a historian at Harvard, published an anecdote-based book, also titled *No Excuses*. The Thernstroms, like their counterparts at Heritage, argued that teachers and students in poorly performing, high-poverty schools should emulate accountability and behavior-control policies common in higher-scoring schools. Segregation and concentrated poverty, in the Thernstroms' view, are little more than "excuses" that educators—and in some cases, students themselves—use to explain away low achievement.

Some narratives about high-achieving schools may represent actual success in boosting test scores, but as Columbia University professor Richard Rothstein pointed out in his 2004 book, *Class and Schools,* and as every first-year statistics student learns, isolated examples of subjective "success" don't empirically disprove that any social condition outside of schools—be it segregation, concentrated poverty, poor nutrition, an overcrowded apartment—might contribute to low achievement. Anyone can frame an anecdote about a heavy smoker who never got cancer; yet that does not prove, Rothstein reminds us, that smoking does not cause cancer.

BACK IN 1999, when I first interviewed James Thompson at Waverly, the political uses for a school like his had yet to be fully exploited. He was quite explicit telling me exactly how he'd pushed his one small school slowly from chaos toward order. He'd spent 17 years as principal at Simpson-Waverly, and by trial and error he'd come up with some effective tools—no magic, just sound and durable ways to harness talent. He'd developed a meticulous teacher-evaluation system. He'd deployed one he called "academic review," tracking each student's progress while developing individualized plans for every kid. He monitored teacher complaints, avoided taking sides, and worked hard to prevent faculty defections. He claimed a good eye for spotting talented teachers and hired well. He looked for confidence, toughness, warmth, passion, experience in a similar environment, and recommendations from principals he respected. Then, even after making a hire, his gut occasionally told him a new teacher had little chance to improve. He'd been quick to fire then, rushing to act before the teacher accrued the months that triggered union protection. And he was obsessively organized—a crucial compulsion, he believed, in an environment teetering eternally toward mayhem.

Thompson felt his teachers did some things especially well. They bore stress with detachment but were committed, deep down, to this place and population of kids. They were masters at classroom control. They did indeed set clear expectations for behavior. Thompson's good teachers also complained increasingly about the pressure of high-stakes tests and the prepackaged scripted reading program Success for All, which the Hartford school system had chosen to purchase and install. Thompson sensed, however, that many of his teachers found the school's strong test results a source of pride. Waverly's numbers, for all Thompson's doubts about the value of "high-stakes testing," were in-your-face stereotype busters.

By 2000, out-of-town experts, in search of transferable answers, made regular pilgramages to study Waverly. Desperate school officials flew Thompson around the country for consultations. He obliged them in his down-to-earth way, helping them compile sensible "to do" lists. But he developed no stump speech. He rejected every chance to create the sort of appealing illusion so many other educators aspired to construct — that one quiet African American principal from Hartford held a secret blueprint that could miraculously transform any racially isolated, high-poverty urban school. The very notion made Thompson look down at his desk and fuss with his neat piles of paper.

"Well, we do some things right," he conceded. "But basically we're establishing order, a system, and within that system, we teach children how to pass the Connecticut Mastery Test. It's *not* mysterious."

Thompson harbored doubts. "I worry about whether this success can be maintained in the larger system, honestly," he said over a quick lunch at Max Bibo's, his favorite downtown deli. "I really worry about that, about what's going to happen after the students leave, what it adds up to, whether we're preparing them. Well, what are we preparing them for?"

Thompson had noticed that few of the people in his field who traveled to Waverly to admire the "miracle" had asked him what he really thought. But his friend and ally John Brittain had.

"John really listened," Thompson said. "He knows the score."

Thompson picked up where John Brittain had left off. "Racial isolation is still the central issue, and the poverty and the accompanying problems with that," Thompson said. But it seemed to him that most people he met these days seemed only to want to hear him brag. And he'd never been very good at that.

Inside the Miracle

D ING. DING. DING. DING. *The school bell rang; it was time for me to go to class. I sat down and pull the chair up to the desk. I look out the window and then I started to day dream that I was a butterfly. I had colorful wings. I had two antennas sticking out of my head and I had six legs. I flew up to see how high I could go but I couldn't go that far so I flew down nice and easy and then suddenly, I realize I was stuck inside of a spider web. I was fighting to come out. But all I tried, I couldn't come out. The spider wrapped me up with his web. I could not move. So I call for help. Someone comes. We waited until the spider was gone. My helper pulled me out and unwrapped me so I could fly. And then the animal that helped me flew away. I heard the teacher say, 'Are you daydreaming?' 'No,' I replied. Ding. Ding. Ding. Ding. The school bell rang . . ."*

"I love it," Ms. Luddy screeched, her hands clasped tight under her chin. "Oh! Martin! I like it. I really like it. I love it."

Her effusiveness and generalized praise ran a bit counterculture for these days. Were she to follow central-office advice more strictly, she'd stick to praising the Hartford Public Schools' prescribed elements of "narrative" writing. Indeed, Martin's piece had a beginning, a middle, and an end. Yes, it had a problem and a resolution. This tidy formula met the expectations of the employees scoring the state's standardized Connecticut Mastery Test. The formula generated reassuringly predictable and logical paragraphs. Kids across the city followed the directions over and over again. After a lot of rehearsal time, a growing proportion of Hartford kids aced the CMT's writing section.

Ms. Luddy admitted to liking the day's exercise. It was one of many "practice prompts" from old CMTs, delivered in stapled packets from the superintendent's office. The booklets even commanded teachers to present specific "prompts" on certain days.

The day before, kids had plugged particulars into an outline, in preparation for actual writing. That prompt had read, "Pretend that you became an animal for a day. Describe how you turned into the animal. Tell about the problems or adventures you had while you were the animal and how you felt when you became a human being."

Martin had established a specific problem and had devised a resolution of sorts. And his essay had an ending, which was a point-scoring good thing. Understandably, a lot of other "timed narratives" (done in sessions equal to the allotted minutes for a writing assignment come test day) halted many a fine piece inelegantly, because the writers, hurrying their crampy No. 2 pencil–clutching hands across the page, simply ran out of minutes. Okay, Ms. Luddy admitted, Martin hadn't covered everything. His dialogue left a little something to be desired. "The animal that helped me flew away"? Ms. Luddy had wondered about that one. And yeah, okay, his tenses were jumbled.

But the piece, Ms. Luddy suspected, was *so* Martin. What a delightful mystery Martin was to her in the early months of third grade. He was a still, calm boy with nerdy glasses and white T-shirts so clean and bright that Ms. Luddy suspected his mother scrubbed, starched, and ironed each one.

Ms. Luddy detected a fine imagination in Martin's sentences. She felt proud of him.

Up on her tiptoes, she asked the class excitedly, "Oh, who likes that one?"

Martin, at the front of the room, put his paper shyly over his face and drank in a hearty round of applause, some hoots, a whistle. Martin inched the paper off his face. He peeked warily at his classmates. The corners of his mouth eased up in a surprised smile. Accepting his fate, he bowed lightly.

The insect theme made Ms. Luddy smile too. Martin had recently requested lessons on the monarch butterfly. His mother had even pleaded with Ms. Luddy on the phone: "He really is interested in that butterfly. Do you think you'll get to it?"

If anyone could teach well about butterflies—monarch butterflies in particular—Ms. Luddy could. She'd long ago designed an entire monarch unit, with donated books and free expert help from a roving naturalist known to local teachers as the butterfly lady.

Back when Ms. Luddy had first taught the unit, several years back, her students had tromped out, magnifying glasses in hand, scouring the ghetto for milkweed leaves laden with tiny eggs. The milkweed did indeed grow, Ms. Luddy showed them, nature unstifled, up through sidewalk cracks, at the edges of vacant lots. Each student had a caterpillar egg, and most of the eggs actually hatched. Even the few kids whose anti-school defenses were already erected lowered their drawbridges for this lesson. They all rushed into the classroom and looked at their jars each morning. In summer, children carried their caterpillar jars home. They reported caterpillar-butterfly progress on postcards and sent them to Ms. Luddy's house over the summer. And later they set the butterflies free.

But butterflies had been off the official schedule in the past few years. Each fall, Ms. Luddy imagined suburban elementary school students rambling around apple orchards on field trips, picking fruit, creaking about on hay rides. Her kids couldn't do that, not with all the mandatory test practice. One weekend in October, Ms. Luddy had gone apple picking herself, and the following Monday, she'd handed each third grader a bright red apple, recounting her experience.

"You don't pull or yank the apples off the tree," she'd advised her students, demonstrating with an already-picked apple and an imaginary branch, just above her eyes.

"You twist," she'd explained, exaggerating the turning of her wrist, smiling. But she couldn't keep dwelling on apple orchards or anything as frivolous as the metamorphosis of caterpillars.

The CMT called.

"Who's next?" she asked the class. "Now remember, Martin is going to be a tough act to follow."

"Me! Me!" Rashida shouted. Her hand grabbed at the air. Barrettes of yellow, blue, pink, purple, and white clipped the ends of her neat braids. She wore pink work boots and dainty gold earrings. Rashida struggled in school, but in the first weeks of third grade, Ms. Luddy had already noticed that whenever Rashida really applied herself, she made "inspiring" progress.

In Rashida's story, someone or something—it wasn't clear who or what—had cast a spell on her. She ran around, animal-like. She got bored. She asked someone or something (again, not clear) to return her to life as Rashida.

"You had some exciting moments in there," Ms. Luddy told Rashida from her sunflower stool in the center of the room. "I liked the way you described your wish to turn back into a human being. It was a good resolution. You had all the important parts in there. But sweetie, you missed some things. Does anyone know what Rashida didn't have in there?"

"Yup," Jeremy said. He raised his hand.

"Jeremy. Go ahead."

"Well, first I want to say it was a good piece of narrative writing that I enjoyed," he said, looking kindly toward Rashida. "But," he continued, wincing, clearly pained by the idea of delivering criticism. "Okay . . . um . . . well . . . Rashida never said what kind of animal she was."

"Right," Ms. Luddy said. "For the reader to have an understanding of what happened—to have it mean something—you need to say you turned into, what? A lion? A frog?"

Rashida took dramatic delight in realizing her oversight. She put her hand to her mouth. She gasped. She released a raucous, raspy laugh. She lay across the desk, still laughing. She sat up suddenly and reread the prompt to herself. She pouted angrily. She pushed her bony shoulders back.

"Hey!" Rashida shouted to no one. "I thought it was just any animal. Nothin' in there say it gotta be a certain one." Rashida shouted in Ms. Luddy's direction: "Hey! See! Look!" She held the prompt up high and stabbed it with her finger. Rashida called out for justice: "Ms. Luddy!"

Classroom chatter drowned her out. Rashida gave up the fight. Eyes on Ms. Luddy, she stealthily unwrapped a piece of pink candy and popped it in her mouth.

Often hidden within Rashida's loud and frequent protests were very good points. She had followed the writing prompt's directions. And she had correctly sensed that in Hartford's schools, that had come to count for a lot.

Replacement

MUCH OF WHAT HAPPENED in Ms. Luddy's classroom, and much of what didn't, mirrored two preponderant national trends. The first, bottom-line tests, increasingly drove urban schools. The second trend often followed from the first: Hartford installed "off the shelf" curriculum models that handed teachers, even great teachers like Lois Luddy, scripts to follow and logbooks to fill. This was, ironically, all related to *Sheff v. O'Neill*.

Responding to the state supreme court's order, the state legislature had allocated millions of dollars to abate Hartford's racial and economic isolation by both building and continuing the operation of "interdistrict" magnet schools, usually, though not always, racially mixed. The small windfall for desegregation had also expanded to other urban areas with the state's voluntary transfer program, allowing urban kids to attend suburban schools. These initiatives, welcomed by the Sheff plaintiffs, still left intact basic patterns of race and class division that had moved John Brittain, Wes Horton, Jack Boger, and the others to action in the first place.

The reform program installed in Hartford—curriculum alignment, intensive test drilling, and a literacy program—had supplanted the *Sheff* dream of integration. The idea of correcting separate and unequal schools fell right off the agenda from the start.

HERE'S HOW IT HAPPENED. After the state supreme court's *Sheff* order in 1996, Governor John G. Rowland made the same move his predecessor, William O'Neill, had before. He announced the creation of a panel.

Rowland's Educational Improvement Panel gathered an eclectic crowd of 21 distinguished citizens, notably light on educational expertise—one school superintendent, one current (suburban) teacher, and one former teacher turned state legislator. It was heavy on suburbanites (13), state politicians (8), and lawyers (7). Two middle-class Hispanics sat on the panel, including Santa Mendoza, a personal-injury lawyer and active Republican from West Hartford. Two of the five African Americans were Republicans and lived in elite suburbs. Eddie Davis, at the time Manchester's school superintendent, was the only panel member with a child in a Hartford school.

Over five months, EIP members argued circles around the circles they'd already argued. They spent a lot of time debating their mission. Did they really have to come up with programs to *desegregate* the schools? Wouldn't it be better if they just made the city schools better?

A few panel members—including Yvonne Duncan, a Hartford lawyer, and Jerry Brown, a union organizer—tried to lead the group to focus on the fact of segregation. They proposed that the schools in the area be regionalized. Mathematically, at least, it was the only way to provide the requisite numbers of various races and classes. They each spoke for 15 minutes. The plaintiffs had their say, also briefly. John Brittain and Phil Tegeler visited the panel, offering detailed guidelines, including programs for teacher recruitment and training, affordable housing, and expanded transfer options for urban children. It was a practical road map. Panel members listened respectfully.

A few months later, in January 1997, committee members settled on 15 recommendations, sorted by category, among them "Improving

Teaching and Learning," "Encouraging Parental Involvement," and "Enhancing a Sense of Community." The last (and according to John Brittain, "the least") category was "Reducing Racial Isolation."

A reflective, soft-spoken man named Jack Hasegawa, from the State Department of Education, served as staff for the panel. He assisted the group, getting papers photocopied, filing unrevealing minutes, scheduling public hearings, talking to the press, and researching panel members' questions.

Before panel members submitted the 49-page booklet of recommendations to Rowland, Hasegawa remembered, a few panel members had expressed a new concern: "They're worrying about when you dropped the booklet down, where did the page open up to?" Panel members, Hasegawa told me, fretted and regretted that "some desegregation-related" program would "emerge" as the center of the discussion. Hasegawa found this "rather ironic."

"*Sheff* was about racial isolation. Right?" He looked genuinely mystified. "That's how I read it. So shouldn't that *be* the center of discussion?"

The suburban-dominated legislature whittled and tinkered with EIP recommendations. Then the legislature's own Education Committee drafted measures even *less* ambitious. Those bills stalled in the Appropriations Committee. In the end, only after the Black and Hispanic Caucus threatened to withdraw support from a budget compromise if *Sheff* measures weren't passed, the legislature enacted a series of laws and grant programs in the closing days of its 1997 session. The legislature officially declared the reduction of "racial isolation" to be one of the state's "educational interests."

No one was ordered to change anything.

One law seemed to establish a statewide urban and suburban transfer program allowing city kids to attend suburban schools and vice versa, but the program didn't actually establish anything. It expanded Hartford's very small Project Concern to cover New Haven and Bridgeport kids too. The legislature also gave the program a new name with

a free-enterprise spin: Open Choice. The law allowed transfers of urban kids *if* (here lay a catch) suburban officials said they had seats
available.

Legislators also established a grant program for charter and interdistrict magnet schools; educators could apply for state money to build, improve, or operate racially diverse schools. This added onto work already
being done. (During the 1990s, the state had paid to build and/or operate 16 interdistrict magnet schools, not only in Hartford but across the
state. Some of these schools were in fact established, in New Haven,
Bridgeport, and Hartford, *before* the 1996 *Sheff* ruling.) Legislators also
increased funding for "interdistrict cooperative grants." These allowed
any school to create small, part-time programs bringing together urban
and suburban youngsters. (This program would allow Jeremy and his
classmates to take some bus trips to a nearby suburban school.)

Legislators also funded "school readiness" programs, apportioning
subsidies to help established preschool programs enroll more low-
income students. More than 90 percent of the $40 million grant was set
aside for the state's low-performing school districts, including Hartford.
But the lawmakers didn't require that these, or any, early childhood
programs be desegregated.

The big *Sheff*-related legislation was Special Act 97-4. In 1997, the
state legislature declared "a crisis" and took control of the Hartford
Public Schools. It fired the local, elected Board of Education and replaced it with a state-appointed board of trustees. The cochairman of
the legislature's Education Committee termed this package "groundbreaking." John Brittain termed it "less than token."

IN 1998, TWO YEARS and five months after the original court
order, plaintiff lawyers felt driven to file yet another set of documents
with the court, complaining that the state's response to *Sheff* had
been "wholly inadequate." The entire team worked at renewing the
case—Phil Tegeler, Dennis Parker, John Brittain, Martha Stone, and

Wes Horton. Marianne Lado had moved on to work on civil rights cases for the nonprofit New York Lawyers for the Public Interest.

In a brief trial before Judge Julia Aurigemma, the plaintiffs showed that the Open Choice program, which accommodated 524 Hartford kids in 1998, included mostly children who'd already joined the old Project Concern program by the time the new legislation package passed. More than 400 new applicants had been turned down for lack of space in suburban schools. The old Project Concern had taken in even more students 20 years earlier; the program's former director, Mary Carroll, testified that she'd enrolled about 1,175 children then. The 524 Hartford kids, Carroll testified, represented a decrease of 223 children even from the school year preceding the 1996 *Sheff* decision. The state retorted, however, that Open Choice served kids across the state now, not just in Hartford. And *that* should be counted as progress.

In 1998 there were three interdistrict magnet schools in Hartford. Two predated the *Sheff* decision and one of them was a part-time program. Only 157 Hartford students out of some 24,000 students in the city system had been able to enroll in those schools. The schools depended on the voluntary participation of suburban districts, which could pull out at any time without penalty.

One of the state's expert witnesses from the first trial, Christine Rossell, showed up again for the new hearing. She called Connecticut a "leader in the nation" on desegregation. Wes Horton contradicted that assessment: "The drop hasn't even reached the bucket here," he said in his closing statement.

In March 1999, Judge Julia Aurigemma, who'd been appointed by Governor John Rowland, ruled in the state's favor.

"The State has acted expeditiously and in good faith," she wrote.

Savior

BEFORE *SHEFF,* HARTFORD sat at the bottom of the state's annual standardized test-score rankings. After *Sheff,* it stayed right there, below other districts with like poverty—New Haven, Bridgeport, New Britain, Waterbury. Connecticut students, overall, consistently scored at the top or near the top in National Assessment of Educational Progress (NAEP), the country's only standardized measure. But on the NAEP—given to a representative sample of students annually—the state recorded notably large gaps between racial minority students and white students. Meanwhile, Connecticut's white kids tended to score higher than white kids in other states.

A month after Judge Julia Aurigemma's decision in the latest *Sheff* go-round, the state-appointed board of trustees for the city's schools spotted a savior. If anyone could get Hartford floating, it was this guy in New York, Anthony S. Amato.

On April 1, 1999, Anthony "Tony" Amato—Mr. Amato to most everyone speaking directly with him—signed on as Hartford's ninth school superintendent in nine years.

Short, with a round, usually unsmiling face and shiny jet-black hair, Amato has a solemn manner and speaks softly one-on-one. Warmth does not emanate from him, but passion on behalf of children does.

"They are beautiful," Amato told me in 2000, a year into his tenure, pacing the floor of his roomy office downtown. "They have so much potential. They are capable of so much, every single one of them. We have no idea the things they can do. My job is to make sure their lives aren't wasted."

Before coming to Hartford, Amato had been superintendent for the 28,000 students of District 6 in New York City, the heavily Latino and poor Washington Heights area. He had started that job with District 6's test scores about where Hartford's were in 1998.

"An abysmal embarrassment," Amato said, looking grief-stricken. "There really was no central office," he remembered. "That had been shut down because of asbestos. But no one knew why the central office hadn't moved to a location without asbestos.

"It was a completely ridiculous situation," he said, shaking his head in disapproval. "I walk in and find no communication linkages. No phone. No fax. There was no way for me to contact any of the schools I was supposed to be overseeing. And then? We couldn't find anybody. People who on paper were supposed to be in charge — they weren't even around. Every school was out there, floating around with no support, nobody paying attention. The schools were like little buoys, floating around in the ocean. Or, you know, ships going around in the night, floating by, just barely. Let me put it this way: A good day for them was not sinking."

Enter the Coast Guard. According to the widely repeated public story, Amato had braved stormy meetings and gotten the district organized. He'd aligned curriculum with the annual standardized tests. He'd handed out "pacing calendars," instructing teachers what to teach when. He'd gotten rid of what he termed "deadwood" — bad teachers and lazy or phantom administrators.

And not long after his arrival, test scores in District 6 had begun to climb. During his tenure, they moved from near the bottom of test-score rankings to just about the middle — 15th out of 32 districts. Equally remarkable, Tony Amato had held on to the District 6 job for 12 years, 9 more than the typical urban superintendent stays put.

In Hartford, Tony Amato hoped to repeat that recent triumph. Months before he officially started work, he'd set about enforcing optimism, pride — and fear — in every dreary, burned-out, passive corner. For decades, Hartford's teachers and parents had suffered through a parade of new leaders, each coming in with moralistic incantations: "All children can learn," "All children will reach their full potential," "Maintain high expectations." Mr. Amato spoke to his new public in refreshing, frightening bottom-line exhortations of his own.

"Come this time next year, we will not be last and we will never be last again!" Amato told crowds of teachers, administrators, and parents. He took to repeating this "we will never be last again" mantra. He paced across stages, a hungry tiger. His singular focus emerged. Teachers and principals were to get those test scores up. Children were to take the test in October. Tony Amato had arrived in April. He had six months.

"Three," he quickly pointed out to me, "if you don't count summer."

Keeping the Promise

Tony Amato fired people, encouraged others to leave, and made some new hires, colleagues who'd followed him from New York and filled out what he called his "cabinet." He called some of them "turnaround" specialists. Members of the state-appointed board supervising Amato confined themselves to uttering praiseful, thankful words about him. The teachers' union, barely credible in the public's eyes and lacking a grand plan of their own, signed on to Amato's early on.

After his round of "never last again" orations, Amato set about taming the central office. He installed an efficient accounting system. In 1998, principals and teachers had suffered through a spending freeze. Many teachers had paid out of pocket, even more than usual, for such basic supplies as pencils and scissors. Principals had cadged donations of construction paper and photocopy toner. A few months after Tony Amato's arrival in 1999, James Thompson noticed that supplies flowed to his school on time and in quantities to last the year. That impressed him right away.

Achieving basic functionality gave Amato little to crow about, though. The media, politicians, and parents awaited action on Amato's pledge to lift Hartford from last place.

In short order, Amato and his staff set up a demanding, relentless training regimen: Power Hour (kids stayed after school, in some cases until nearly 5 p.m., drilling for tests); Power School (October's test takers in the fourth, sixth, and eighth grades drilled right through the prior April vacation); Super Saturdays (imminent test takers drilled on weekends). And fall's test takers had to attend summer school. Kids filled Ms. Luddy's windowless, stuffy classroom in July.

Amato soon compelled school-department receptionists to chirp, "Hartford schools on the rise!" when answering the phones. Callers heard clipped, weary voices mismatched with the hopeful-by-policy greeting. Memos also bore that same official motto: "Hartford Schools on the Rise." "On the Rise" pins appeared on lapels. Tony Amato delivered eloquent motivational speeches telling and retelling the allegory of his own rise — he'd grown up poor, Puerto Rican, and ghettoized, in the Bronx.

The central office kept busy. Amato frequently declared emergency meetings. New descriptors for initiatives were *hot, power,* and *super.* Waverly's principal, James Thompson, said, shrugging, "A lot more adjectives now."

Amato's face glared from SAVE OUR SCHOOLS billboards at two entrances to the North End — by the highway beyond Upper Albany, and above a littered sidewalk and battered chain-link fence in Clay Arsenal. The signs urged yes votes on an upcoming school bond referendum. They stayed up long after the yeses had carried the day.

"He has his own sign now, Mr. Amato does," sweet, dainty Naia whispered to me, her pretty brown eyes growing wide. "I even seen it once!"

THE KEY STATISTIC in Connecticut's test-score accounting, Amato understood, was called the "index." It reflected the portion of students meeting the state's "goal" and also the portion not meeting it. The highest possible index was 100 — all students met the goal. The lowest possible index was 0 — no students met it.

Anthony Amato's first year of judgment was 1999. The files of test-score results arrived in his office, near Christmas, he later remembered.

He knew just where to look. Hartford's new index, he saw, was 52.3—
good news. Hartford's test scores had improved, with the index jumping 11 percentage points. A big gain, but had he kept his promise? Were
Hartford kids last again? Well, they continued to rank far worse than
most. But yes, they'd climbed enough, scoring better than kids in a few
other cities. Hartford stood third from the bottom among Connecticut's
163 school districts.

The news flew across the educational landscape. In September 2000,
a feature story on Hartford's "improvements" graced the cover of the
American Federation of Teachers' widely circulated magazine, *American Teacher.* The following month, that group issued a policy brief her-
alding test-score gains in urban school districts, including Hartford.
That same year, even the education field's paper of record, the widely
read *Education Week,* reported Hartford's test-score improvements.

The next year, state testers devised a new exam, CMT Third Generation, reportedly a bit tougher. Education officials cautioned the media
not to compare old and new test results. Yet, any way you considered it,
Hartford held steady, still near the bottom, but now ahead of Connecticut's other high-poverty urban districts.

Several months later, with Ms. Luddy's third graders ensconced in
Power Hour, an *Education Week* headline read, UNDER AMATO, HART-
FORD SCHOOLS SHOW PROGRESS. Later that year, the American Federation of Teachers sponsored a conference, "Overcoming the Challenges
of Low-Performing Schools." In a press release, organizers wrote, "Hartford is the site of the conference and serves as a model for how to overcome the challenges of low-performing schools and see results. Over
the past few years . . . Hartford has recorded significant increases in
test scores." Reporters attending the conference, another press release
said, may "visit public schools in Hartford that are using successful
school reform models."

In all the excitement, few dared acknowledge that Tony Amato's
prideful pledge implied something incredibly depressing about the state

of urban schooling. Anyone whooping it up about coming in third or fifth from the bottom—at the expense of other children and educators freshly tarnished with the "last place" stigma—was celebrating a dreary miracle. Hartford's rise to "best of the worst" brought an unintended consequence. The dizzying quest to nudge up test scores overshadowed far-off visions of equal, integrated schools. The *Sheff* cause drifted even further to the margins of public concern.

"People are happy in their neighborhood schools," Connecticut's education commissioner, Ted Sergi, told a legislative committee that convened, in part, to discuss fulfillment of the *Sheff v. O'Neill* mandate. "The Hartford schools are getting better," the commissioner said.

Ms. Luddy, meanwhile, did what she could. All hands on deck, Jeremy and his classmates, with tired eyes, sore butts, and stir-crazy souls, set about helping Mr. Amato keep his promise never to be last again.

Reform: The Idea of Ice

"ONLY FIFTEEN MINUTES MORE," Patrick whispered to me near the end of a Power Hour. "I don't know if I can hold out here." Even though Ms. Luddy's third graders weren't scheduled to take the big CMT until fall of fourth grade, they had to start prepping in the fall of third grade. By spring of third grade, they had to log extra practice hours four afternoons a week.

"This is too long," Shasa said. She stood and stretched. "My butt's killin' me here."

Ms. Luddy's hair fell in sweaty half-inch panels over her forehead. She sighed. The whites of her pale blue eyes had reddened. Her delicate face, usually pinkish around the cheeks, was a bit ashen.

She stayed on task, resigned and loyal to her central-office test-prep book. She fretted about the day's reading comprehension passage. It was on dogsledding. The topic had engaged the kids before, but the topic wasn't really dogsleds this time. It was the "main idea" of the dogsledding passage, the "appropriate title" of the dogsledding passage, the "details" that could and could not be gleaned from the dogsledding passage.

This Power Hour trucked along like the others. For the kids to really, truly "get it"—not merely to pass the test, but to learn, to understand—Ms. Luddy had to clarify dogsled terminology. Her chalk clicked, writing out definitions on the board. She drew little sketches.

"Here's a 'lead' dog, yes, who *leads* the team," she explained.

There was a "lead," which fastened a dog to the team. Ms. Luddy drew a leash that ended in contact with a vaguely doglike blob.

Hamilton slumped. His head fell into the crook of his left arm, set on the desk. He closed his eyes. His arm slid off. He awakened himself, head shaking, startled. He coughed and blinked rapidly.

"Hamilton, sweetie," Ms. Luddy said, winking. She walked over and rubbed his back. "Try to stay with us," she whispered in his ear.

Rashida groaned.

Ms. Luddy flashed her a hard look and softened it.

"I know, honey," she said. "But we don't have much longer to go. Help me out here, Rashida."

Shasa shut her eyes for a few seconds, then opened them wide and sucked her thumb.

Patrick forced his eyelids open with his fingers.

Owen, across from him, bewildered, surveyed Patrick and laughed.

Patrick whispered to Owen, "I ain't tryin' a be funny. I'm keepin' myself awake here."

Owen pushed his own eyelids open with his fingers.

"It work!" he exclaimed.

"Owen! Patrick!" Ms. Luddy admonished. She looked perplexed, observing Patrick. "What are you—? you know? Don't tell me. Just stop."

Aisha swayed as if about to faint.

Keesha drew a snowman on the back of her hand.

Dominique doodled on her packet.

Kayla rocked back and forth.

Test-prep book in one hand, chalk in the other, Ms. Luddy paced. The runners of a dogsled, she explained, are grooved. "Grooved?"

"They have grooves. That grip the ice?"

She looked over the room. Ms. Luddy sensed by the quality of silence, by the state of eye glazing, when the children understood.

"No?" she asked the children.

A few heads shook no. Aisha looked devastated. She hid her face in her hands.

Rashida groaned again, snagging everyone's attention.

"Rashida," Ms. Luddy said wearily.

Shasa cracked her knuckles, stretched her thin arms into a high arch, scrunched her face, yawned.

T.J. massaged his shoulders and flexed his feet under the desk.

Patrick put his fingers in his eyes again.

Owen dozed.

Kayla yawned. She picked at something in her right eye. She bit at her fingernails.

"Okay," Ms. Luddy said perkily. "Well, otherwise, the dogsled, it would slip and slide, see. If the runners were flat, there would be nothing to grip onto that ice? While the dogs are pulling it."

Ms. Luddy attempted to draw a sled runner with grooves.

Shasa nodded, thumb in mouth again.

Rashida squinted at the drawing. "Huh?" she said.

Ms. Luddy slogged through the mandated curriculum, which stipulated that she deconstruct a deadening passage about dogsledding. Many of the New England children in this room had never skated over, slid upon, nor seen a frozen lake.

School finally let out. Jeremy had missed that Power Hour. His social worker had driven him to see his little brothers. I told him about the dogsledding exercise and he told me he had once seen a lake. But he'd seen it in spring. He'd never seen a *frozen* lake. I told him that others in his class hadn't either—not Patrick, Owen, Hamilton, Aisha, Martin, Jinaya, or Keesha.

"But I should tell you," Jeremy said, interrupting my tally. "I did freeze something once in the winter. In cups. I put some water in cups. I wanted to see how fast it would freeze and I kept looking at it. And I made these little notes, like, my aunt, well, she told me I needed to keep track of what I was doing? So at the same time, we put one in my freezer and then we went on and put one out on the stoop? The steps? And I wanted to see what one froze faster? And it was the same time! It was great for us to make that ice. I think that even if I haven't seen the frozen ponds, I have had a little bit of ice that I made."

The Next Race

Throughout most of third grade and throughout the hot, dull month of summer school, the students stacked up hour upon hour, session upon session, of writing prompts, math drills, and "degrees of reading power" passages peppered with blanks. Photocopied answer sheets with miniature circles labeled *a, b, c, d,* accompanied assignments, which looked increasingly like the test. Sample CMT questions got tacked onto worksheets. Booklets arrived from the central office, labeled by the skill to be tested on the CMT—"Cause and Effect," one label read.

Those writing and reading exercises, heavy on passive voice and littered with ambiguous reference pronouns, were "boring," Owen complained. In the first days of fourth grade, a lot of the kids complained. But they also inched pridefully toward a clear goal. They'd internalized CMT lingo—DRP (degrees of reading power), RC (reading comprehension), PNV (place number value)—early in third grade. They slogged through Power Hour, usually without complaint.

"DRP. DRP. That's bad. That's boooooring!" Shasa said.

"I'm nervous," Jeremy said. Ms. Luddy noticed Jeremy's new tic: he'd started blinking and contorting his face. The tic would cease after the tests.

"What if I have a bad day?" Jeremy asked. "What if I mess up bad?"

Patrick was terrified. "Man," he said, "I be workin' hard as I can. But

I don't know. It could be bad, and if it's bad, that's not something I can think about."

Aisha had nightmares. "My grandma says, 'Don't think about it,'" she told me. "But I can't help it. I sit down at night and I fall asleep, but I'm worryin' in my sleep, I guess."

The test drills came easily to T.J., who practiced steadily and without difficulty.

"You gotta do what you gotta do." He shrugged. "They tell us to do it. We do it."

Rashida felt sick of it and bold about saying so. "If I gotta do one more CMT thing, I just throwin' it back," she told me, biting into a bruised apple at lunch. "It's got to be over with."

"Every day I wake up and I want to go to school and I think it's gonna be good?" Jeremy told me. "But then it's the same thing, all about the CMT. And I don't want to put all negatives on this. But I have to agree with everyone. It's really boring."

A recent practice-reading passage about "raw materials" had begun, "Many things are used to make other things . . . Wood is the raw material from which tables and chairs are made. Trees are changed into lumber or smooth wood, and furniture is made."

The directions asked students to underline "key" words, "the words with big ideas . . . the words that make pictures in your mind."

Ms. Luddy, mildly irritated by such directives, took them in stride. But as the test drew closer, she grew sadder. It had "become impossible," she told me, to "squeeze in those little extras like science and social studies."

One afternoon, for example, yet another writing prompt asked Ms. Luddy's students to describe what they "find" after a meteor lands in their backyard, making a crater.

Hands shot up.

"Ms. Luddy, what's a meteor?"

"Ms. Luddy, what's a crater?"

She went off message and taught an abbreviated science lesson.

"Okay, everyone have an idea of a meteor? A crater? A crater's a big hole in the ground."

The questions buried her.

"What happens if a meteor lands on Hartford, Ms. Luddy?"

"Is a meteor going to land on Hartford?"

"Ms. Luddy, Ms. Luddy. How often does a meteor land on us?"

"Has a meteor ever landed on Hartford?"

"Ms. Luddy, have you seen a real meteor?"

The chaotic barrage of eager, human curiosity thrilled Ms. Luddy. But the lively eyes before her reminded her of the clock.

She put an end to the questions; the eyes deadened.

"They did very poorly on the meteor prompt," she told me the following week.

She sighed heavily and blamed herself.

"Maybe if I'd explained it more fully, maybe found some pictures for them, brought that in," she said. "They shouldn't get punished because they don't have a clear idea of what meteors are and what they look like. That's not their fault. They should have a chance to study meteors or at least see pictures, don't you think? Don't you think studying meteors would be great?"

Sophistication

HARTFORD'S UNDEREXPOSED KIDS had to learn not only the skills and the content that the test covered but also the skills of taking tests.

"The suburban kids know how to take tests," Tony Amato said to me confidently in 2000. "Our kids need that level of sophistication."

Amato and his staff had built "test sophistication" instruction right into the mandated CMT lessons. Children were instructed, for example, not only to "fill in the blanks" but also to "read the following paragraphs. Before you circle each answer, REREAD and READ MORE."

Tony Amato sent the *Literacy Enhancement and Test Sophistication Program Teacher's Resource Guide* to schools. It reminded the experienced Ms. Luddy to "be sure that you are . . . EXPLAINING and MODELING appropriate test-taking procedures," and "point out to students that they can find the right answer without knowing every single word in the passage," and "tell students to skip names of people and places," and "keep up an intensive business-like pace."

Tony Amato sent home test-taking "enhancement" memos to parents. They mostly sailed right over Nina's and Anna's heads. "The mathematics test uses multiple-choice, grid-in and open-ended items . . ." And, "Each grade level also includes extended problem-solving tasks designed to assess integrated application of mathematical understanding." Parents were also encouraged to "reward your child with praise, hugs and kisses" after she or he demonstrated skills in "editing and revising."

PERHAPS Ms. LUDDY WAS able to forge onward because she actually did respect the CMT.

"Really, I do," she said. The children, she insisted, need "every one" of the skills the CMT tested.

But Ms. Luddy added that kids' CMT scores often didn't match how well they did on other homework and assessments. In educational research parlance, the scores didn't generalize to other domains. Still, to Ms. Luddy, the CMT was revealing. The so-called "off level" CMTs kids took in third grade—the run-up to the big day—showed her that although Patrick was improving, he still had trouble multiplying big numbers, and that in word problems, Owen often mixed up subtraction and addition, division and multiplication. It confirmed her instinct that she needed to challenge Shasa's great competence more. And Jeremy might as well skip the too-basic math lessons, go to the library, and read about whatever he wanted to read about.

And Rashida—she had that writing formula down pat. But she too had difficulties beyond the CMT.

Thing, Ms. Luddy said. "That's Rashida's word for too many objects. Simple objects. Like an eraser? That's a thing. And verbs? *Go.* Her verb is *go*. As in 'He goed to the store, then he goed home.'" And, she continued, "ask Rashida to write several sentences about a book she read? She needs a lot of support. Sure, she can do the formula. But she's stumped by pretty much anything beyond that."

Owen also had posted solid CMT writing scores in third grade, but Ms. Luddy didn't feel he could write well at all. Patrick, by far the most imaginative and poignant writer in the class, had barely met the state's writing goal in third grade. There was no way, Ms. Luddy said, that a test could capture the depth of Patrick's talent and sensibility as a writer.

T.J., meanwhile, had scored high in math, reading, and particularly writing. But Ms. Luddy found most of his essays dull, formulaic, and lacking in verve. He rarely wrote anything clever. T.J., a hard worker with "good support at home," was a child whom, "given more time and freedom," Ms. Luddy supposed she might help "open up a little bit, really flower." He was successful by one measure, she said, but he got no joy from learning the way Jeremy and some other kids did. He had a difficult time admitting even small mistakes. She worried about T.J.'s stamina over the long term.

"And so I feel like the mind-set out there is that he's okay. You don't have to worry about kids like T.J. But of course I see he does have potential to work hard, to catch on quickly, and then I want to take that next step in helping him find a passion that's going to keep him going. But in this environment, it's pretty difficult to do."

For two out of five days each week, in fourth grade, Ms. Luddy's students didn't attend "specials," such as music or art, any longer. From about 8:30 a.m. until nearly 5 p.m.—finally the end of Power Hour—they sat and drilled for the test.

Even one of the old "specials"—computer lab—had morphed into more test drilling by spring of third grade.

Late one morning in the first week of autumn, the kids had sauntered into the cramped but functional computer room and flicked switches. A cartoon—of a placid lake, green trees, and little people—filled each screen.

"Welcome to the July 4th picnic," a message read. "You will be asked to count the people at the picnic from across the lake. Each tent holds 100 people. Each boat holds 10 people."

Students were to load boats and tents with picnickers. The games had been developed to match skills the CMT tested. For 45 minutes, the children were locked into on-screen test prep.

The children grew loud. Owen kept popping out of his seat. Rashida bickered with Jinaya. Hamilton wandered aimlessly. T.J. and Patrick argued loudly. Ms. Luddy shut the corridor door. She had private words with them. They settled down, but most kept fidgeting and poking. A few plotted escapes.

"Ms. Luddy?" Jeremy asked, lumbering over glumly. "Umm, I don't want to be negative, but, umm, well, see? I've done all these already?"

"I know, honey," she answered. "Everyone has done these already. You're not alone. But what, you wanna read a book? Then read a book. Go get a book. Hurry back."

"Really!" He perked up, his smile deepening his dimples.

Shasa had snuck in a Harry Potter paperback. She held it up, caught Ms. Luddy's eyes, and raised her eyebrows coyly, asking, "May I?"

Ms. Luddy nodded.

Shasa pushed her chair against the wall, opened to a page, sucked her thumb, and lost herself in a place of magic.

Martin shuffled over, holding up a book about bats. Before he asked, Ms. Luddy answered, "Yes. Go ahead." He smiled and hopped a little, gleeful.

MATH CAME NEXT. For the review on linear measurement, the children handled no actual rulers. They gazed at inches depicted on a worksheet. Ms. Luddy wished they'd held real rulers and measured actual objects.

For "estimating measurements," Ms. Luddy would have divided the class into groups, given each a half-gallon jug, and had them estimate how many cups of liquid they'd have to dump in to fill it. Studying probability, back in third grade, they'd flicked handmade spinners, and written down number frequencies. They'd had a blast. Fourth grade's review of probability consisted of worksheet exercises.

Ms. Luddy complied with the "CMT aligned" curriculum. But she also hunted for diversions. And some things, she said, she'd never sacrifice.

Take class council. On Friday afternoons, even during the height of CMT fervor, Ms. Luddy and the children sat on the floor in a cozy circle and practiced democracy. They debated classroom policy. T.J. had suggested the previous year that if your name was on the board more than three times for misbehavior, you should miss recess—if in fact there "were recess at our school." The kids hashed out conflicts, peaceably. Martin, the prior fall, had complained of Patrick, "He was laughing at me when I couldn't say the word 'asterisk,' and it made me feel bad." And they always had great fun counting up votes for student of the month.

During fourth grade's first class council meeting, children secretly scribbled votes on scraps of paper and stuffed them into a slot in a baby blue shoebox. Cross-legged on the floor, Ms. Luddy flipped open the lid. With a flourish she pulled out the first paper.

"This vote is for . . ." She teased them with a long pause. Her eyes scanned the room. Children leaned forward.

"Ohhhhh!" she exclaimed. "Patrick!"

"I voted for him because the last time we did writing, he was really on task," Owen said. "He really got a lot done. I saw it!"

Patrick covered his face with his hands. A few cheers went up.

The third and fourth votes. Patrick.

"Patrick," the fifth note read. "Because he's nice."

Patrick looked around at his classmates, amazed.

"Me? Nice?" he said. "Nahh."

"You are nice, Patrick," Shasa said. "You are always nice to me," she added, nodding steadily. She glanced around at the others, seeking public confirmation. A few other girls nodded.

Squinting at Patrick, Rashida asked him, "Who say you ain't nice? You nice."

Index finger to his lips, Patrick sat on his haunches. He considered the label as though it were a priestly collar he wasn't sure he wanted.

Ms. Luddy unfolded another paper.

"It's Patrick again," she said, looking straight at him. Her stare had asked him to make a decision.

"Okay," Patrick said, spreading his arms wide. "I'm nice."

Two hours later, beaming over coffee and cookies at a local café, Ms. Luddy rehearsed the afternoon's big event.

"Did you see how he put that certificate into his backpack? How excited he was? The smile on his face? What a victory for him!"

What a victory for her.

Turned out, Ms. Luddy wasn't alone in her faith. The kids hadn't forgotten about the old Patrick. They'd seen him push desks, have tantrums. He'd even thrown a chair across the room. For a time, he'd made learning difficult for everyone. Then, right before their eyes, the children had witnessed something remarkable. They'd seen Patrick change. And in their close circle that Friday afternoon, Ms. Luddy's class wasn't merely a struggling tangle of cute kids, but a collectively hopeful team, bestowing ritual honor upon their most deserving member.

IN THOSE EARLIEST DAYS of fourth grade, Ms. Luddy showed me the index cards she'd recently taped to each student's desk. Back in third grade, she and James Thompson had scoured that year's so-called "off level" test results and detected patterns. On index cards, she'd recorded skill areas in which each child had yet to reach either "mastery" (the highest level) or "goal" (the second highest) on the upcoming CMTs.

Many of the kids, she'd noted, had slipped up on "integrated understandings." Here, students had to choose a method—say, subtraction or addition, or usually both—for solving a simulated real-life challenge. Some slipped up on estimation. But the surprise weakness was "place number value." Hartford's kids had practiced this since first grade. Too many children still had trouble. "Place number value" became a central-office priority. In fourth grade, with only several weeks to go before the CMT, Luddy was still drilling it into the kids.

"On problem number five. Everybody on problem number five? You had to borrow? Correct? And you had to borrow from the what column?"

"Tens!" On it went for 32 minutes. Ms. Luddy's shoulders dropped.

"Okay, now, we are done with place value. You may not see it again until when?"

"The CMT," the children chanted.

"And when you see place value, it is going to be like an old friend, right?" Ms. Luddy suggested, nodding fast. In less than a month now, on test day, they would indeed see it again. "You'll open up that test booklet and you can say, 'Oh, hello there, place value. How are you today? It's so good to see you!'" Ms. Luddy waved in the manner of royalty before a crowd.

The children giggled.

"Let's all kiss place number value good-bye!"

Kids kissed their test-prep packets. Ms. Luddy kissed her hand and blew. "Bye-bye, my old friend place value," she said cheerily. "I won't forget you."

"I ain't kissin' good-bye to no place value," Patrick said, turning up his lip. "This is some crazy, man. You's all gone crazy."

Tests of Two Varieties

SEPTEMBER 11, 2001, ENCROACHED on Hartford's finely drawn testing plan. The southwestern section of the state—the portion of Connecticut most linked, economically and emotionally, with New York City—lost many residents. Testing would be delayed two weeks, the education commissioner, Ted Sergi, declared, out of respect for students who'd lost family. The children of Waverly watched the news at home. In the days after September 11, like other Americans, they'd repeatedly seen those images—the planes crashing, the towers crumbling. The scenes repeated in Jeremy's dreams "for days," he said. Owen, Ms. Luddy observed, "is obsessed with the event." "But," she added, "in a good way."

"The child wants to understand," she said. "He is trying to really grasp the politics, the religious aspects to it, the people involved, the science of it."

Many students asked questions that even Ms. Luddy couldn't answer. T.J., usually militant about learning, groped around in intellectual and spiritual darkness.

"How do you? I mean, how do you? I mean how do you stop thinking about this?" T.J. asked. "This is something that the whole world is going to be thinking about for a long time."

Patrick added, "Those kids aren't going to be able to get over something like that in two weeks. Why not just let them take the test when they feel like they're ready?" Ms. Luddy thought Patrick had made a good point.

The central office expressed a different sentiment. Teachers, central-office administrators suggested, might want to spend some time talking about September 11 but should use most of the extra two weeks for still more test preparation.

Ms. Luddy did feel the children needed time to "talk through" September 11. They wanted, she said, "to feel useful," as if they were doing something "constructive" related to the event. She and the students devised a project: They'd send out support letters to New York. And they'd decorate the bulletin board outside their door with a patriotic theme—red, white, and blue construction paper hands and flags.

Most of the children wrote to September 11's obvious, public heroes—the firefighters, the mayor. Several wrote to President Bush. Jeremy, though, wrote to an unnamed "citizen of New York City, U.S.A."

"I wanted everyone to have a fair chance of getting my letter," he explained. "I didn't really want to do it so that only if you are important you are going to get my letter, like if you are the president or something. Anyone could get the letter and say, 'Hey! A letter from Jeremy Otero, a kid in Hartford, Connecticut!'"

The equal-opportunity letter read, "Hi. My name is Jeremy Otero. I'm in fourth grade. I hope that none of your family members have gone away. Please be safe during this tragedy. I'm sorry I can't help, but the one and only thing I could do right now is hope. Your friend, Jeremy Otero. P.S. May God bless your hearts."

The afternoon activity made Ms. Luddy tense. There *was* much to accomplish before test time.

"Okay, let's go now," she said reluctantly after a while, as the kids traced their hands onto red construction paper. She'd do some of the cutting and pasting herself, after-hours.

"We've got to get this done," she told the class. "We have to clean up now and move on."

STUDENTS SAT FOR the CMT each morning, starting in the last days of September and continuing into October. Then the school days proceeded normally—with more drilling—through the afternoons.

Per central-office directive, Ms. Luddy dismantled her cozy, clustered communal desks and repositioned them in conventional rows.

A colleague stepped into Ms. Luddy's room the next day, eyed the rows and declared: "Oh. No. Oh. No. I'm sorry, but this is disgusting. This is really disgusting."

Ms. Luddy told me state regulations prohibited me from observing the test taking. Thompson jokingly overrode her: "Look. Sit in the back. Don't say anything. Don't talk to anyone. Don't ask any questions. You can be a volunteer monitor, let's say. You see someone cheating? Turn them in."

No one cheated. But during the reading comprehension exercise, a lot of the kids, Patrick especially, visibly sweated. Jeremy's nervous tic, rapidly blinking eyes, got set off. Rashida looked sad. Shasa tried to bite her nails but couldn't because they were already down to the quick. Children read through bland passages, including one about the historical significance of button placement on men's shirts. They filled in circles with No. 2 pencils.

The annual *Hartford Courant* story about the district's scores wouldn't hit the streets until spring. But the central office was scheduled to get the results just after Christmas. They'd trickle out to principals, then to teachers, and finally in report cards carried home.

On the final day of testing, in October, the children helped Ms. Luddy shove their desks out of "those cold, hard, awful rows" and re-install the familiar table arrangement. Ms. Luddy usually allowed the kids two minutes or so of quiet chitchat at their desks before they lined up for dismissal. On that day, though, she requested silence. She had something important to say.

"I'm proud of you," she told the children. "I'm proud of what you did and how you rose to this challenge of the CMT. I saw you put forth your best effort. And I saw you help each other and support each other. Every single one of you has reason to go home tonight feeling very good. Okay now? We're done."

Success for All?

THE TESTS WERE OVER—until next time. But as the months wore on, Ms. Luddy still had to bear another of Tony Amato's directives. Soon after he'd arrived, Amato had asked principals and teachers to vote for the packaged literacy program Success for All (SFA) or else come up with another "proven" literacy program. The catch was there were no "proven" literacy programs. SFA and a similar one, Direct Instruction, boasted impressive research results (though most studies of SFA had been conducted by employees or former employees of the program's creator, Robert Slavin, or by Slavin himself). Still, many findings by unbiased evaluators concurred. Generally, SFA children seemed to make steady progress in reading, often better than similar children not in SFA programs. During the years I visited, SFA was used by teachers in every Hartford elementary school but one.

Success for All's complete curriculum package had kicked around America's low-performing schools since the late 1980s. In the early 1990s, many more urban school administrators, desperate to improve reading scores, adopted it. By 2000 it had become the most influential educational reform program ever. (But with so many urban education reforms touted as magically effective, only four years later, in 2004, new programs, heavily marketed as even *more* surefire test-score enhancers, would move in on SFA's market share.)

SFA itself grew out of research and observations that Robert Slavin and his wife, Nancy Madden, had undertaken with associates in the 1970s. The program is driven by one basic, well-documented, commonsense finding: that learning to read in the early grades is a key to later school success. SFA emphasizes correcting reading problems early, through quick "interventions," such as tutors and family support. Cooperative learning—splitting of children into teams that discuss, evaluate, and answer questions—is part of the program. So are drills on vocabulary, word sounds, and deconstructed stories. The program requires intensive teacher training. During the first year, SFA trainers visit SFA schools and evaluate and coach teachers.

SFA Foundation sells schools a tower of paper materials: storybooks, worksheets, tests, logbooks, and even festive, seasonal banner ads for decorating hallways and classrooms. Schools purchase teacher manuals with step-by-step, minute-by-minute instruction. Simpson-Waverly had to give over a classroom to storing all the materials. Hartford paid about $4.3 million for the program in its first year. (According to its Web site, as of 2003, more than 1,500 schools in 48 states serving a million mainly poor children used SFA. SFA's Web site says the foundation employs 400 people and vends about $61 million worth of programs a year.)

SFA classes are supposed to be relatively small, so all across Hartford, music teachers, librarians, teachers' aides, and art teachers trained in SFA methods. They would teach their own SFA classes or tutor kids. Children in Ms. Luddy's class had sadly said good-bye to their own enthusiastic music teacher. He left for the new "interdistrict *Sheff*" Montessori Magnet School, he told colleagues, after learning that SFA class duties would steal prep time for his music lessons.

EVERY MORNING, AS PER SFA guidelines, Ms. Luddy's regular students, ranked by reading level, dispersed to various SFA teachers. For 90 minutes, Ms. Luddy taught a new group of students. Jeremy, Shasa, and T.J. went off with sixth graders and read at a seventh-grade level. Rashida stayed with Ms. Luddy.

Teachers then tested students on reading every eight weeks. Any student who reached a standard moved up. SFA was supposed to offer those "interventions" to struggling readers—tutors and support teams that explained strategies to use at home. The home-support idea, though, presupposed that Hartford parents could show up for meetings and had consistent phone service. Neither was the case.

Ms. Luddy and other experienced teachers often told me they resented the SFA teacher manuals, which dictated to the minute what teachers should be teaching and how they should teach it, even how they should position their fingers and hands and what rewards they could offer for what sort of behavior. Ms. Luddy had to tape a sign to her door indicating which book and skill she was teaching. Ms. Luddy had to fill out her SFA logbook every day. In it she had to report what pages and what skills she'd taught. She had to confirm that she'd adhered to time limits. The log sheets said things like "Partner Reading (alternating sentences) Part I (9 minutes)" and "Silent Reading (8 minutes)."

The bottom of one log sheet read, "The Two Minute Edit has been deducted from 20 minute Listening Comprehension total. Result: The Two-Minute Edit plus 18 minutes Listening Comprehension equals 20 minutes. The Two-Minute Edit is not included in the 55 Minute Reading Together block and is presented after the Reading Together block and before the Last 15 Minutes." Ms. Luddy went along with it. She mastered SFA lingo quickly and even helped confused colleagues decode it.

A core concept that Tony Amato told me he especially liked about SFA was "uniformity": Ms. Luddy would teach SFA Level 3.1 at Simpson-Waverly at 9 a.m. She'd read from the exact same page in the exact same book, teaching the exact same skills and using the exact same hand signals used by some Level 3.1 SFA teacher at Kinsella School, far across the city, at the same time. Standardization would, according to Tony Amato's grand plan, guarantee that a child transferring from Simpson-Waverly to Kinsella would not miss a curricular beat. Hartford families weren't only moving around Hartford but, increasingly, also fled to suburbs, whose teachers rarely used Success for All.

Ms. Luddy, though, did appreciate many of SFA's elements—the intensive vocabulary review and the carefully monitored reading with partners. But SFA, she complained, left her no room to rest, compose, reflect, pause, veer, intuitively answer students' curious, off-point questions. It left no time for disruptions or for serendipity. For better or worse, SFA enforced order, harnessed chaos, instilled predictability. It kept the lid on tight.

"ONE," Ms. LUDDY said to her students, who sat in a circle on the floor below her chair. She held up her index finger.

Like a squad of well-trained SFA soldiers, the children stood, chattering.

"Two," Ms. Luddy said. She held up another finger. The children quieted.

"Three," she said, raising a third finger.

The children moved briskly to their seats.

"Kinda scary, huh?" Ms. Luddy asked me, raising her eyebrows. "That always feels a little creepy."

The children settled down with the day's story. It was one Ms. Luddy especially liked: *Music, Music for Everyone,* by Vera B. Williams. The SFA manual said children should read a bit, look at the pictures, then predict what will happen later in the story. The predicting part was tricky. Children who had stayed back and hadn't climbed to the next SFA level were hearing a story they'd heard before. Predictably, they aced the prediction. Ms. Luddy had warned me that she'd sneak in some unscripted part today. In the story, a little girl puts on a show to cheer up her ill grandma. Ms. Luddy hoped the children would realize that it's the granddaughter's narration—her voice—that makes the story evocative and poignant. These kids, Ms. Luddy mused, could understand that, since many had deep, loving relationships with grandparents.

"When someone is telling a story, what do we call that person?" Ms. Luddy asked, looking around. "The person who is telling the story here, telling the story from her point of view," she asked, "what do we call that? What's the name we give that person?"

"Storyteller!" Darin yelled.

"Speaker!" DeAndre tried.

"Good guesses," Ms. Luddy said. "Let's keep trying. It begins with an *n*."

"Nun!" Rashida yelled out. Ms. Luddy giggled.

"Nice person," Nicholas shouted.

"No," Ms. Luddy said.

"'No'?" Patricia questioned. "We call them a 'no'?"

Ms. Luddy closed her eyes. She was able to suppress her giggle this time.

She didn't have all day.

"Nar-ra-tor," Ms. Luddy said slowly. "Narrator." She wrote it on the board. She tapped the word with her chalk.

"Narrator," they chanted, following SFA training.

Ms. Luddy glanced at the clock. No time for more literary criticism.

AFTER YEARS WITH SFA, Hartford's reading scores would remain among the state's lowest, even lower than in similarly poor school districts that did not use SFA.

"What's up with that?" Ms. Luddy asked me.

Robert Slavin and others have often blamed poor results such as Hartford's on shoddy district- or school-level "implementation" of their program. But urban public schools are forever buffeted by uncertainties, budgetary and otherwise. Principals, vice-principals, and teachers in urban schools have become masters at choosing among priorities and at cutting, pasting, scrimping on this or that, in order to retain some other program. Considering this environment — the very environment with which *Sheff* took issue — SFA's weakness may have been an unrealistic dependence on reliable funding, consistent leadership, orderly educational settings, and parents with phones and time on their hands. There were indeed tutors at Waverly, but "not enough," James Thompson said. There were "interventions," Ms. Luddy affirmed, "but they don't always get followed up."

After three years with SFA, Ms. Luddy would say, exasperated, "I'm getting kids coming in from other Hartford schools, some of them, who are in fifth and sometimes who are the age of sixth graders, who've been held back once, maybe twice, and barely reading at a third-grade level according to other assessments — and they haven't had interventions. You have kids moving up in SFA who are supposed to be at grade level according to the SFA tests. Then they bomb on the CMTs. So what does that tell you?"

A FEW MONTHS AFTER the CMT, the central office had inexplicably asked that teachers temporarily abandon SFA and try out some new reading texts and materials. Ms. Luddy got to keep her own kids all day long.

"You gotta check out the new book," Shasa told me one morning. "I gotta show you it!"

Ms. Luddy liked the book because its topics — heavy on natural wonders, animals, and history — "dovetailed," she said, with her self-crafted mini science and social studies lessons.

"This is so exciting," Ms. Luddy said, hugging the book.

The children read aloud a story about an unsure boy who sailed a long way by ship. The author built the tale upon a teaching of the ancient Chinese philosopher Lao-tzu: "A journey of a thousand miles must begin with a single step."

During this precious week, children didn't have to "underline the main idea," "skip names and places," or "look for clue words." And Ms. Luddy didn't have to rush. For the first time in months, she opened a wide-ranging discussion.

"What do you think Lao-tzu meant?"

"That first you need to try, even if something seems impossible?" Jeremy started off.

"Oh, that even if something that looks really big and hard, you can start slowly?" Keesha suggested. "My mother calls it baby steps . . ."

"Okay. Good," Ms. Luddy said, nodding. "Anyone else?"

"Like if you have a goal for something," Shasa said, "you make a plan? You check things off, one by one?"

"Excellent. Now, can anyone tell me what a journey is, in your own words. Is a journey just a trip? Or is it something more? Can you think of examples of journeys?"

"The CMT!" Jeremy yelled. "That's like something we work at a little at a time and then reach the end."

Ms. Luddy looked shell-shocked.

"Yeah, and it's like the DRP is one step and then other parts and then you take all the steps and you know it all together," Martin added, looking thrilled with himself. "That's not a thousand miles, but it takes a lot of different steps."

"Well, okay," Ms. Luddy said. "But can you think of anything else?"

"The CMT was a journey," Owen insisted.

"Yeah," Patrick agreed. "That's a journey for me. A journey up a big ole mountain!" Ms. Luddy and the kids laughed. Ms. Luddy winked at Patrick.

"Okay. The CMT. But are there other things?" Ms. Luddy pushed gently.

Ms. Luddy bit her index finger.

"Now, there's a difference between a journey and a trip," she began. "Let's think about that. I'm going to tell you a story about a trip that I made, a trip that turned into a journey." She was going to end up talking

again about her trips to Africa, to Japan, about the adjustments she'd
had to make to new cultures and the life-changing lessons she'd learned
along the way.

"I don't have any journeys," Jeremy interrupted.

"I know, honey," Ms. Luddy answered softly. "But you don't need to
have traveled the world in order to get this idea. You'll get it. You'll all
get this. I'm sure of it."

Another Country Somewhere in Connecticut

IN ORDER FOR ME to get it—to fully appreciate what was and wasn't happening in Hartford—I took a break from my routine and visited with a third-grade class in the suburbs. The teacher was Mike Larkin. I'd run into him during one of the Hartford kids' "interdistrict cooperative program" field trips to their sister school out in Marlborough, a small town just 14 minutes down the highway.

CMT prep dominated studies in Hartford, but out in Marlborough, to my surprise, Larkin assigned his class no reading comprehension passages ("Yuck!" he declared). Larkin and I chatted quietly. His students read silently from novels—good ones. One group read *Stone Fox,* by John Gardiner, a "save the farm" narrative that the *New Yorker* had called "superb . . . the most exciting and moving book of this season."

Another group read *The Cricket in Times Square,* by Rene Auberjonois, runner-up for the Newbery Medal. A musical cricket is displaced from—of all places—suburban Connecticut but adjusts to urban life.

A list of Spanish vocabulary words ran down the side of the bulletin board. Students had Spanish lessons twice a week, learning vocabulary through conversation.

"It's not intensive," Larkin explained. "The idea is exposure, exposure, exposure."

Larkin taught science two or three times a week. The children studied animals, habitats, and adaptation. He'd designed his own environmental

curriculum—ecology, recycling, and pollution. Larkin also fit in social studies two to three times a week. The children "do a whole lot of
work" with maps and geography, he said.

"I think it's important for kids this age to have their bearings," he
whispered. "And my sense is that they want to understand where they
are in relation to everything else. Their eyes and their minds are open
to that."

On Friday afternoons in the spring, parents and professionals in the
community came in and offered minicourses. Children chose among
such offerings as railroads (by a retired train engineer), American Sign
Language, and conversational French. A cooking class featured "foods
from around the world." One man taught the history of lacrosse. A
children's literature buff deconstructed Harry Potter.

Larkin's kids had genuine recess outdoors, usually twice a day. I
joined him on the playground. His students ran, slid, jumped, kicked
soccer balls, and hung on a jungle gym.

"I could not believe it when Lois [Luddy] told me that the kids do
not go outside," Larkin said. "That's unthinkable here. The parents
would be on the phone in five minutes. And you bet the kids would be
outside, fast."

Marlborough also used a curriculum called Talents Unlimited. Like
SFA, Talents had emerged from scholarly research on teaching and
learning. Both offered exercises that employed a variety of skills. That's
where the similarity stopped. Talents aimed to teach, not measurable
skill development, but the development of widely applicable thought
processes and intellectual habits. On the first day in a new school year,
a teacher might request "many, varied words" describing a student's
feelings. Larkin might ask students to pantomime a child walking
down the hall on her first day and predict what could happen in home-
room or recount memories of entering new situations. Perhaps they'd
read a story on the same subjects and note parallels with their own
experiences.

Goals of the Talents Unlimited curriculum, Larkin explained, included helping students think critically and creatively by fostering articulate communication, forecasting, decision making, and planning. Talents Unlimited didn't dictate content; a teacher could bring its methods to lessons on volcanoes or poetry or horses.

"As with any program," Larkin said, "if a teacher uses it too much, day after day, then kids get bored. A teacher's got to have some authority to decide when enough is enough. We all know there's no miracle program out there that's going to work every time with every child. But I will say that these children don't worry all the time about being right or wrong. They understand that there are a variety of solutions, a variety of ways to understand and experience a situation."

Larkin's goal, "in addition to skill building," he told me, "is for my students to be open to ideas, be inspired learners, see and appreciate all the different ways of conveying knowledge . . . so that they can see things from a lot of angles. I want to give them the opportunity to see how fascinating it is out there."

A community's school officials favor one educational program over another not just because of objective efficacy, but also for more subjective reasons too: values, cultural norms, and memories of the decision makers' own schooling. Our diverse nation keeps revising its patchwork of choices about public schooling. The pendulum swings.

But the most recent federal legislation of Jeremy's childhood—the test-heavy No Child Left Behind Act—shoved underperforming schools that enroll a disproportionate share of the poor toward test-aligned, rigidly prescribed curricula.

So Jeremy drilled dutifully. During SFA sessions, he too rose at the teacher's cue of "one," quieted at "two," and sat at "three." Meanwhile, a few towns away, in Marlborough, the kids thought critically, creatively, jumped around huge maps, practiced foreign languages, studied lacrosse and railroad history, appreciated the fragility and beauty of the natural world, wrote novellas, and felt entitled to recess.

Band-Aids

BACK IN HARTFORD, Success for All—and those CMT test-prep booklets—appeared sensible to the people in charge. Research tells us that urban schools suffer disproportionately from high rates of teacher turnover and teacher burnout. Elementary, middle, and high schools with large proportions of racial minority and poor children are far more likely to employ underqualified, uncertified teachers, and new teachers at such schools are less likely to stick around long enough to get good at their jobs. High-poverty schools are more prone to neglect and interruptions of work on curriculum and teaching methods.

The unstated attractiveness of SFA is that it provides a mere consenting adult—with or without teaching skills—clear instruction for what to do every minute of every lesson. Both SFA and the CMT stipulated clear accountings, tangible proof, tables of numbers, logbooks, scripted manuals, pretests, posttests, more tests, test results to demonstrate that children got something from somebody at least some of the time.

But if the curriculum packages adequately treated symptoms, they also caused side effects. How long would good teachers tolerate the demotion? In controlling for bad teaching and nonexistent teaching and neglect, SFA and CMT sacrificed the skilled work of the profession's Ms. Luddys.

"It's a bit of a trap, see?" James Thompson observed. "Or—what's the term? Catch-22."

SFA and "CMT alignment," though, were only the latest of the many magical school reforms Ms. Luddy had lived through in 28 years of service. With each innovation, new rubric, or method, she still allowed herself, miraculously, to feel hopeful.

Hernan LaFontaine, one of Hartford's previous superintendents, had once outlined, with great specificity, what each child should know at each grade level. Ms. Luddy had considered his list reasonable and educationally sound. LaFontaine had departed more than a decade back.

Then a superintendent named Ben Dixon had lasted long enough to print his own color-coded schedule of attainment. The chart was never really enforced. But Ms. Luddy checked kids' progress against it anyway. A lot of teachers still kept that chart hanging near their desks.

"I look at that and I think, 'Okay. Thank you. I can do that,'" Ms. Luddy said, staring up at her old copy. "But the guy who made it resigns and someone else comes in. Maybe you get a new chart. Probably you don't. Maybe you get ten charts."

In 1995, Hartford's school board had pinned faltering hopes on "private management." The school board turned over control to a for-profit corporation called Education Alternatives, Inc. EAI representatives had promised not only improved achievement but, amazingly, a profit for investors. The relationship, shaky from the start, ended in acrimony a year later with no achievement jump and no profit. Miami and Baltimore terminated EAI contracts around the same time.

"Something inside me does make me hope, still," Ms. Luddy said, her grown-up self scrunched into a child-size chair in her classroom. "I'm willing to try, always. If you start out thinking, 'Oh no, not a new miracle, again!' the kids will feel that attitude. So I figure, what's the harm of trying, really?"

She laughed about some consultants not long ago, who'd shown up from Australia "with terrific accents" and wandered the corridors chatting up teachers about their new reading program, First Steps.

"Oh, they seemed like really nice people, and someone must have paid for them to come all the way out here," she said. "This was the talk of the town. Everybody had to go and get trained in First Steps."

Ms. Luddy had gone and gotten trained. She'd found it intriguing.

"What the heck," she remembered having thought—for "probably the fifteenth time"—"why not give it a chance?"

Ms. Luddy pulled out a nine-inch pile of First Step materials—booklets, sample exercises, a teachers' guide. She'd been all ready to give it a shot when First Steps had died mysteriously.

Each program that was presented to Ms. Luddy over the years had arrived with its own exotic, legitimizing narrative. Some Hartford schools, years ago, had bought into a program called Words in Color, invented in 1957 by a Unesco official, Caleb Gattegno, who'd worked on literacy in Ethiopia. Converts' testimonials explained that Gattegno considered brain functions that earlier, narrow-minded reading experts had overlooked. Gattegno was a mathematician by training and applied "algebraic principles" to reading. The method required teachers to shade like sounds with like colors.

They tried this in Hartford for a while, as they'd tried so many other methods and will try so many more. School officials reinvented, adopted, restructured, implemented, all the while hiring and firing school superintendents, searching for the magic—for *the* hero administrator and *the* program—that might unglue the mess of poverty piled atop poverty. By the time Tony Amato arrived, the curriculum had become a hodgepodge of techniques and texts jumbled up with little oversight. The variations in programs and in teaching quality, said Edwin Vargas, a former teachers' union president, were "startling."

"You had teachers working their tails off, taking kids on their own field trips, running homework centers after school," he told me. "I mean, the most dedicated, talented people you could imagine. Then you have teachers coming in, reading the *Hartford Courant,* letting kids color all day."

Some elementary school teachers did a lot with science or math or literacy. Some did nothing. Social studies became another coin toss for students. In 1995, local teachers had put together a new social studies text with help from the Connecticut Humanities Council. The text-book they developed, *Migration,* contained units on European, African American, Latino, and Asian movement to the United States. But five years later, teachers and principals across the district tossed out the bright yellow hardcover.

By 2002, even the savior Tony Amato was looking like last year's solu-tion. Eleven months into his tenure, he'd sought the superintendency in San Francisco. And less than two years later, he applied for the school chief job in Portland, Oregon. Then the teachers' union, already bris-tling about Amato's management style, ousted its president, Ed Vargas, who'd been Amato's seeming ally. Back in 2000, during Amato's brief honeymoon period, an article in the American Federation of Teachers' magazine had boasted of the union's help enacting Amato's reforms. The vote against Vargas signaled Amato's demise.

Ed Vargas, though, was no headless comrade. His actual, nuanced views of Amato and his reforms had been shaped by disappointment, not blind faith.

"See, before, it was like a lot of kids were getting nothing. We're talking here about the most powerless members of our society, being served by a nonfunctioning, broken system," Vargas told me. "We had gotten to such a low, low point that you have leadership coming and go-ing and the Board of Ed couldn't get it together. No one was in charge. Whether or not kids got anything at all was left to chance. So Amato comes in, and so he's not perfect, but you *can* say the kids are getting something."

Vargas had ceased waiting for deep structural changes that might, in theory, open the educational resources of suburbs like Marlborough to city kids. He still believed in "civil rights" solutions that might, he said, "equally distribute problems of poverty and the problems that poverty causes." *Sheff* had matched Vargas's broad social vision, and Vargas had supported John Brittain and *Sheff* from the beginning. Even before it was called *Sheff,* he'd been on John Brittain's original watch team. After years of reflection, protest, and bureaucratic finagling on behalf of Hartford's disenfranchised, Ed Vargas had decided to settle for Amato's imperfect compromises.

"How long do you wait for revolution?" Vargas asked me, driving through deserted downtown Hartford late one blustery afternoon. "Waiting around for revolution that's not showing any signs of coming? When does it really mean giving kids nothing at all? Just leaving them sitting there waiting? When do you give that up and say, 'Okay, pal, give me something. Give me something that's better than nothing'?"

Revolution—of the sort the *Sheff* plaintiffs might have hoped for—was most definitely not coming. In 2001, at the start of Jeremy's fourth-grade year, according to calculations made by Phil Tegeler, only 5 percent of Hartford's kids had been touched by the *Sheff* movement either through attending magnet schools or through going to suburban schools. (Only 457 minority students in Hartford would attend interdistrict magnet schools that year.) In neighborhoods like Jeremy's Northeast, ordinary people had no hint that a big case had been fought and won for their benefit. In the 2001–2 school year, Hartford's schools would be more, not less, segregated than they'd been in 1989, the year *Sheff* was filed. That year, 94 percent of the 23,000 children in Hartford were members of racial minority groups compared to 89 percent in 1989.

"The nation, Connecticut included, is no longer trying to get to *Sheff* or to *Brown,*" John Brittain remarked irritably after delivering a frank speech at an upbeat education conference in Waterbury. "We are trying to get to *Plessy*—to 'separate but equal'! And let's not fool ourselves. We aren't even *there.*"

SFA and CMT might very well have been better than nothing. Perhaps they were even superior to all the previous acronyms. But they weren't the elusive solutions for which Ms. Luddy prayed. And they weren't the "problem" either.

The *Sheff* lawyers, toiling at the margins, never saw themselves in opposition to Amato's reforms. But throughout the years of good press about Hartford's purported "turnaround," the lawyers continued to focus on their own conception of "the problem." They believed the problem was exactly what Wes Horton had said back in 1996. The problem was then, and remained, the system—the separate, unequal, overwhelmed, isolated system. The system itself.

PART SIX

The Suburbs

"I wonder if I shall fall right *through* the earth! How funny it'll seem to come out among the people that walk with their heads downwards! The Antipathies, I think"—(she was rather glad there *was* no one listening, this time, as it didn't sound at all the right word)—"but I shall have to ask them what the name of the country is, you know. Please, Ma'am, is this New Zealand or Australia?" (and she tried to curtsey as she spoke—fancy *curtseying* as you're falling through the air! Do you think you could manage it?)—"And what an ignorant little girl she'll think me for asking! No, it'll never do to ask: perhaps I shall see it written up somewhere."

—Lewis Carroll, *Alice in Wonderland*

"What's the Suburbs?"

"Ms. Luddy, what's the suburbs?" Kayla asked, out of the blue, derailing a midafternoon transition to math.

Kayla's thick braids bumped off her high cheekbones. She fiddled with an elastic band and moved restlessly off her butt, onto her knees. She stared at Ms. Luddy. All eyes looked up at Ms. Luddy.

Ms. Luddy popped off her sunflower stool and stood at attention, as if following a command. She faced rapt silence, free of chattering, paper rustling, whispering, foot tapping, chiding. Ms. Luddy knew this type of silence. Every child present wanted an answer. She considered Kayla intently. "Well. The suburbs," she began. "A suburb is a town that's close to a bigger city. Hartford is a big city, a major city. The suburbs are built around Hartford."

"*This* is the city, here," she said, pointing to her fist, shaking it in the air above her eyes.

"And all around it, *these* are the suburbs." She sketched, with an index finger, an invisible orbit around her fist.

"Like, the suburbs are nicer?" Kayla asked.

"No," Ms. Luddy said. "No. Not better. Different. Okay. Hartford? It's also called an 'urban' area. The houses are a little closer together. There are a lot of apartments. You can usually walk places. You can walk out of your house and maybe your neighbors are out and you can visit."

This was sometimes true. Twenty years ago, people say, it was true more often. These days, though, there wasn't much hopscotch, double Dutch, pleasure walking, or public socializing on porches. A few older boys still played chess on their stoops. But recently that teenager Gary Little had been shot in the head while playing chess across from Waverly. Talk on the streets called Little's killing part of a street beef, not a stray bullet. Still, most parents had stuck to the ban on playing any sort of game on any stoop.

Ms. Luddy reached for a positive spin.

"If you live in a suburb, you need to drive everywhere. Even just to get milk. A lot of times, you have to get in your car and drive and drive and drive."

"So, but . . . ," Kayla muttered, seemingly unsatisfied. "But Mrs. Johnson—" Kayla stopped short. She stared at the elastic band she'd woven around her fingers. Her eyes darted from classmate to classmate. Mrs. Johnson taught SFA to some of the children.

"What?" Ms. Luddy pushed. Math had been derailed. They'd lost eight minutes.

"Well, why's Mrs. Johnson always sayin' a us, 'You gotta do better because the suburbs are beatin' us'? 'You gotta see how the suburb kids be doin' so good on the CMT and Hartford's way down the bottom'?"

Ms. Luddy stood there, gathering herself in.

"*What* did she say?" Ms. Luddy asked, squinting.

"Sounds like she say we stink, is what she say," Rashida declared from the front. "She say we no good and that the suburbs are better."

"I don't think she said that," Ms. Luddy answered, raising her eyebrows.

"Sorta," Patrick interjected from behind. "Ms. Luddy, that's sorta like what she said."

Rashida threw up her hands and scrunched her face, as though she'd just sucked on a lemon.

"Why she be all, 'You gotta beat the suburbs. You gotta beat the suburbs'? I mean, we come in, we do our work. I mean . . . ," Rashida said, adding a grandiose, theatrical exhale. "It's wrong. We don't need to be hearin' that!"

Shasa's eyes moved between Ms. Luddy and Rashida as though she were watching tennis. Shasa stayed out of this one but nodded from across the room, agreeing with Rashida.

Ms. Luddy pursed her lips.

"Rashida," she began softly, "it's possible that Mrs. Johnson said that so students would have motivation to work harder. In fact, I think there's quite a bit of room for you to work harder, honey. You have a lot of potential, and the teachers in this school know how smart you are."

Rashida seethed, frown fixed.

"I don't need to be hearin' that," she said again. She smacked the table with her fist. "It's not fair what she said." Rashida began to cry.

Jeremy piped up. Mrs. Johnson wasn't his SFA teacher, but when he sensed tension, he tried to dissipate it.

"Umm. I have an opinion about this. I think that she was trying to inspire you, to give you a little challenge by saying we could do as well as any kids."

Rashida sobbed louder.

Patrick opened his mouth to respond to Jeremy's goody-two-shoes comment, saw Rashida crying, and, with his eyes fixed on her, said nothing. Tears streamed down her cheeks. Her shoulders jumped. She wiped her wet nose with the back of her hand, sniffled, and crumpled on her desk. Her skinny arms were a tent over her head. The rebel Rashida, facing her fated place in the world.

"Nah. Nope," Patrick finally said. "I don't think she was doin' that at all." He folded his arms across his chest. "I think she tryin' to make the Hartford students feel stupid."

"Patrick," Ms. Luddy scolded, "I'm quite sure she was not trying to do that."

"Nah, forget it," Patrick said, almost shouting. "Forget the suburbs, man." It was an order to his classmates.

Jinaya rubbed Rashida's back. Kayla slipped her a tissue. Rashida dried her tears.

And on to math they went.

THE PHYSICAL DISTANCE between city and suburb was short. But for Ms. Luddy's students, the psychological distance was long. The suburbs, as Naia and Patrick had said, were "out there." Suburbs were abstractions, unseen, vague locations—white faces and high test scores adrift in the great beyond. Relatives of some of the kids lived in the nearest suburbs—the older, often moderately poor, largely working-class communities demographers termed "at risk." Beyond these half-known areas lay unknown Avon, Glastonbury, Farmington, Canton, Simsbury, even West Hartford.

There was one state-funded *Sheff*-inspired program that allowed Ms. Luddy to lead her students to the suburbs for a visit. No matter how tired, how socked in with responsibilities, she would "never, ever" sacrifice the sister-school program that took her kids for a day to the tranquil suburban hamlet of Marlborough nearby.

The few hours of urban-suburban harmony that unfolded each year revealed the potential for connection. The clumsy distance between black and white, rich and poor, urban and suburban, closed enough for minimal comfort. Then it was over.

Many *Sheff* remedies that were more substantial had drawn fire. The state's designs (as the plaintiff lawyers had pointed out to Judge Aurigemma in the brief 1998 hearing following the 1996 decision) were structured to siphon money from local education budgets. Every time a kid from, say, Simsbury wanted to attend an interdistrict magnet school, Simsbury had to throw some of its money into the pot. Even suburban school superintendents who believed in racial diversity had testified at hearings before state legislators that *Sheff* programs pressed them when their own budgets were already thin.

But state education officials, including Commissioner Ted Sergi, always praised the uncontroversial "interdistrict cooperative grant program"—the umbrella category of allocations that included Ms. Luddy's sister-school visits. It didn't take cash away from suburban districts. And it didn't force the suburbs to educate poor black and brown children from the city for more than a few hours.

No one wanted to knock innocent exchange programs that sprinkled positive feeling around. Still, the plaintiffs' bottom-line argument rang true for Simpson-Waverly's suburban trips and the scores of similar outings. At the end of the day, everyone had to return to their segregated schools. Ms. Luddy shrugged off the trite oaths uttered on these visits. She termed the platitudes "the 'we are all connected' stuff." But she also believed third and fourth grade wouldn't be complete without a sister-school visit. The kids "out there" in suburban Marlborough gained too. And Ms. Luddy reasoned that at least on the trips to Marlborough, her kids would get recess out of the deal.

Getting in Line

RASHIDA, HALFWAY TO THE BUS, had already wandered out of line. She wrestled her backpack off her body. She double-knotted the laces on her pink work boots. She dashed to catch up with her classmates. They'd all lined up by a yellow bus at Simpson-Waverly's curb.

Rashida stumbled into Jeremy. He barely noticed. She grasped his shoulder for balance, and Jeremy peered expectantly over his classmates' shoulders for a look inside the bus. He shook his arms, freeing his hands from his long sweatshirt sleeves, and grabbed the bus railing, hauling himself aboard. Rashida flashed a huge grin at Ms. Luddy, who laughed and shook her head in wonder.

Rashida hoisted herself up the bus steps and flopped into a bus seat. Stepping up and peering down the aisle at the rowdy crowd, Ms. Luddy looked a little dismayed.

Owen and Patrick tossed a pink eraser back and forth. Rashida patty-caked with Naia, chanting, "I left my bra in my boyfriend's car . . . Oh, Miss Suzy had a baby, a baby, a baby."

Ms. Luddy overheard and flashed a shocked glance at the girls.

They averted their eyes and stopped.

Jeremy rubbed his hand underneath his seat, as if he'd lost something. T.J. kneeled, inspecting the floor.

"How do they get the seats to stay on?" Jeremy asked. "Ms. Luddy, do you know how they get the seats to stay on? Ms. Luddy?"

"What?" she asked, cupping her ear. "I'm sorry, but I can't hear you."

"Oh, man!" T.J. yelled, popping up. "I figured it out. There's bolts!"

"Bolts," Jeremy yelled. "Ms. Luddy! Bolts!"

"Oh, interesting," she shouted. "Yes."

Martin breathed fog onto the window. In looping script, he wrote his name and pondered his art.

Keesha and Aisha bounced.

Rashida shrieked.

"Oh, bye-bye, my school," Naia crooned, waving to Simpson-Waverly.

Kayla and Shasa argued with Owen. "Nope," Shasa told him. "We ain't movin'. You go find youself another one." Owen slogged away, outnumbered.

"Ms. Luddy?" Jinaya said, too quietly. "Ms. Luddy?"

Jinaya dug in her backpack.

"Oh," Jinaya said to herself, "where did I . . . I know I have it. Ms. Luddy, I made you something. Ms. Luddy?"

"One moment, Jinaya," Ms. Luddy answered. "Hang on, sweetie. I'll be right with you."

"Well, it's a happy noise," Ms. Luddy said to the middle-aged woman who drove the bus. "They're just excited, is all."

The bus roared out the back way, joggling gingerly over speed bumps. The children released loud, exaggerated "WHOOOAS!" They pretended to lose their balance and fell into each other gleefully. The bus crawled past the Jewish cemetery, by the police cruiser that kept daily watch, past a trim neighborhood of single-family homes.

Jinaya finally found the gift in her backpack and pulled it out. She tapped Ms. Luddy on the shoulder and held up a necklace. With tiny black-and-white blocks of the sort found on old-fashioned baby brace-lets, Jinaya had spelled out "Ms. Luddy." Ms. Luddy handled the plastic beads like diamonds. Jinaya's intense eyes and sly smile anticipated praise.

"Oh, Jinaya!" Ms. Luddy shouted, fastening the necklace, touching it gently with her fingertips. Jinaya's symmetrical dimples showed up with her smile. She lifted her arms for a hug.

"I love it, Jinaya!" Ms. Luddy said, tearing up. "Thank you!"

"Ms. Luddy, I'm excited because this is my first field trip in a long time," Jinaya said. Jinaya's last field trip, two years ago, hadn't gone well.

"We's went to the theater, not the movies but, like, a stage? See, and the performers, like, the dancers, they come out on the stage and they's in, like, skin-color tights, and the boys, I think the boys in our class, they be thinkin' the dancers was naked and so they start yellin', 'Oh, look! He's butt-naked!' And they asks us to leave."

Back at Waverly, the vice-principal at the time, Jinaya remembered, had spoken harshly to the exiled children.

"She said we was an embarrassment," Jinaya said, looking down at her knees.

Jinaya perked up suddenly. "Ms. Luddy, you know? I liked it, going there that day. You should have seen them dancing! The way they could move themselves all around." She arched her arm over her head.

"Oh, Jinaya," Ms. Luddy said. "You are so fabulous."

"I wanted to go back and back again, a lot of us was likin' it a lot. But we couldn't stay," Jinaya said, "because we was an embarrassment."

It might have seemed culturally condescending, were a teacher to have instructed the black children to file quietly into the theater and never to cheer or hoot, and warned them that yes, the costumes might make it appear that the performers were undressed, but here's why they did it that way. "You can't make assumptions that they know these rules," Ms. Luddy whispered to me. "We know them so well, we don't even know how we know them, these rules."

"What a shame," Ms. Luddy said, that an, "open, sensitive, nice" kid like Jinaya had gotten shortchanged. The bus veered left onto the highway, out of the North End industrial-warehouse ghost land.

"Ms. Luddy!" Owen yelled. "Look!"

"What?" Ms. Luddy asked, turning to him. "What is it?"

"The river!" Rashida screamed, hand over beating heart.

"Land and water, Ms. Luddy!" Martin yelled. "Ms. Luddy, we're passing land and water."

The muddy Connecticut River trickled through cement barriers. The children gasped and cheered. Faces jockeyed for good views. Noses pressed against bus windows.

"Whoa," Kayla said, pointing, a hand over her mouth.

"Ms. Luddy, can she slow down the bus?" Jeremy asked. "I want to look closer. Please? Ms. Luddy?"

"Ms. Luddy? Can we get out on the way back?" Owen begged. "Explore around? Ms. Luddy?"

During the first *Sheff* trial, 10 years ago, the schoolteacher Gladys Hernandez had testified that she'd brought first graders on a field trip and the children had given the Connecticut River a standing ovation. In the 10 years since the *Sheff* trial, many standards for judging the outcome of the *Sheff* movement had been offered by interested parties. Some measured positively by the millions spent. Others looked pessimistically at the city's rising segregation rate. Education officials saw promise in new suburban diversity. But Ms. Luddy felt defeat at that moment, a decade after Hernandez's testimony, seeing little boys and girls once more screaming with astonishment about a river that flowed just beyond their homes.

"Now, you all know what river this is," Ms. Luddy shouted above the exultant noise, "don't you?"

"Oh, please," she thought in long seconds before their reply. She bit her lip. "Let them know this."

"Connecticut," they sang out together.

"Very good," Ms. Luddy said, clapping. "That is the Connecticut River. Connecticut. That's your state. So that's *your* river."

A FEW MINUTES LATER, the children settled down.

Then Naia walked to the front of the bus, hand to hand, gripping the seat backs.

Her brown eyes wide and her lips clenched tight, Naia, in embroidered lavender fleece, her hair in an exquisite updo, looked near tears.

"Ms. Luddy?" she asked in her high soprano voice.

"Naia, honey, what is it?"

"Um, Ms. Luddy?" Naia moved in close to Ms. Luddy's ear. She whispered, "Is this a *white* school?"

Naia was newer to Simpson-Waverly and was making her first visit to Marlborough. Most of the others had made this trip the previous year and had visited with Mike Larkin's third graders.

"Well, Naia, I think that most of the children who attend this school are white, yes. I believe there are some Asian children who attend this school. But, yes, Naia."

Naia nodded. "Oh," she said, turning to go. "I didn't know."

Naia shuffled back.

Ms. Luddy closed her eyes for a few seconds.

"It is the new millennium here. And that child just asked me, 'Is this a *white* school?' Did you hear that? Did you hear what she asked me? Maybe I should have said, 'Yes, it is a white school, honey. And you go to a black school. Don't you think that's crazy?' But where do you begin? I worry that I didn't give her the right response."

THE KIDS HAD BEEN old enough for a while to notice separations by color and class. In their scattered unpredictable ways ("What's the suburbs?" "Is this a *white* school?") the students frequently begged for help sorting the implications of what they were figuring out. Ms. Luddy wished to be flawless on a topic that bore much sad news.

On this clunky yellow bus, she'd put herself in the middle of America's gaping race and class divide. In her crisp chino pants, plain blouse, sensible, flat, navy blue shoes, gold-rimmed eyeglasses, and new black-and-white "Ms. Luddy" necklace, she made the going look easy. She giggled girlishly with Jinaya. She tamed the noise level with strategically placed admonishments. She draped an arm around Jeremy, who, she noticed, looked bus sick.

But Ms. Luddy's smile masked anxiety. She was scared for the lot of them, she told me. "Maybe I'm ready to protect these kids before I really have to?" she wondered. "You know, I just worry about them. I worry about them being misjudged."

Jinaya, Patrick, Kayla, Rashida, Owen, James, and Shasa spoke with the cadence, phrasings, and grammar of their neighborhood. They pronounced *hold* "hoed." *Asked* was "axed." *Their shoes* was "they shoes." *Where is Shawn?* became "Where Shawn?" or else "Where Shawn at?" or "Where Shawn be at?" "Be" often substituted for various conjugations of *is,* as in "He be good at math." The grammar of what's referred to as "black English" was as complex and nuanced and agile and expressive as the dominant American grammar, but to the sheltered white ear, Ms. Luddy knew, it would sound strange or wrong or dumb. The judging went the other way as well. To her kids' eyes and ears, those white kids would look and sound strange too.

Folks in Marlborough, especially the children, had been so welcoming, so nice, so "wonderful" to work with, Ms. Luddy had often said. "But I know people tend to notice if the black Hartford kids start acting up. There's a burden there. I feel like everyone's watching them. And you know something? It's not fair."

THE BUS PULLED OFF the exit into Marlborough, a town of about 16,000. Newish midsize cars and minivans traversed unclogged streets. Out the bus windows, the children eyed the town center—an unpretentious convenience store, a coffee shop in rustic-lodge motif, a bank, a pricey restaurant, and a real estate agency.

Marlborough is what a broker might call a "growing bedroom community." Residents' professional jobs were elsewhere, but close by. Recently rural, Marlborough had sprawled, uninhibited, into a suburban identity. Since 1950, the town's population had increased by 533 percent.

Modest ranch houses and funky Victorians dotted the established residential parts of town. Newer developments with cul-de-sacs, young plantings, and scattered children's toys seemed destined to outnumber the old places. Neither glitzy nor snobbish, Marlborough still had far more in common with its pricier neighbor, Glastonbury, than with Hartford.

In 2000, the median household income in Marlborough was $80,000. It was less than $25,000 in Hartford. Two percent of Marlborough's population was poor, making it the 145th poorest of the 169 cities and towns in Connecticut. Hartford was first, the poorest. Forty-four percent of Marlborough's adults held a bachelor's degree or higher; remarkably, that made it only the 33rd best-educated community in the state. Just 12 percent of Hartford's adults have a bachelor's degree or higher — 166th of 169.

The median home value in Marlborough in 2000 was $180,100 (58th). Hartford homes averaged $93,900, the lowest.

Two and a half decades before, in a period of great suburban growth, a state-commissioned report had named the town of Marlborough as one of the most highly restrictive communities with regard to zoning. The report showed that Marlborough required a minimum lot size of 20,000 square feet for a single-family house that would have a minimum floor area of 1,000 square feet. The town had separate special-review processes for construction of multifamily housing and even had restrictions on the number of bedrooms a house could have, potentially excluding large families. Hartford had no such restrictions.

• • •

THE BUS TURNED SLOWLY onto School Street, past a quaint public library. Bulldozers growled in a nearby field, making room for more subdivisions.

"Water!" Kayla yelled.

A postcard-perfect pond on the left reflected orange, yellow, and red leaves. Tree branches formed a canopy over the water. Sun streaked through.

"Ms. Luddy! Look! Quick! Out the window!" Owen shouted.

Rashida asked, "That the ocean?"

"No," Ms. Luddy answered. "That is not the ocean."

"What? That's the ocean?" Martin asked, looking confused. "Is it?"

"No," Ms. Luddy said. "That is not the ocean." She pointed to the pond. "Everyone understand? That is *not* the ocean."

"What is it?" Owen asked.

"Umm, I think it's a lake or a pond," yelled Jeremy, who, a year before, had himself made the ocean error.

"Yes, it's a pond," Ms. Luddy said.

"Oh," Owen said to himself, appearing saddened.

"But this one ain't ours," Rashida declared. "Not like that river was."

The bus pulled up at their destination. Ms. Luddy took a deep breath. The children, even those who'd come before, strained to look out at the school. It was an unremarkable, flat building. Like Waverly, it was nicely landscaped, and like Waverly, it was nestled in a quiet corner, back from main roads.

"Remember, we are here in someone else's school," Ms. Luddy reminded the kids. They stood silently facing her. That look of confident expectation arrived on Ms. Luddy's face.

"When we walk in there, the whole school will be watching," she said, making eye contact with child after child after child. "We are guests. Just like when you go to someone's house and you're a guest. This is a chance for you to show how very proud you are to be from

Simpson-Waverly School. When we go in there, we will walk quietly.
And we will be on our best what?"

A low-volume chorus: "BEHAVIOR!"

"Okay. Now," she said, "let's go."

Urgently, Patrick peeled off his baseball cap and stepped forward.

Jinaya pushed her shoulders back.

Shasa cleared her throat.

Rashida's stomach growled. "Oops," she said, grimacing. "I'm sorry."

They filed silently down the stairs.

Naia's delicate three sneezes sounded loud. A few classmates' faces,
full of judgment or perhaps fear, turned toward her.

"Bless you," Jeremy said. "Bless you, Naia."

Jeremy stepped down last. He joined the silent—and surely con-
spicuously black—children mustering on the walkway. Jeremy fell behind his classmates. Two shyly waving blond girl greeters held open
the doors. Almost there now, Jeremy began tiptoeing until his big body
became too much to bear. He returned to his natural waddle, and the
long legs of his shiny athletic pants brushed together, hissing with each
step.

"I'm trying to make my pants stop the whistly noise they make? The
legs rub," he whispered to me. "I don't want to disturb things. But I
try to walk slow, on my toes, and it stops the whistlingy sounds? But it
doesn't feel so good. It doesn't feel so right to myself. So if I try it too
hard to keep my pants quiet, well, okay, I know this sounds strange,
but I get a headache."

Welcome

I SEE SOME FAMILIAR faces from last year," Ms. Luddy said, shepherding the last kids into a classroom. "Well. Hello everyone!"

The white children sat in rows, watching the Simpson-Waverly kids file in.

Naia hid behind Shasa. "It's okay," Shasa whispered to her. "It's not a big deal."

The Marlborough side waved first, then tried a few faint "hi's." Waverly's students volleyed uneven "hi's" back. Jeremy began waving exuberantly, as if he were the mayor on a parade float.

"Now, let's see," Ms. Luddy said. "Who was here last year when we worked with Mike Larkin's class? In third grade?" More than half the children raised their hands.

Marlborough's fourth-grade teacher, Ms. Rose, stood behind her desk. "Welcome, everyone," she said. "We've been looking forward to this day."

Ms. Rose was tall and slender, with straight brown hair. She spoke with a British accent.

She and Ms. Luddy conferred quickly.

"Pairs, I think," Ms. Luddy suggested to Ms. Rose. "We'll match them up."

Patrick hung back, arms crossed, foot tapping. He inspected the scene as if he were appraising a used car.

"I ain't doin' this," he declared. "No way."

Jeremy fell in easily, gabbing with a boy he remembered from last year's trip.

"I think I know you," he said to the boy. "Do you know me?"

Rashida, hands on hips, didn't budge.

Ms. Luddy and Ms. Rose plucked children from the separate groups, enforced introductions, nudged children together.

"Jared, you go with this boy, here," Ms. Rose said, pulling gently on Patrick's shoulder. "What's your name?" she asked Patrick.

"Joey," Patrick lied, and immediately he looked terrified.

"Okay, then, Joey, you'll go with Jared."

"Man, wha'd you say?" Owen asked Patrick. "What's this Joey?"

"Shut up," Patrick said. "Shhhh." He formed a fist, lifted it over Owen's head. Owen ducked but kept laughing.

"I don't want these people knowin' my name," Patrick told him.

"Why?" Owen asked. "You crazy."

Ms. Luddy whisked Owen over to a boy named Sam.

Ms. Rose walked toward the Waverly flock. She paired Naia and Mallary.

Ms. Luddy guided Shasa toward Brenna.

"Okay, now, you and you, there," Ms. Rose said, pointing to T.J., then to a blue-eyed boy, Jason. The boys sized each other up, shook hands, and sat on the floor together, silent.

Ms. Rose and Ms. Luddy nodded to each other.

"Now, everyone? Everyone? We're going to do introductions," Ms. Rose announced. "Shhhhhh."

Patrick, eyes down, walked toward Ms. Rose. The room hummed with chatter.

"I'm sorry, I have to tell you, my name's not Joey," Patrick mumbled to her. "It's Patrick. My name's Patrick."

Ms. Rose's hand landed on Patrick's shoulder. He flinched. She cupped her ear and moved it toward him.

"Sorry?"

"I said my name was Joey? Really, it's Patrick."

"Well, okay, then, Patrick," Ms. Rose said, not picking up on his brave confession. She patted him on the back and smiled. "Joey is just a nickname then? Welcome to Marlborough! Now have a seat. Go take a seat now, Patrick. Go, join everyone, there! Just join in. Join in."

Patrick stood still, a desperate, just-before-tears look on his face. He spied Ms. Luddy. Gaze fixed on her, he sat down cross-legged and dragged himself across the carpet closer to his mandated partner, Jared, who extended a hand. Patrick stared at it skeptically for a few seconds too long.

"Oh!" Patrick finally got it. He laughed nervously, pursed his lips, nodded to Jared, and shook. And so it began.

Separate but Equal?

MS. LUDDY FELT GOOD about the way the Marlborough visit had started.

It's "great," she said to me, that these kids could come to "feel a little more comfortable with one another." But still, she conceded, "standing around and saying, 'We are all connected,' doesn't make it so." And, she added, "even starting with the assumption that all children are equal, which is an assumption I believe people in Marlborough start with, doesn't erase the advantages their kids have."

People sympathetic to the inherent inequalities of urban schools still talk a lot about inadequate and unequal funding, as if their hearts and minds seem not to know where else to reach. But inequality—the unmentioned elephant in the room during the Simpson-Waverly–Marlborough field trip—actually includes a constellation of characteristics that go far beyond not having enough money or as much money as the suburbs do. Equal funding for schools, while instrumental in true reform, hasn't alone proven sufficient. Comparing urban and suburban schools—or privileged and disadvantaged schools—requires more than a glance at balance sheets.

But the numbers show that in 2003, Hartford spent $10,848 per elementary school pupil, almost all of it coming from the state. Marlborough spent $7,053, most of it raised through local property taxes. It is not uncommon, in fact, for a high-poverty school district, such as Hartford, to spend more per pupil than a district that enrolls a wealthier student body. That's not to say that funding disparities between school districts have been eliminated entirely, either in Connecticut or in the nation at large. Big gaps between urban and suburban schools remain, even in some states where courts had ordered more equal funding schemes. As of 2002, plaintiffs in 45 states had brought funding-related cases, intended to benefit either property-poor districts or districts with large numbers of poor children. And courts in 21 states have, since the 1970s, ordered state legislatures to even up funding formulas to benefit poorer school districts and poorer children.

Much testimony in that first *Sheff* trial, in fact, explored physical deterioration and neglect in the city schools. Some problems remained a decade later. But the most dramatic—collapsing ceilings and dead pigeons—had been fixed by the time I showed up. Simpson-Waverly surely didn't fit the underfunded urban school stereotype. No Hartford school I visited did. At Simpson-Waverly there was no falling plaster, no ripped-out light fixtures, no rats, not even any overcrowding. The roof was tight, the paint was new, the hallways didn't smell of urine. There wasn't a dust bunny afoot anywhere. Floors gleamed. Custodians vacuumed fastidiously and shined already-shiny stairwells. The bathrooms reeked, but only from floral deodorant. The receptionists smiled and kept good records.

The textbooks weren't old or tattered. Each classroom had a computer. The library was small by suburban elementary school standards, and the well-trained librarian was resentful because she'd been drafted to teach Success for All. But the library, with its pink beanbag reading chair, was well organized, spotless, cozy, and good enough.

Dogwood trees trembled in the breeze outside. A rosebush bloomed in spring. A clean, huge American flag flapped in the wind. Graffiti marred just a few signs in the parking lot. Waverly's play area, part of a city park, was usually littered. A series of violent crimes had scared most families away. But except for the graffiti and dearth of kids playing outdoors, few visible differences separated Hartford's Simpson-Waverly and Marlborough's elementary school.

Marlborough's and Simpson-Waverly's test scores in past years—the most commonly used and misused comparison—weren't terribly far apart either. Hartford's scores, generally, were far, far lower than you'd find in middle-class suburbs, but Simpson-Waverly was catching up. The achievement gap remained, but the good numbers inspired hope, not despair. To discern the differences between a school like Simpson-Waverly and one like Marlborough required a closer, honest observation. Look carefully, and the numerical illusion of equity (or even of near equity) collapsed.

"Did you see here how kids can just walk around this school? There's a kind of trust," Ms. Luddy commented to me in Marlborough. "If you see a child walking down the hall at Simpson-Waverly? I'm automatically asking, 'Ahh, excuse me, exactly where are you supposed to be?' You'd want to hear from that child who'd given him permission to leave. The freedom here? It's different."

Order, predictability, and obedience were important at Simpson-Waverly.

"Why," Ms. Luddy asked me one day, "do the lines have to be straight? I don't know. I do it, but I don't know."

Quiet, straight lines reflected schoolwide culture. Ms. Luddy kept straight lines, not in response to an explicit rule, but to honor a crucial convention. She could justify the quiet. "The quiet teaches them consideration for others," she'd said. "But the straight thing confuses me."

Marlborough's hallways were less quiet. Teachers permitted children to cluster into social groups. The kids could whisper. Simpson-Waverly's silent, arrow-straight lines didn't inspire imitation in Marlborough. Mike Larkin, the third-grade teacher I'd spent time with there, had said, "They have to be quiet, respectful, and I have to keep track of them. But I never think about the lines, in fact. Never."

The rigidity outside Ms. Luddy's room aside, her class was more than a decorous, functional room. It was a reliable sanctuary within a chaotic, unreliable neighborhood. But what happened in Simpson-Waverly out beyond Ms. Luddy's safe haven? What kinds of things happened at Simpson-Waverly that didn't happen in Marlborough?

In the corridor at Simpson-Waverly, the dour (white) chaperone lightly but repeatedly slapped the hands of first graders who sucked their thumbs. A (black) former vice-principal hollered at a second grader, "You should be ashamed to say my name. Don't you speak my name. Don't you dare. And get that foolish hat off your foolish head." A (black) substitute teacher hurled insults at a fifth grader: "lazy, rude, foolish." Another substitute (black) screamed, "Shut up." A third substitute teacher (Asian) declined conversation with children. A visibly exasperated, young (white) teacher pushed a whiny, jumpy child against the wall (hard) and back into a line. I overheard a teacher (black) say scoldingly to a child in the hallway, "What is *wrong* with you? There is something *very* wrong with you."

A school's culture, I'd long found, reveals itself most discernibly far from the classroom.

At 12:20 each day, Ms. Luddy stole a 20-minute lunch break after escorting the kids downstairs to the lunchroom. Occasionally, though, she left earlier for a noon planning session. On one of those days, a middle-aged (white) lunch escort materialized, leaned in the doorway, and frowned. After Ms. Luddy left, the silent escort turned the lights off in an effort to quiet the unruly children. It always did the opposite.

The children, already out of their chairs, attempted to navigate in near darkness. The shrieking built up. The children bumped each other and stumbled over chairs and desks. They shouted irritably: "Ow." "Ouch." But within minutes they tucked themselves into a neat line. Patrick yelled, "Everybody, SHUT UP!" They quieted. The woman, whom I'd never seen utter a word to the kids, flicked on the lights.

We descended the stairs noiselessly, a centipede strolling to dine.

The lunchroom, this day, was full and shockingly quiet. The children joined the line, selected cheeseburgers, ketchup packets, bruised apples, milk cartons, Tater Tots. They sat at brown foldout tables. Several muttered grace. The windows, made of thick plastic, didn't open. One Hartford administrator explained this with the term "vandalism-challenged neighborhood." Unbreakable plastic was a must. But over a few years, it scratched and clouded over.

"What's wrong with you?" the white janitor hollered at a slim fifth-grade boy, who'd just rinsed the tips of his sticky fingers in the water fountain.

"You are an animal. An animal," the janitor yelled.

The little boy, in pressed jeans, clean sneakers, and a starched button-down plaid shirt, pointed to himself and asked meekly, "Me?"

"Yeah, you!" the janitor screamed. Under the gaze of his peers, the boy walked with small, gingerly steps back to his table, eyes down.

"Whaddid I do?" he whispered to his friend, who shrugged.

"What did you DO?" yelled the janitor, face flushed, towering over the boy. "What did you DO? You acted like an animal, is what you did!"

His belly protruding below a filthy white T-shirt, the janitor spelled it out for the boy: water fountains are for "drinking out of," not "for washing dirty little hands."

On some days, the janitor permitted children to speak with one another during the short lunch period. Sometimes he didn't, and on no-talking days he played enforcer. After an unspecified number of infractions for talking, an offender stayed after school for detention. The lunchroom often grew too loud for conversation at other times. In that case, a uniformed security guard turned off the lights and yelled, "Shut up!"

On one no-talking day, my presence inspired the janitor to grant Ms. Luddy's students the exclusive right to speak—but only to me. I became the designated conduit for communication among the children. It was a defiant game, a prison game. Other children weren't as fortunate.

"You were talking. YOU," the janitor bellowed at a small boy, "AFTER SCHOOL!"

"But I wasn't talking," the boy pleaded.

"Well, now you're talking!" the janitor retorted.

The boy slammed his fist on the table.

"After school!" the janitor hollered.

Witnessing injustice, Patrick growled through gritted teeth.

"Patrick," Shasa said, catching her friend's anger. "No! He ain't worth it."

A FEW DAYS LATER, Ms. Luddy left her class with a substitute, sacrificing a science lesson, to attend a workshop on incorporating "CMT objectives" into SFA curriculum. ("God help us all," she'd declare afterward.) A grumpy-faced, middle-aged black man covered Ms. Luddy's absence.

Patrick dallied too long at the pencil sharpener, then poked at Hamilton on the way back to his desk. He chided T.J. about dirty sneakers.

"Sit down," the substitute teacher barked at Patrick. "Sit down and shut up."

"I'm goin'," Patrick snapped back, palms out to ward off the words.

"You a fool," the substitute said, staring challengingly at Patrick. Patrick's eyes narrowed. He hunched his shoulders and looked ready to pounce. Then he forfeited the staring contest, dropped into his chair, and pouted, looking more sad than mad.

Kayla walked over to the teacher.

"Umm, excuse me. What does this word mean?" Kayla asked, blinking her big brown eyes. She held her booklet open and pointed.

"Sir? *Aquava* . . . ? *Equiva* . . . this word here?" she asked again, tapping her pencil on the page.

The teacher took the booklet, looked at the word, and didn't answer. He handed back the booklet.

"Sit down," he ordered. "Stay in your seat."

Kayla sat. She looked across the table to Shasa, who'd whipped through the assignment. Shasa sucked her thumb and read. Kayla kicked Shasa under the table.

"What's this word?" Kayla whispered.

"Oh. *E-qui-va-lent*," Shasa answered slowly.

"What's it mean?" Kayla asked.

"Equal to," Shasa responded.

Kayla set to work. She added. She multiplied. In a minute she was done matching equivalent equations. She and Shasa gabbed brightly about horror movies.

"Shut your mouths," the substitute barked at the girls.

"Sorry," Shasa said, her hand going up in front of Kayla, as if to block any protest.

RIGHT ALONGSIDE THIS harshness, other adults at Waverly, of course, demonstrated a deep, daily appreciation for the kids.

The muscular and sweet physical education teacher regularly burst with joy. "You all should be very proud of yourselves," he exclaimed to Ms. Luddy's kids one day after an intense racing game. "Each and every one of you today. You played your best and I saw great sportsmanship."

The cheerful music teacher put together an all-school performance featuring dancing from around the world. Ms. Luddy's students, abashed, suffered through an Irish step-dancing routine. Then the music teacher indulged T.J.'s break-dancing solo. The crowd erupted into cheers. The music teacher clapped hard and draped an arm around him. Brow beaded with sweat, T.J. beamed.

But seasoned observers of urban schools will recognize the manifest disrespect that defined many child-adult interactions. Many teachers and administrators in Hartford acknowledged it — mostly in private. Perhaps scholars who visit schools to carry out specific studies assume such abuse comes from a few rotten apples, not the system. And anyway, foundations do not confer grants for the study of janitor behavior. Why did nasty culture thrive in parts of Simpson-Waverly in just the form I'd seen at so many urban schools? For one thing, the low status of the children and the relatively low level of parental involvement may license susceptible adults to treat kids contemptuously. With the exception of Patrick and Rashida (who'd earned reputations for insubordination), Ms. Luddy's students accepted, as a matter of course, treatment that would bring suburban parents and even students themselves down on school authorities within minutes.

After I'd witnessed the janitor's gonzo reign of nastiness, I told the kids I was going to speak to Dr. Thompson about it.

Shasa advised me, "No, you know, I wouldn't do that. Why get all bothered up about it?"

And Jeremy said, "Ms. Luddy's nice. The other people don't matter so much."

Even Ms. Luddy had grown accustomed to such incidents.

"It is wrong," she said. "It starts to feel normal sometimes. But it's not okay."

The poorer the school district, the less parents generally engage with schools. Nonengagement isn't fated, and it's not the case in every poor, urban school. But it's typical. And it's understandable. Corral the most disenfranchised, least education-savvy, least entitled-feeling, most stressed-out and exhausted members of society into one isolated social institution and they'll be less likely to oppose whatever's on offer.

I decided that as an outsider and guest who needed continued good access and whose own professional training conveniently encouraged strict boundaries, I might best shelve my complaint about the janitor. The following week, though, I brought along my son, Will, who was six then, to visit. Patrick was the first to approach him, hand outstretched.

"You need anything, young man, you just come to me," Patrick told my son soothingly. "Your mother's got work to do here. So you come, you sit down over here with me."

At noon, in the cafeteria, it was a no-talking day. The janitor's insults were angrier than ever. "I'm sick of you, sick of you . . . now shut your mouth!" he shouted. Will began to cry. After only a year of kindergarten in a racially, culturally, and linguistically diverse but solidly middle-class suburban public school, Will was already certain that he and his classmates shouldn't be mistreated. Indignation quickly followed. He was dismayed by my detachment.

"Mom. C'mon. We *have* to tell on him," Will insisted. "Where's the Dr. Thompson guy?" The next week, I told. Not long afterward, the janitor got transferred to a high school.

IT WAS NO DOUBT HARDER, more stressful and unhealthier in Hartford (and for heroic people of a certain special constitution, more rewarding) than it was over in Marlborough.

Ms. Luddy not only filled her logbook and drilled kids for the test, but she also worried about a student's father who'd been beating the student's mother, who then fled to a safe house with the boy in tow. Ms. Luddy picked up a packet of marijuana in the hallway, eyeing it, then sniffing it to be sure. She fretted about how to deal with it because she liked the parent who'd dropped it. She would have trouble shaking the memory of the sixth grader who'd shot a classmate in the neck around the corner from the school and got hauled off to juvenile detention.

Local police had recently raided Patrick's house and found a cache of illegal weapons hidden by his uncle (another of Ms. Luddy's former students) beneath mattresses and inside the television console.

"The kid is still worried about going outside . . . afraid of being a victim in a revenge killing," Ms. Luddy told me one afternoon. "How is it that we've managed to convince this child that division is something he really needs to take seriously? Look at him. Look at that child." Patrick, pencil in hand, labored over a worksheet.

Ms. Luddy drove around after school, calling on parents who

wouldn't answer the phone. She caught up with one father on the roof of a nearby bodega, hammering nails.

"I have some concerns, sir?" Ms. Luddy had shouted up to him. "I'm quite worried about your son."

So THE JANITOR, who by the way was a superlative cleaner, was clearly not cut out for supervising youngsters. (Incongruously, he'd successfully tutored individual children, including Patrick, who were having trouble in math.) Should James Thompson have fired the teacher I saw shove a student? She was normally great in the classroom, it was said, and other teachers hadn't ever seen her shove. "School got better," Jeremy said, after the harsh vice-principal was transferred and the grumpy lunch escort retired. But like SFA and CMT, such individual personnel difficulties were symptoms too.

Concentrated poverty poured challenges on the Waverly community but spared Marlborough. Semisaints like Lois Luddy and James Thompson bore it brilliantly. More ordinary people stumbled, tripped, fell, and quit.

Into a Suburban Rain Forest

IN MARLBOROUGH, THOUGH, the Hartford kids and their suburban partners kept trying. Stuffed monkeys dangled from the ceiling of Ms. Rose's classroom. Construction paper palm trees grew in one corner. Papier-mâché snakes and pastel creepy crawlies slithered in another. Vibrant photographs of rain forests brightened a bulletin board. Between introductions and snack time, the kids clumped together. Some of Ms. Rose's students told the Hartford kids and me about what they'd been learning in recent weeks.

Elise explained that her class had "learned all about the rain forests of the world."

"Everything," Elise said, "from the animals that inhabit the rain forest, to the materials that we use every day that the rain forest provides," as well as "cool facts and stuff, like about how long different creatures will live and how long they get." Elise said she and her classmates "conduct our own science experiments" to discern relationships between plant growth, humidity, rainfall, and nutrients.

Sam told me his class studied "cultures and communities that depend upon rain forests or who have depended upon rain forests in the past."

In Marlborough the classroom windows opened. A huge map of the United States, dappled with colored pushpins, hung on one wall. Strings led to postcards taped along the map's perimeter. Jared said the class had mailed letters to "people we know from across the country." The contacts had sent these postcards back to the class, pictures of their states, on-the-ground reports of American life elsewhere.

"Basically, pretty much every state was covered, or at least all the major regions," Jared said. The suburban families' social networks were up to that test. Jared himself had written family friends in Colorado and Florida. A classmate, Kate, got back postcards from the "Midwest, near Chicago," and from "the northwestern part of the country, which included Oregon and Washington—not Washington, D.C., which is somewhere else, but up here, see?" Kate said, her finger dabbing Seattle.

"The climate is a bit different there," she explained, "and this is one of the reasons why certain plants will grow there and won't grow, or won't grow as well, here, in our part of the country, New England. Or you can call it the Northeast."

"Right," Sam added, "because when you say 'the Northeast,' you think of New York and then Delaware and maybe Pennsylvania," he said. He pointed to each state. "And of course, that's not New England." And Marlborough wasn't Hartford.

Marlborough's children, who had more exposure to other places, worked with a school curriculum package offering even more exposure. Hartford kids worked with a mandated curriculum that didn't add much.

Horace Mann, humanitarian and abolitionist, said, "Education, then, beyond all other devices of human origin, is the great equalizer of the conditions of men—the balance wheel of the social machinery." Not only did Hartford's and Marlborough's contrasting educations fail to correct disparities, but they exacerbated them.

Ms. Rose called out, "Snack time!" And the well-orchestrated suburban-urban exchange hit some subtle snags.

Patrick, despite that promising handshake, turned his back on his suburban partner and moved over to Owen. They munched corn chips together, made nasty faces behind the suburban kids' backs. Mallary tried to chat with Naia, who giggled shyly in response and soon walked away to Shasa, who hung back, her usual self-assuredness given over to focused thumb sucking. Jeremy chattered merrily. "No, I'm not really into baseball, but I'd like to hear about it," he told a boy.

Meanwhile, Jinaya and Rashida looked out the window at a big playground and giant green play structure. Parents had raised $80,000 for it. Swings swayed in the light breeze. The girls saw slides, a stand-and-pedal trapeze, monkey bars. It rose from the newest and safest playground surface—a spongy black material that eased children's tumbles.

"Isn't that nice?" a classroom aide asked the girls sweetly. Jinaya and Rashida kept staring. The aide moved in.

"And you see our butterfly garden?" She pointed toward a circle of perennials and a dangling hummingbird feeder, with a bench nearby. "Our parents did that. They planted that butterfly garden," the aide said, meeting Jinaya's eyes. "They looked in a book and learned what sorts of flowers would attract butterflies, and they put them in." The girls glanced at each other. They looked back out the window and again at each other. Jinaya giggled and stared at the floor. Rashida's mouth hung open.

"Here, let me open the window," the aide continued helpfully. "Here, you can look right out." She bent to their level, putting her hand out and feeling the air. "Isn't that wonderful? Nice fresh air! And it's a nice day. Such a nice day for you to come. We're so happy to have you here."

"We don't have as much stuff," Jinaya said.

"Oh. Well . . . ," the aide responded, literally wringing her hands, smiling closemouthed. The girls walked away.

MIKE LARKIN, THE THIRD-GRADE teacher I'd visited in Marlborough, had reflected, "Simpson-Waverly might not be the real world, but we are not the real world either. I mean, we are *so* white out here." He'd recounted an event that had disturbed him.

He'd started a routine lesson from the Talents Unlimited curriculum, offering a prompt: "Let's try to come up with many varied words to describe a city."

He'd expectantly held a Magic Marker in his hand, prepared to record the words on an easel. Usually this went smoothly and quickly. But not that day.

"All the words were negative. 'Dirty,' 'dangerous,' 'scary,' 'ugly,'" Larkin recalled, his hand over his mouth. "Terrible! I just stood there for a minute, hearing words like 'crime,' 'traffic,' 'polluted' . . . So where do I begin? When they are getting these wrong ideas and negative images from who knows where, but from a variety of sources for many years already. I had expected to hear 'busy.' Or perhaps 'crowded.' I mean, these are really nice kids! Really very open, good, caring kids! It's not *their* fault."

Larkin suggested that the children think of positive words about a city.

"I talked about the theater, the arts, museums, and I used the word 'exciting' a lot. And I say, 'Now, in the city, at night, near museums and restaurants, might there be people around there who could help if you were lost? Perhaps it would be less scary, hmm, than being in Marlborough?'"

Larkin's prodding brought forth some neutral adjectives.

"But basically, it was a flop," he recalled. "How can you teach diversity when you don't have it?"

In Larkin's view, the visit his students had made last year into Hartford was, "crucial, if only because they could get to the school, see that it's a nice, pleasant environment. They could see that if they were given more time somehow, maybe if they were together more, the children in the city would become their friends."

Working Together

FRIENDSHIP MIGHT HAVE COME with time. But after snacks, many of Ms. Luddy's students lingered with one another after Ms. Luddy had firmly told them to find their suburban partners. Several kids—Owen, Patrick, Rashida, T.J.—looked resigned. Patrick, though, finally offered a friendly nod to his partner, Jared. Naia delivered a cheery, "Hello, again!" to Mallary. And Shasa, her thumb out of her mouth, smiled politely, but only faintly, at Brenna, who grinned back heartily.

"Okay!" a lithe, exuberant woman, Lisa Taylor, shouted to the urban-suburban partners spread across the floor. Ms. Rose and Ms. Luddy had brought in Taylor, a poet and fiction writer, to teach a writing lesson. She smiled warmly, spoke loudly, and exuded confidence.

"How many people in here like to write?" she asked the kids, nodding in agreement with herself. "I really believe that writing should be fun!"

Shasa didn't look so sure. She looked about warily. Patrick, cross-legged, stared at the floor. Jeremy, though, yelled back, "Me too!"

Taylor, Ms. Luddy, and Ms. Rose passed out brown lunch bags—one to each set of partners.

"Now, you are probably wondering . . . what's in the bags? Is it alive? Is it going to crawl right out?" Taylor asked, her hand slithering.

"No," Shasa said quietly. "I was not wondering that."

"You know what's in the bags? Ideas. Ideas are in the bags."

"Huh?" Shasa murmured. She rolled her eyes, suspicious of showy enthusiasm.

Ms. Taylor shouted mischievously: "Your mission is this: Dump the contents out of the bag. I want you to make up a story containing things that are in the bag. You can split up the work. One person can do the physical writing. And use your imaginations. Something pretend can become something real with your imagination. I love imagination."

Shasa turned the bag upside down. Fake dimes and quarters glistened. Plastic lizards, a whistle, some shells, rained down between Shasa and her partner, Brenna. The resistance fell from Shasa's face.

"Ohhhh," she exclaimed, "*this* is gonna be good."

Naia's writing partner, Mallary, had long eyelashes and shiny brown hair cut in a perky pageboy. Like Naia, she was soft-spoken and smiled a lot. Naia tapped her pencil on a blank piece of paper snapped onto a clipboard. On their knees, the girls stared at their small pile of plastic fish, fake money, and shells.

"I think we should have smooshed fishes," Naia said thoughtfully. "Like that's our problem, that there's this lake? So the problem is that fishes are getting smooshed? People are swimming in the lake, and they are finding that fishes are getting smooshed?"

Naia transformed declarative sentences into questions.

"Great," Mallary said. "Perfect."

"Yeah?" Naia said, leaning forward. "Okay. We become inventors. Kid inventors," she continued. "We invent a thing, some thing that can see underwater and tells people with a beep, beep, beep, or by making a big splash, when they are smooshing fishes. Then we save all the little fishes! We're fish savers!"

"Ohhh. Ohhh. That's so cool," Mallary said. "Awesome. Let's write it . . . We need to call your device something."

"The underwater thingy?" Naia asked. "How about underwater seer?"

"Oh, no. No," Mallary said. "An underwater pirate device. Or an underwater robotic device. That's what you're imagining."

"I am?"

"Yeah," Mallary answered impatiently, as if she'd said something obvious. "Why don't we say that this underwater robotic device has the power to detect when human beings put too much pressure onto fish, and then the device alerts everyone to the problem?"

In Hartford, a writing session like this would have had no play to it and would have been aided by a structure chart, or "pillar," into which children would plug the main idea, supporting details, resolution. Marlborough kids had also learned "prewriting" skills. They mapped out or diagrammed stories. But even though Marlborough kids wrote out story plans—jotting down setting, characters, plot summary, problem, and resolution—the work flowed more freely. CMT-aligned writing exercises, however, plodded. Some encouraged kids to pick "exciting beginnings" from a list of choices. The bulk of Waverly writing assignments came with rushed, CMT-inspired time limits.

Marlborough's third and fourth graders, as a matter of course, spent weeks on one story, which they mapped, drafted, remapped, wrote, revised and revised again, illustrated, and typed on computers. Mike Larkin's third graders each wrote a novel by year's end. Marlborough kids did have deadlines, just not 45-minute ones.

"What do you want to have in the story?" Shasa asked her partner, Brenna. "Should the fish eat the fake quarter or what?"

Brenna laughed. Shasa laughed.

Shasa: "What about chameleons and a lake. Do we have to do it about a lake?"

Brenna: "I don't know. But, like, if you look at this, right? Well, like, these are all things that are in a lake or near a lake. Like, a fish and a chameleon and a lizard, those are all things that could be around a lake."

Shasa: "Chameleons are in a lake? I don't know—I'm just askin' 'cause I never seen a chameleon, so I don't know."

Brenna: "More likely, I'd say, they'd be in a tropical environment, or in a humid woodsy environment."

Shasa looked puzzled.

Brenna: "A hot place?"

Shasa: "Like a jungle?"

Brenna: "A hot jungle."

Shasa: "So . . . this could be about a lake in a hot place?"

Brenna: "Actually, I could ask. I know a lot of lizards live in tropical environments, so this is just an assumption I'm making. But I shouldn't jump to conclusions, just generalize. I don't know specifically about chameleons."

THIS WAS NOT A CONTEST. Still, the question hung in the air: Side by side, how did the groups compare?

Oral reading skills? The same. Imaginative capabilities? The same. Ability to stay focused? Save for Rashida—who rolled around on pillows and popped candy in her mouth—the same. The ability to work cooperatively? The same. Willingness to take risks? The same. Ease at fitting in? Excuse Patrick his initial fears and Shasa her brief resistance, and they're the same too.

Well, not *exactly* the same. The Waverly students lacked the subtleties that, fairly or not, cue mainstream folks about a person's education level and sophistication. Take vocabulary: "tropical environment," "generalize," "pirate device." Take the store of trivia that denotes worldliness and promises for easy conversation with people from beyond the neighborhood: the Northeast versus New England; the climate in the northwestern United States; the "Midwest, near Chicago." Take habitual turns of phrase that denote ease conceptualizing: "alerts everyone to the problem," "I shouldn't . . . generalize." Patrick's partner, Jared, had declared, "These sneakers tend to irritate my Achilles tendon." And Patrick had responded, "Wha?"

THE CHILDREN LINED UP after the writing exercise.

"These kids hardly ever go outside," Ms. Luddy whispered to Ms. Rose. "This is a very, very big deal for them."

The heavy doors opened onto a small picnic area. The children flew out like freed birds, over grass and over the twisted, clean, green metal play structure that had called to them since morning.

"Look at this," Ms. Luddy said, mouth open, eyes wide. "Look. Just look, would you? Look at them. Look at them playing."

It was as if Ms. Luddy had taken the kids to Disney World.

Play revealed character. Patrick hurriedly organized a touch football game with Owen, T.J., Martin, and four suburban boys. Two racially mixed teams emerged without adult prodding.

"We ain't keepin' score," he told me proudly. "The idea, here, is to have a good time."

Jeremy made a spirited go at recreation. He got in line to try a new-fangled slide—just two slanted parallel bars. The Hartford children had never seen such a thing. Shasa's partner, Brenna, demonstrated.

"You, like, hook your arms over it," she said, an underarm over each rail. "Then let yourself slide." Knees to her chest, Brenna whisked down and landed elegantly, flipping her arms up, as if nailing a perfect 10. Shasa, Jinaya, Rashida, Naia, and Jeremy applauded. Brenna bowed and blushed.

Shasa positioned herself at the top of the slide. Brenna stood below. "You got it," Brenna shouted.

Shasa slid and screamed, eyes wide with fear.

Down came Rashida, screaming louder.

Jeremy took a deep breath, positioned his arms, and fell several feet to the ground through the bars. Thud.

Mallary shouted down to him from the top of the slide: "It's very difficult to do, actually. I needed to practice quite a bit before I got it. Everyone had to learn. Come on up. Really, it's okay! Try again!"

"No, but thanks," Jeremy said. "That's it for me."

He hoisted up his pants and limped away, rubbing his butt.

"Maybe I should try swings," he said.

No one had ever taught Jeremy how to pump. He watched others swinging. Keesha pumped high, eyes closed. She shouted out to no one: "I want to touch the sky!" Jeremy's body didn't yet know the physics of swinging. His legs flailed but he couldn't replicate Keesha's moves. His swing jiggled, earthbound. He walked away.

After 20 minutes, the children ran back in, refreshed. Even Ms. Luddy looked rejuvenated. It was time to start for home. The urban-suburban exchange program wasn't going to change much, but Ms. Luddy's kids had shined in Marlborough, merely writing, playing, trying.

"I am walking on air," she told the kids before they boarded the yellow school bus for Hartford. "I can't tell you enough how very, very proud I am to be your teacher."

Judgment

Ms. Luddy's students had sat through the big Connecticut Mastery Test in the fall. In spring 2002 they awaited their final report cards. At the same time, the *Sheff* lawyers were preparing a judgment day of their own.

For the second time since their 1996 victory, the plaintiffs returned to court. Once again they had filed documents informing Judge Julia Aurigemma that the state's remedy had failed to benefit an adequate percentage of Hartford children. The plaintiffs hoped the court might finally order the state to devise a remedy that would allow more children to attend less overburdened, less segregated schools. The lawyers agreed that the state certainly had made some constructive progress. Several excellent, new magnet schools were up and operating. But the plaintiffs planned to argue that the state's efforts touched far too few of Hartford's isolated students. Those successful and surprisingly popular new schools, the lawyers would contend, should be models for expansion.

The legal team for this round had both familiar faces and new ones. John Brittain was present, although only by conference call. He'd moved to Texas in 1999 to teach at Houston's historically black Thurgood Marshall School of Law.

While Brittain and the other lawyers had been preparing the *Sheff* case in 1991, the U.S. Supreme Court had quietly leeched more life from *Brown.* In a decision called *Board of Education of Oklahoma v. Dowell,* the Court had allowed the Oklahoma City school board to dismantle its existing court-ordered desegregation plan and knowingly re-create extremely racially segregated schools. In *Dowell,* the Court established that once a lower court had declared a previously segregated school "unitary," or free of the vestiges of its prior "segregation," then the school district might be released from its court-ordered desegregation plan, even if throwing out such a plan returned a district to segregation levels as high as those that existed before *Brown,* if not higher.

The next year, in 1992, the U.S. Supreme Court struck at *Brown* again. In a case from Georgia, *Freeman v. Pitts,* the Court ruled that school districts could be partially released from court-ordered desegregation plans even if the district *hadn't* complied with all the parts of its desegregation order. Then, in 1995, the Court, in *Missouri v. Jenkins,* went even further. It ruled that education-related remedies to segregation—remedial programs, for example—need not demonstrate that they've ameliorated inequalities or even improved student achievement.

Perhaps the biggest blow to *Brown* was that in *Jenkins* the Court defined desegregation as a temporary punishment, not as a worthy goal. By the time Wes Horton had stood up and argued *Sheff* on appeal, federal courts, once civil rights allies, were no longer likely to advise school districts how to create desegregation plans, but how to dismantle them legally.

These decisions were to Southern desegregation what *Milliken* had been to Northern desegregation. The South, America's most integrated region since the 1970s, slipped slowly toward more segregated schools after these decisions. In 1954, before *Brown v. Board of Education,* the percentage of black students in majority-white schools in the South had been 0. In 1988, it reached a remarkable 44 percent. It dwindled slowly each year, down to 30 percent by 2001.

For John Brittain, the case that brought what he called "the *Brown* reversal" into clear relief had been the Fifth Circuit Court of Appeals 1996 decision in *Hopwood vs. University of Texas Law School*. The *Hopwood* decision banned any use of race or ethnicity—aka "affirmative action"—in admissions to public law schools.

Hopwood shocked the American civil rights community, and John Brittain "hoped very hard" that the Supreme Court would overturn it. But the Court refused to hear the case. *Hopwood* stood. However, in 2003, the U.S. Supreme Court did essentially uphold affirmative action—under some circumstances—in the Michigan case *Grutter v. Bollinger et al*.

Right after *Hopwood,* Brittain suspected that more black and Latino would-be lawyers, especially from Texas, would seek out the Thurgood Marshall School of Law, the state's only historically black law school. That's when he took their job offer. He moved south and awaited the students. The year before *Hopwood,* Thurgood Marshall had enrolled about 78 percent of Texas's black first-year law students. In 1999, a little more than two years after *Hopwood,* 90 percent of Texas's 212 black first-year law students went to Thurgood Marshall. *Hopwood* had worked its damage. In his small way, Brittain tried to counteract it. In 1999, trustees at the law school named John Brittain dean.

Meanwhile, Phil Tegeler had become the legal director at the Connecticut Civil Liberties Union. He'd also inherited the less-than-glorious tasks of watching the numbers, keeping up the files, collecting information, worrying, and getting incensed about what wasn't happening in Hartford.

Tegeler seemed like John Brittain's opposite. He's white, with a mop of brown hair and a boyish, open face. He'd grown up on Boston's suburban South Shore. His father was a liberal Lutheran minister; his mother, a public school principal. He'd excelled as a scholarship student at the elegant, mildly progressive Milton Academy. He'd driven a van for his father's summer camp, which brought white South Shore kids and black and Latino kids from Boston together.

"The positive impact it had on both groups of kids, and how incredibly easy it was," Tegeler recalled, "made me think, 'What is the big deal? We should be able to do this.'"

At hearings, meetings, working lunches, Phil Tegeler usually stayed poker-faced. He wasn't a charmer; he won his notice and respect through steady, hard work over the long term. The *Sheff* lawyers agreed that Tegeler was *Sheff*'s most unsung hero.

"Everyone has an idea of whose case this is, of who represents this case, of who is the lead attorney," Dennis Parker, the LDF attorney, told me near the start of the trial. "Well, there is no lead attorney. There never was a real lead attorney. It's been a cooperative effort all the way. But in terms of day to day work? Consistency? It's Phil."

Phil Tegeler always looked comfortable enough before a crowd, but he left most public speaking to his colleagues.

"I'm not good with that sound-bite sort of thing," he'd told me. "It's not me."

But his decades of legal work followed directly from his kind and seemingly innocent heart. In the face of losses, setbacks, and nonstop resistance, he'd somehow preserved an inviolate trust in human goodness. Given half a chance, he insisted, his fellow man would come through in the end. *Sheff,* he said, had the potential to demonstrate the goodness of human nature.

"This will work," he'd assured me. "I don't believe that anyone is in opposition to what this case represents."

Tegeler's former supervisor at CCLU, Martha Stone, had moved from the Connecticut Civil Liberties Union to the University of Connecticut. She ran a children's advocacy law center there. She'd faithfully kept track of *Sheff* with Tegeler and the other lawyers. Martha Stone also had the doggedness and passion to keep *Sheff* alive. And

Chris Hansen, a longtime staff lawyer at the American Civil Liberties Union, had been with *Sheff* from the start. He regularly joined in conference calls and consultations. In the late 1980s, he and his boss at that time, Helen Hershkoff (later an NYU professor), had compared state constitutions, looking for the right door to pry open.

Dennis Parker, LDF's lead *Sheff* attorney since 1995, was burly, with prep-school diction and eyeglasses, which he often pushed back up the bridge of his nose. He'd grown up in working-class Mount Vernon, New York. In the 1960s, a public elementary school teacher had noticed his potential, and the teacher (the school's only black male teacher) had pulled Dennis's mother aside and suggested that her son might benefit from a more rigorous school nearby.

The next year he had won a full scholarship to the exclusive, preppy, white (he stressed "progressive") Rye Country Day School. Although Country Day was full of rich kids, Parker had "a really positive experience, though there was this feeling, a little bit, of being the other—being the only black person there."

"I knew all kinds of people, growing up in Mount Vernon, whose paths went in very different directions from mine," he said. "And it wasn't because I was smarter. It certainly wasn't that. And it wasn't because I worked harder. That's not true. It was because, by chance, we had very different opportunities in our lives. And when I talked with people who worked in law, it seemed to me that was the best route to try to correct for those inequalities on a big scale."

Dennis Parker also saw *Sheff*'s potential for bringing out the best in people. He'd traveled the country fighting similar battles in many courtrooms. His sighs and glares revealed a man chafing at slow progress.

"It's amazing just watching people here," he'd observed one morning in the posh Legislative Office Building. Snappily dressed state politicians had strutted up and down the elegant curved staircase, gabbing on cell phones. "Look around this place. There's a kind of fraternal air . . . like there's a party going on, and less than a mile away, there are children who don't have enough to eat. When we get to talking about *Sheff,* the way some of these guys react, the things they say? Either they don't know what's going on, or they don't give a rat's ass."

Parker had brought in a young protégé from the new generation of black civil rights lawyers. Derek Douglas wasn't quite 30 when he joined the *Sheff* team. He'd graduated from Yale Law School, shunned big money from corporate law firms, and applied for a grant-funded $37,500 fellowship at the Legal Defense Fund. He'd already been an LDF intern and wanted back in.

Douglas's law school buddies started first jobs at salaries that were, he'd said, "high, very, very high, six figures." His LDF salary barely covered his law school loans and New York City rent. For Douglas, racial, economic, and cultural diversity had come naturally. He'd attended racially and culturally diverse Seventh-Day Adventist schools. He'd found the racially defined social groups on the University of Michigan campus unsettling.

"I didn't completely realize that the rest of society lived with this tension and separation," he said. "For me, living and learning with people of different backgrounds was just the way it was. It was how you existed."

At Yale, Douglas's professors had included Justice Flemming Norcott, who'd cast a pro-*Sheff* vote in 1996 on the Connecticut Supreme Court. Douglas had learned about *Sheff* in one of his classes.

"I remember being fascinated by it," Douglas said in the bustling cafeteria of Connecticut's Legislative Office Building. "To convert the victory into something—I wanted to help with that."

In the proposal that had landed him the prestigious Skadden Fellowship at LDF, Douglas attested that he'd told funders he'd like to revitalize *Sheff*'s community mobilization effort—which Nina Morais and Marianne Lado had headed up years back. His proposed project had to pass review with a partner in the intimidating New York law firm Skadden, Arps, Slate, Meagher, and Flom, which had funded the grant. Douglas had heard whispers that the partner who would interview him—a white labor lawyer, Michael Connery, from suburban Greenwich—had opposed *Sheff*.

"I imagined what his worries were, and they were legitimate," Douglas recalled. "I knew he'd want to know *Sheff* wasn't out to hurt fine suburban school systems, that its objective was to widen opportunities for parents, kids, who didn't have equal chances.

"He listened. And then he said he supported what I was doing and best of luck," Douglas said, smiling. "He funded me. So go figure." Maybe *Sheff* actually did encourage human virtue.

Dennis Parker had set Derek Douglas to work on the very mission he'd named in his grant application—fanning the embers of community support. Douglas had scheduled a long round of meetings with clergymen, educators, and activists. He'd driven around the Hartford region, regarding the ravaged city for the first time. He'd seen what John Brittain had in the late 1970s and what Marianne Lado had in the 1980s.

"People say, 'Yeah, you're right, segregation is such a terrible thing . . . We need to find a way to get this back on the agenda.' So I don't understand. Why are the Hartford schools *more* segregated than when the whole case began? People tell me they've been talking about these issues for twenty, thirty years. I don't understand why nothing changes."

Tussling

O N APRIL 16, 2002, the *Sheff* lawyers drove the 10 miles from Hartford to Judge Julia Aurigemma's modern courtroom in New Britain.

Judge Aurigemma was a pert 48-year-old suburban Republican appointed by Governor John Rowland. She was known among lawyers for running a tight, orderly courtroom.

"But you know," Wes Horton added, "you can't predict how she'll rule. You really can't." Back in 1998, though, Aurigemma had ruled against the plaintiffs after they'd complained that the state was moving too slowly and enacting a *Sheff* remedy that was too small.

This was Derek Douglas's first trial ever. He'd prepared by getting his hair trimmed close. He showed up in a perfectly fitted blue suit. Chris Hansen from the ACLU, Phil Tegeler, Martha Stone, and Dennis Parker gathered again at the plaintiffs' table. Wes Horton was a touch grayer since the supreme court argument seven years before.

The court marshal's opening cry died away, and Wes Horton began to outline the familiar arguments. He was quick and efficient. The existing programs — Open Choice and magnet schools — had great potential, but they were tiny. Their funding mechanisms and transportation problems needlessly reduced their appeal, he said. He ended on a personal note that was widely covered in news accounts.

"I was born on April 16, 1942. When I was thirty-one, the plaintiffs started *Horton v. Meskill*. When I was forty-seven, the plaintiffs started *Sheff v. O'Neill*. Today I am sixty and this is my birthday wish: that before I die we will end the racial and economic isolation that destroys the dreams of Hartford's children."

THROUGHOUT THE PROCEEDINGS, Judge Aurigemma tapped furiously on a laptop computer. The sides tussled for two weeks. Was there enough money to support more desegregation programs? Were other educational programs more important than integration? Were new reforms really improving the city schools? Had similar desegregation programs worked in other cities?

For the first time, the plaintiffs offered their own plan for delivering more programs to more kids by increasing enrollments in the suburban transfer program and in interdistrict magnet schools.

"The test of a desegregation plan is not how much it costs or how much effort was put into it, or how many activities are established in pursuit of it," a seasoned desegregation architect, Len Stevens, testified. "The test of a plan is its results. If you look for results, you see the concentration of black and Hispanic students in Hartford remaining."

"Do you have an opinion about what the ultimate goal should be?" Dennis Parker asked Stevens.

"Well, I think the ultimate goal should be what the 1996 opinion says, and that is to eliminate racial isolation in Hartford."

THE PLAINTIFFS' LAWYERS had believed from the start that their aspiration for a more integrated region could really happen. They'd seen proof with their own eyes. One school in particular impressed them. A few months before trial, Phil Tegeler, Derek Douglas, and

Dennis Parker had visited what would soon become the most popular and one of the most successful of the racially integrated magnet schools in the city: the University of Hartford Magnet School. The school culture at UHMS was relentless in its enforced earnestness, but it was a constructive relentlessness and probably a necessary one, as it had to overcome the barriers to human understanding and interaction that decades of unacknowledged segregation had set up.

The school's warm, energetic principal, Cheryl Kloczko, had led the lawyers through sunny classrooms and a big, round common room with floor-to-ceiling windows. The lawyers had nodded a lot, perused tacked-up lessons and artwork, thumbed through children's books, and smiled at the kids.

UHMS had opened its doors in 2001. It was handsomely built and funded, mostly, with state dollars that flowed after the 1996 *Sheff v. O'Neill* decision. The school had enrolled 350 children, pre-K through grade five. Like the other magnet schools, UHMS drew kids from across school district boundary lines. That made it of special interest to advocates of desegregated schools, which in many metropolitan areas outside the South would have to draw students in the same way. Half came from Hartford. Half came from nearby suburbs. A little more than one-quarter of the students were poor—probably about as high a percentage as schools can typically handle without being overwhelmed by the issues of poverty themselves. Sixty-one percent were members of minority groups. Kids were selected by lottery. In 2002, 85 suburban and urban parents applied for 16 openings in the new kindergarten alone.

The school sat on the border between Hartford and West Hartford on the campus of the University of Hartford, a small liberal arts university. Above UHMS's entryway, a banner on which painted children stood side by side proclaimed, WE ARE ALL RELATED. Did the politically correct banner reflect more wishful thinking?

Kloczko, the principal, thought not.

She told the lawyers, "We *are* all related. The school really is built around that fact." After a few hours at the school, they came to believe her. Children's self-portraits, in peach, mocha, and coffee skin tones, hung outside Kloczko's office. Students had brought in cloth and leather—an African necklace, South American embroidery, an Asian belt—and woven them around the school's railings. This tapestry project, Kloczko said, "represents the interrelatedness of cultures." It's there "so the children can share with us something they love."

But it wasn't as if running UHMS was easy and harmonious all the time. Kloczko had been a principal in a far less challenging town, Canton. "I found it was different here," she said. "We had low-income kids in Canton. But there's more here. We had single-parent families there too. It's just that there's more here. But you get a teacher here from Hartford? From their perspective, it's a more workable situation." Former Hartford teachers are less overwhelmed at UHMS and can fill in the "experiential" differences between wealthier suburban and poor urban kids. One winter day, for example, a class read a story about sledding. The teacher saw that many of the children had never been sledding or even seen a sled up close, hadn't heard the word *toboggan,* and could not picture a snow fort.

"These children live in New England, for goodness' sake," Kloczko said, looking horrified. "You bet we got them out there, on sleds, going down the hill right out there."

She was frustrated, not by the school's cultural differences, but by her test scores, which weren't yet even near her goal. She told the lawyers that she and the teachers were committed to a curriculum based upon Harvard professor Howard Gardner's "multiple intelligences" theories. "MI" classifies eight intelligences, none of which a test score could sum up.

Kloczko's MI curriculum offered children a rich education, full of science, music, art, expression through drama and literature. The math lessons focused upon understanding concepts, not just on mastering multiplication tables. The curriculum obviously wasn't aligned with the state's tests. Kloczko was proud of this but had to worry about it too. Nationally, urban schools were dogged by teaching to tests. It may have been purist to ignore the pressure. But doing so would jeopardize her school.

At UHMS, many Hartford kids continued to struggle on the CMT. They scored, in most categories, only slightly better than their counterparts in traditional city schools. That may well have indicated success, Kloczko suggested, as the city schools drilled hard and UHMS didn't. The suburban children at UHMS, meanwhile, scored the same as suburban kids in regular schools.

"We're searching for balance," Kloczko said. "We know what these kids can do. They show us every day. Incredible skills, understanding, coming from these Hartford kids. But we can't have low test scores. We can't."

Kloczko watched a multicultural crawl of children walk down the hallway between classes.

"You know, we could have the highest test scores in the state. But we just would not be as good if we didn't have the racial diversity and see that as our strength, as a precious, nonnegotiable characteristic," Kloczko said, eyes on the students. The children waved. She waved back, winked, made a few funny faces.

"No. No," she said, "let me restate what I just said, could I? You know, it's not only that we would not be as good. It's that without everyone included, all races, backgrounds, without wanting that and doing it that way on purpose, we wouldn't be a good school, period."

AFTER A FEW HOURS at UHMS, the lawyers piled into Phil Tegeler's car. They were of course delighted with Kloczko's exalted philosophy. But they also felt frustrated.

"Could you believe that place?" Derek Douglas exclaimed. "That place was amazing. But we're talking three hundred kids? Only three hundred kids."

"I know," Phil Tegeler answered. "But no one can say, now, 'Oh, you can't do it.' The argument that no white parents are going to buy into this is useless. Did you hear her waiting-list numbers? It's phenomenal."

"Okay," Derek Douglas said, eyeing the late afternoon bustle along Hartford's Albany Avenue. "But think about all of Hartford. Twenty-three thousand kids. There's three hundred kids at that school, and one hundred fifty from Hartford. So yeah, it's great. But in terms of numbers, it can feel like not much."

AT THE TRIAL, the plaintiffs' lawyers set out to prove exactly Douglas's point, highlighting several examples of successful racial integration and arguing that more children should have access to such experiences. The Montessori Magnet School was a modern elementary school in a gleaming complex in what was one of the city's roughest, ugliest neighborhoods. In 2002, the principal received 362 applications from across the region for 35 openings. The Metropolitan Learning Center, an international studies school out in Bloomfield, had 242 black and Latino students on its waiting list.

"It's pretty cool seeing three different children all sitting and working with each other," testified Timothy Nee, principal of the Montessori Magnet. "Knowing the children as I do, I know that this kid comes from one of the poorest homes and this kid comes from one of the wealthiest families," he said, adding exuberantly, "so you see a lot of that just naturally going on in the classroom, or outside the classroom."

In addition to creating more magnet schools, the state could also easily increase capacity in its public school choice program, a woman named Susan Uchitelle testified. She'd overseen St. Louis's far-larger voluntary transfer program, in which 12,400 city kids traveled voluntarily to suburban schools in its peak year. Hartford's public school choice program, Uchitelle said, could accommodate more children, with additional advertising, targeted recruitment, better transportation, and a rule that suburbs enroll a specified number of students.

From 1981 until 1999, the proportion of St. Louis students in integrated schools, Susan Uchitelle testified, rose from 14 to 62 percent. At that, Judge Julia Aurigemma raised her eyebrows and tapped on her laptop.

Two lawyers represented the state. The lead attorney, Ralph Urban, was slight and genial, with a gray crew cut. His colleague, Holly Bray, seemed cheerful enough and certainly friendly. She gushed openly over Elizabeth Sheff's photographs of her grandchildren and asked after Milo. She'd won the affection of opposing counsel. The courtroom maintained a cozy, tame atmosphere.

"Oh, we love Ralph and Holly," Derek Douglas said. "Too bad they're on the wrong side—good people like that."

Ralph Urban and Holly Bray competently and dispassionately poked holes in the plaintiffs' plan. It was too costly, their collection of high-ranking state officials testified. In 2002, Connecticut, like many other states, projected an overall budget deficit.

The state called the education commissioner, Ted Sergi. Sergi was stocky, with close-cut, jet-black hair and enormous eyeglasses. He wore plain suits and white shirts that set off his olive complexion. He'd grown up in Queens, playing stickball and attending public schools. He'd worked in public education for 32 years, much of it in politicized positions that required not merely street smarts but a knack for picking battles wisely. He was a lawyer too. Wes Horton had been his teacher at UConn.

Ted Sergi looked comfortable in the spotlight. His big hands sliced the air elegantly while he spoke. He was rumored to have a short temper and a sentimental streak. On the witness stand, he didn't so much talk tough as emanate the sense that he was a brave if occasionally affable messenger of hard truths. His funding initiatives and speeches over the years had demonstrated his concern for urban kids. But he needed to get his plans through a suburban-dominated legislature. He was a Democrat serving a Republican governor.

"Ted Sergi is a good man," Phil Tegeler insisted. "He's in a tough spot. But I've gotten to know him. I really think he's with us."

In the courtroom, though, Ted Sergi positioned himself firmly against Phil Tegeler in cross-examination.

"And other than your duties now imposed by the legislation, do you consider yourself, as commissioner, to have independent obligations to comply with the supreme court decision?" Tegeler asked.

"No, I do not," Ted Sergi replied.

"And you don't have any opinion as to when the state will be in full compliance with *Sheff v. O'Neill,* do you?"

"No, I do not."

"Or how many years it will take."

"No, I do not."

THE PLAINTIFFS' PLAN, Ralph Urban and Holly Bray argued, rested upon a wrong assumption—that families would continue to volunteer for desegregation programs. For the third time, the state trucked out Christine Rossell, the Boston University professor who had argued against desegregation at every trial so far. She testified that Len Stevens's voluntary plan could "transition into" one that includes forced busing.

"Forced busing!" Dennis Parker exclaimed after her testimony. He knew a code word when he heard one. Busing, of the mandatory sort, had never been on the table. For decades, Parker had seen foes of integration invoke the word *busing.* For many people, it conjured up ugly images of race-based violence and urban tumult. Even parents who might be in favor of sending their child to a more diverse school, Parker understood, tended to shudder at the word *busing,* which, rightly or wrongly, suggested disruption of comfortable routines and a loss of parental control. Parker viewed Rossell's use of the word as a tactic devised to scare Judge Aurigemma away from even voluntary desegregation.

"Ridiculous," Parker said, sighing and shaking his head, during a break in testimony. "It's so old and so boring."

Parker had come up against Christine Rossell many times in other cities. And once again he set out to discredit her. During her deposition before trial, his frustration with her had been palpable.

"Is it significant for students to have contact with people of different races? Is that important educationally in your opinion?" he'd asked Rossell during the deposition.

"We don't have any evidence that it is," she'd answered.

Dennis Parker: "And as an educator, do you believe there is a benefit?"

Christine Rossell: "I can see benefits and I can see important costs."

Dennis Parker: "And what are the important costs?"

Christine Rossell: "That a child leaves a school in which they are — in which they belong, in which they are considered smart, in which they feel successful, and they go to a suburban school where the students there are smarter than they are, they are considered less successful . . ."

Dennis Parker: "Do you think that suburban students are smarter than the African-American or Latino students in Hartford?"

Christine Rossell: "You know, I don't know about native ability, but I do know this, that social class explains virtually all of the differences in achievement."

Parker, who'd come from a humble background himself and succeeded brilliantly at a prestigious white prep school, had asked Rossell if she'd read earlier studies suggesting that black children who went to integrated schools were more likely than their previously segregated counterparts to live, work, attend college, and succeed in white-dominated settings.

Yes, Rossell had answered, but "the problem" with such studies was that "it doesn't look at possible costs."

Dennis Parker: "And the costs are the ones you referred to before about finding out that you're stupider than suburban kids?"

During trial, the question of which kids were smarter didn't reappear.

But Rossell, ever poised on the witness stand, did testify about the purported failure of mandatory desegregation plans. Dennis Parker objected, pointing out that plaintiffs had never proposed a mandatory desegregation plan. Undaunted, Christine Rossell testified (accurately) that suburbs generally aren't as uniformly white as they used to be. The Hartford area, Christine Rossell testified (inaccurately) "is not that racially imbalanced."

Elizabeth Sheff, sitting in the second row, narrowed her eyes.

"Disgusting," she whispered to me. "What planet is *she* living on? Not mine. Mine's real segregated."

DURING TRIALS, LAWYERS expend much fretful energy divining the judge's thinking. A judge's questions are subjected to wild analysis. It was true in this case too. Judge Aurigemma's every nod, smile, grimace, raised eyebrow, tap on her laptop, set the anxious plaintiffs' lawyers speculating. Useless guessing often went hand in hand with suspended disbelief. The lawyers worked at convincing themselves that politics and personal ideology didn't influence the process—that sheer logic counted. They proceeded under the assumption that the best arguments, most cogent legal theories, would win. They all knew better.

Derek Douglas, still easing himself into his role as a trial lawyer, had a lot of questions. He dared to ask them all the time, offstage.

"So, say Judge Aurigemma rules in our favor," he speculated to the far more experienced ACLU lawyer Chris Hansen over sandwiches midway through trial. "She's not going to be getting any supreme court appointment from John Rowland, right?"

"I would doubt it," Hansen answered. "I don't think a Republican governor would be thrilled with her."

"So then—" Derek Douglas began. "Sometimes you wonder, 'What are we doing? Are we just wasting our time?'"

"Well," Chris Hansen answered calmly, "we're doing what we do."

"I know you have to just keep at it," Derek Douglas said, tossing his napkin onto his empty plate. "But think about it. Why's she gonna rule in our favor? She's young. She's smart. Doesn't she *want* to be on the supreme court?"

"You never know," Hansen said. "We don't have a lot of choices. Anyway, we're right!" Chris Hansen smiled encouragingly. Lunch recess was over. He walked outside.

"Oh, I know we're right," Douglas answered Hansen as they strolled toward the courthouse. "But the more I learn here, the more I'm worried that isn't enough."

Derek Douglas had reason to worry. If they lost here, any appeal would go to the state supreme court, which might be cooler to *Sheff* than it had been in 1996. Ellen Peters had retired. So had *Sheff*'s staunch supporter, Justice Berdon. Governor Rowland—he'd never warmed to *Sheff*—had appointed three new justices to the court. And Justice Borden, the passionate dissenter, and Justice Palmer, who'd voted against *Sheff*, still sat on the court.

After two weeks, in the final minutes of the trial, Wes Horton asked Judge Aurigemma what she'd "like" in the way of final briefs. Did she want them to focus upon alternative remedies, for example? And in reply, she did proffer a clue to her thinking. Perhaps she didn't think what the state was doing was appropriate, she told Wes Horton. But perhaps, she added, she didn't think that the plaintiffs' plan was necessarily the way to go either.

"What I'd *really* like is for you to settle it," she told him forcefully.

The following week, conference calls commenced.

"I don't like that word, 'settle,' so much," John Brittain told me from Houston. "I don't love the idea. But you don't want to lose the whole thing."

Since the start of *Sheff*, back in the late 1980s, Greater Hartford, like most of America's metropolitan regions, had grown more complicated. The region didn't fit a simple model of what social scientists had once termed "chocolate cities and vanilla suburbs." All over, the closest suburbs absorbed the overflow of urban challenges. Nearly 15 years after *Sheff* was filed, arguments about harms of isolation and concentrated poverty surely weren't invalid, as Christine Rossell had implied they'd become. Rather, the harms of racial isolation and poverty had spread to ever more schools in more communities, such as Bloomfield, East Hartford, and New Britain, right near Hartford.

Meanwhile, racial integration barely inched forward in the fancy white suburbs slightly farther out. As for Jeremy Otero and his classmates who remained in the Northeast neighborhood of Hartford—from which even working-class minorities were fleeing fast—isolation had grown far *more* extreme than it had been 15 years earlier. The team of lawyers didn't often meet up with the kids there, but they were exactly the sorts of children they worried about most.

Results

As the most recent *Sheff* trial wound down, Ms. Luddy again sat studying her students' test results from the fall. Before she knew it, she'd be putting together final report cards. In September, her kids would enter fifth grade, devoting much of the year to CMT prep for the sixth-grade round of testing. In her final two months with them, she hoped to get a little more inventive in the classroom and "challenge them, push open their minds a little bit more." She said they'd "blossom if you just give them a chance." And anyway, she said, handing me the test results, "these numbers are solid. No one can say we didn't prepare for this test."

The story about Hartford's test scores showed up in the *Hartford Courant*. Once again, Waverly's numbers stood out.

In math, 56 percent of the school's fourth graders had met the state's "goal"; only 29 percent in Hartford overall had. In reading, 56 percent of Waverly's fourth graders met the goal, about matching the overall state average of 58 percent. In writing, Simpson-Waverly's fourth graders had done even better than far more affluent counterparts across Connecticut. Eighty percent of Simpson-Waverly's fourth graders had met the state's writing goal. In all Connecticut, 61 percent of children had. Ms. Luddy's kids scored higher in writing than their counterparts in West Hartford and even in Marlborough. And Hartford, overall, cranked up one more notch in the state standings — they'd climbed to sixth from the bottom. Ms. Luddy was most pleased, though, with good results that could not be quantified.

First off, there was Patrick. In third grade he'd announced to his classmates, "I decided to change." He'd certainly shown everyone he'd meant it. Back then he'd scored far below level on his CMTs. By fourth grade, head down in his books and will strong, Patrick reached state goal in reading and writing, though math still tripped him up. He had endured the torture of long division drills, but he'd also decided that Ms. Luddy's classroom was a safe place to lay down his anger and trust in his bright, witty self.

Ms. Luddy felt hopeful looking at Shasa and thought that she might, against all odds, actually become a trauma surgeon. Near the end of third grade, Ms. Luddy had begun calling her "Doctor." By fourth grade, Shasa had grown accustomed to the honorific. Dr. Shasa even won the school's science fair for her tests on the varying viscosities of homemade slimes. T.J. still nearly always came up with right answers. A few times, Ms. Luddy had seen him lighten up and not take himself so seriously. In those short discussions about September 11, she had seen a little "bit of a spark" in T.J. Not only had he displayed deep moral concern, but he'd also been willing to admit to not knowing all the answers all of the time.

Jeremy's curiosity had survived the months of rote CMT drills.

Owen had plugged away, increasingly earnest. He wasn't always successful academically, but he'd grown more curious about science.

Martin read nature books and stayed true to his artistic spirit.

"I saw the most beautiful Mexican colors today in art," Martin wrote in an e-mail to me that spring. "We learned about colors in art that are Mexican and I didn't stop staring at how beautiful they look. Someday, we will paint paper mashay with them and I will write to you again that day but you can know today that the future day of Mexican color painting will be a good day for me! Your friend, Martin."

By late April, Ms. Luddy was indeed teaching more boldly. She'd always loved doing science lessons. A colleague had peeked into her classroom recently, and exclaimed, "You're actually *doing* this?" Ms. Luddy was standing happily among the children, who twisted wires, screwed in lightbulbs, and debated electricity.

Ms. Luddy also bravely steered around the shoals of the SFA reading list and taught a series of books by the children's author Avi. *Poppy* followed a mischievous, endangered troupe of mice. The fanciful, suspenseful story snuck in loads of natural history and animal habitat lore. The children couldn't get enough of it. The books sparked fine discussions about bravery, the suffocating effects of fear, and the challenges of standing up for your beliefs. The best part of all, to judge by the kids' shrieks, was Ms. Luddy's displaying a real mouse pellet that had once been ingested by an owl. Shasa had exclaimed, "Oh. Oh. Oh. So cool."

Near the end of the school year in 2002, Ms. Luddy found herself nominated for the city's Teacher of the Year. That was a far bigger deal for her students than their good test numbers.

Her colleagues at Waverly had nominated her. And to Ms. Luddy's surprise and horror, she'd been selected as one of three finalists. She had to write self-promoting essays for the final round. Her Irish Catholic humility made this assignment excruciating. A cameraman sent by the selection committee videotaped her teaching a lesson. She chose to teach science that day. The kids squeezed water out of eyedroppers onto mystery substances and then tried to identify the powders and crystals.

"We was good. I especially was good. And Ms. Luddy, she was hot. Yup, she was good," Patrick recalled. "We put liquid into baking soda. Did you hear? It bubbled up, all fizzly like."

By choosing to teach science, Ms. Luddy had taken a risk. She knew (and was delighted) that during science her kids got all worked up by what they saw, felt, smelled. They expressed awe (loudly), moved around (a lot), pumped arms, gasped, screamed in surprise, got grossed out.

Whenever Patrick had a small scientific discovery, he belted out "Oh YEAH! Oh YEAH!" Shasa, gleeful, often shook and shivered as if she were about to wet her pants. Kayla moved her hand up and down in front of her mouth as if she'd eaten something spicy. Keesha said, "Wow," over and over. The toughest student to engage — Rashida — was fully engaged with science classes, which had drawbacks. Rashida squealed over fizzing chemicals. One day she hopped from chair to chair and loudly announced that she'd wired a glowing lightbulb. In science, the children seldom understood everything, and they took their time realizing exactly what they were supposed to be doing. They shouted urgent questions at Ms. Luddy. Jeremy, usually respectfully quiet, could hardly contain himself in science. He talked incomprehensibly fast and muttered his every observation.

"One at a time," Ms. Luddy had to say. "One at a time, please."

Even though the science-demonstration kits came from the central office with step-by-step instruction, the children soon flew off course. That was why Ms. Luddy loved it. Teaching science felt to her "like opening latches, setting minds free."

Soon after the taped science lesson, she'd sat through a dinner honoring the three award finalists. Tony Amato had addressed the crowd. He'd met Ms. Luddy's fellow teachers, he said, who'd mentioned her close-knit "community of learners." Amato kept mispronouncing Lois Luddy's first name, calling her "Lewis." Those fellow teachers had snickered and rolled their eyes. Lois Luddy had shrugged and smiled.

In June, a woman told Ms. Luddy over the phone that she'd won. James Thompson got on the school intercom and, sounding very happy, announced the news. Ms. Luddy's room erupted. The kids cheered, whistled, screamed. Ms. Luddy shut the door. They shared a group hug, then danced a little.

"I never had any doubts about Ms. Luddy," Jeremy told me later that afternoon. He was still elated. "We knew in our hearts she was gonna win. I think we all had more faith about this than she did."

At the year's end, Jeremy circulated a petition asking James Thompson to please give them Ms. Luddy for another year. Every member of Ms. Luddy's class signed it.

"She has done a good job," the petition read. "But she is not finished with her work."

"I couldn't," Thompson told me sheepishly, reading the petition in his office. "It wouldn't be fair, see. There are other parents expecting their kids to have her, who are counting on that experience for their kids. These kids will move on to fifth grade with that solid foundation she's given them. They'll be great."

New Numbers

IN OCTOBER 2002, with Jeremy and his classmates several weeks into fifth grade, Anthony Amato stood at a podium before local reporters and announced his resignation. Partway through his statement, he burst into tears and walked away.

Teachers had long grumbled about Amato in acronyms: CMT, SFA. At one school, teachers had watched accounts of the press conference on TV and had strutted around the teachers' lounge, chanting, "No more SFA. No more SFA."

Ms. Luddy, watching the same news accounts, said she felt bad for the guy despite her discomfort with his curriculum. Tony Amato, she'd felt, had pointed Hartford in a "clear" direction. She hadn't much liked it, but it *was* a direction.

It seemed that Hartford's mayor, Eddie Perez, had pushed Tony Amato out gently. *Hartford Courant* reporters speculated that Perez, a well-liked, up-by-his-bootstraps local, wanted a fresh face for the city schools. Others close to Perez said they'd plain resented Amato's intermittent public search for a better job elsewhere and his brusque management style.

Had Tony Amato demonstrated that he'd committed to Hartford for the long haul, he might have endured. But even in his case, purity of intention wasn't manifest in numbers.

Some of his bottom-line numbers looked good. He'd boasted that he'd lowered the dropout rate. In 1999, only about 54 percent of students who'd been freshmen four years earlier had stuck around to graduate. Amazingly, the following year, 71 percent of freshmen had stayed the course. Amato credited his new Save Our Seniors program, which forgave absences and, in some cases, failing grades in return for attendance at Saturday school sessions.

But the following year, the *Hartford Courant* had reported that 90 of 136 graduates from Hartford's schools had failed a recent exam for jobs on the city's police force. The test had purportedly been calibrated to pass those at a 10th-grade level. Then, in 2002, only 2 percent of Hartford's 10th graders reached goal level on all four portions of the required state exam—reading, writing, math, and science.

Hartford's typical numerical contradictions, unlike its dramatic test-score spikes, attracted no national media stories.

As it would turn out, the final tests students took under Tony Amato's tenure would never get ranked in the manner by which he'd measured his success. State Department of Education officials, complaining of vaguely termed "misuse" of the school rankings by CMT scores, stopped compiling such rankings, and the *Hartford Courant* pledged to stop publishing the list.

The *Courant's* incisive education reporter, Robert Frahm, noted that because educators agreed on the importance of early reading skills, the newspaper would still publish school districts' fourth-grade reading scores.

And there, at the bottom, languished Hartford. Last again, right where Tony Amato had started and where he'd pledged never again to be. A measly 16.9 percent of fourth graders had met the state's reading goal in 2002.

Tony Amato had left by then to take a new $200,000-a-year job as school superintendent in New Orleans—a district that, at the time, was two and a half times the size of Hartford's. The City of Hartford also paid Amato a severance package worth more than $200,000.

"Amato's most dramatic success has been the reform of the Hartford schools, earning him national acclaim for urban school reform," wrote an optimistic reporter for the *Times-Picayune* in New Orleans. "His achievement there was a key reason Orleans Parish School Board members chose Amato out of more than 40 applicants."

PART SEVEN

Settling

A boy put his hand into a pitcher full of filberts. He grasped as many as he could possibly hold, but when he tried to pull out his hand, he was prevented from doing so by the neck of the pitcher. Unwilling to lose his filberts, and yet unable to withdraw his hand, he burst into tears and bitterly lamented his disappointment. A bystander said to him, "Be satisfied with half the quantity, and you will readily draw out your hand."

—*Aesop's Fables*

The Plaintiffs

NEARLY A YEAR AFTER the latest court hearing with Judge Aurigemma, nearly a decade and a half after the lawyers had filed the case bearing young Milo Sheff's name, the *Hartford Courant* headline shouted, in monster type ordinarily reserved for disaster or the end to long wars, SHEFF V. O'NEILL CASE SETTLED. Lawyers hastily organized a press conference.

Since 1989, Milo Sheff had always been a central figure at such events, even after the boy had grown into a man. Back when he was thirteen, peering over the edge of a witness stand, his big eyes had held not a flicker of self-doubt. There was equanimity still in the face of the 24-year-old when he fell under the *Sheff* spotlight again in January 2003.

Milo wore a casual gray sweater to the press conference. A plain rubber band bound neck-length braids off his face. Before reporters filed in, he flashed his mother an admiring grin. Elizabeth Sheff, regal and relaxed, a triumphant contessa, sat at the long table in the Connecticut Civil Liberties Union's first-floor conference room. This was where it had begun. And today, it would end here—at least for a little while.

Officially, Milo and Elizabeth were still lead plaintiffs in the case. But Milo, who'd been, in his mother's words, "emotionally devastated" by the first *Sheff v. O'Neill* loss, had long since dropped out of high school. He'd gone on, though, earning his diploma in a program for adults and attending Eastern Connecticut State University. It had been years since he had had much practical contact with the case he'd come to represent. For a long while, though, Milo, like so many others involved, had believed in *Sheff* with all his heart.

In recent years, though, Milo had been content to be beside the point. He'd become a singer and songwriter, a hip-hop artist. His band, Harsh Reality, had a hot single playing on local airwaves.

"Life's good," he told me the morning of the press conference. "I have my own things going now."

Reporters crowded the stuffy conference room. They'd been trained to pick up on human interest, so they turned away from lawyers and focused once more on the photogenic, abiding Milo. Cameras clicked. Reporters positioned microphones near him. Pencils scribbled.

Before the press conference officially began, a tanned, blond male television reporter asked, "Now Milo, you have a son of your own, don't you?"

"Yes, sir, I do," Milo answered. "That's correct."

Reporters' heads turned.

"And now, Milo, how old would he be?"

"My son is seventeen months old."

"Seventeen months, you say?"

"Yes, sir," Milo answered. "My little boy is seventeen months old."

"Oh, ho, well, ever think of making him a plaintiff?" The television reporter laughed heartily at his own joke. Fellow reporters laughed heartily along with him.

"No," Milo answered, not cracking a smile, his gaze steady.

Reporters scribbled, "No." No more laughing.

With that austere reply, no-nonsense expression, and stern eyes, grown-up Milo reminded reporters that *Sheff*'s long history was not a joke.

AFTER MILO'S IMPROMPTU interview, Wes Horton, who, with Dennis Parker and Phil Tegeler, had been on the front lines of settlement negotiations, took over as host. He invited his legal adversary, the attorney general, Richard Blumenthal, to sit at the table. He even urged Ted Sergi, the education commissioner, to make remarks and take questions. But all the details and quotes that came out were secondary to the fact of settlement—dull compared to the mannered minidrama of long-overdue agreement between adversaries.

The details, Horton explained, went like this: By 2007, the state pledged to create eight new interdistrict magnet schools within the city of Hartford. Each school would enroll about 600 students. The state would also expand enrollment in the urban-to-suburban transfer program to 1,600 kids and increase funding for interdistrict grant programs, such as sister-school partnerships. The agreement called for 30 percent of Hartford's students to "experience an educational setting with reduced isolation" within four years. In the year before the settlement, 2002, less than 10 percent of Hartford's students had such an experience.

"Is this the vision that we held so dear years ago when we started out?" Elizabeth Sheff asked rhetorically when it was her turn to face the reporters. "The answer to that is no. But is it a reflection of the vision? The answer would be yes. Today is a celebration in my heart." All the reporters knew her. In 1999 she'd been voted into office as a city councillor. She was outspoken and widely quoted. "We think this is the way that Connecticut will show that the problem of de facto segregation can be solved . . ."

To Elizabeth's left, Dennis Parker, elbows on the table, looked wrung out, but he put a positive public face on the wrangling that had stretched on for six months.

Connecticut's renewed efforts on behalf of *Sheff,* Dennis Parker told reporters, could be a "beacon for the rest of the nation." "I represent the office that brought the *Brown v. Board of Education* case," he said. "And I'm very proud to have brought this case too."

A television reporter asked Milo to speak some more.

Other television and radio reporters adjusted microphones again and they all edged in close, stood on tiptoes. Television cameras hogged the space up front and center.

"Go ahead," Milo said, folding his hands.

"*You* go ahead," a reporter urged from the back. "What do *you* have to say, Milo?"

"I guess I'd say one thing. If you start too late with integration, there are only going to be problems. Because too late, like, by high school, that's too late, see," he said. "Already you have stereotypes all built up. The only thing I would say is that kids should start with integrated education in elementary school, as young as possible."

Phil Tegeler, characteristically quiet at the end of the table, nodded in agreement. He looked at the floor. He said nothing, although his legwork and commitment may have kept the case from fading away. Tegeler's colleague and friend Martha Stone, long overshadowed by John Brittain's eloquence, Wes Horton's congenial charm, and LDF's noble cachet, did speak up.

"It's very important that the court retain jurisdiction," she said, leaning toward the microphone. "None of us are going to go away. This is a commitment that is very deep-seated in all of us."

Only a few reporters later quoted her. Her soft voice might have obscured her challenging message. This wasn't a final settlement, after which books would close, deal done. This was a temporary settlement, in effect for four years. Then plaintiffs and the state would revisit the agreement. Until then, if there were a "material breach"—if the state dropped its end of the bargain—the plaintiffs could return to court.

The press conference fragmented. The participants mingled and schmoozed. Dennis Parker sat pensively in a corner.

"You could ask about the other seventy percent. The kids not covered by this agreement," he suggested to me. "What about those seventy percent?"

He shook his head. That was the nature of settlement. No one was supposed to come out of one happy.

"But we've all been feeling as if there's been a court decision, a real victory, and it's just been floating around out there," he said. "After fourteen years, you need to think about remedy and looking at what you can do for at least some children right now."

John Brittain understood the logic. And still, his disappointment ran deep. He and Martha Stone had been holdouts during settlement negotiations. They both wanted the state to offer far more. "No, I'm not happy," he told me by phone from Houston that morning. "The masses are still stuck."

Inadvertently, his colleagues had left his name off the official settlement documents. "I don't care," he told me. "I don't want my name on that thing."

Ms. Luddy

L ATE IN THE AFTERNOON, after the press conference, and after school, Ms. Luddy sat atop a kid's desk and frowned. She'd heard the news from James Thompson.

If there "had been the will here . . . ," she said, "it could have moved us in a better direction. Everyone separate? It's not working. People think *this* is working? Please." She did her exasperated eye roll.

She pulled her heavy teacher's bag up onto her lap.

"In terms of living a world apart? That's getting worse. I'm telling you. It is. But who's going to listen to me?"

Ms. Luddy saw no cause for celebration in the new stipulation and order the lawyers and state officials had signed hours before. She didn't know any of the *Sheff* lawyers personally except for Wes Horton, whom she'd met through his wife, Chloe, who'd been a revered teacher in Hartford. And Ms. Luddy "certainly" didn't think that "with all the poverty and problems in the city," a desegregated school would be a "miracle cure."

"I can't solve the problems of the world. But, c'mon, now. Fourteen years, and this is it?" She scrunched up her face and echoed Dennis Parker's concern. "I'm sorry, but what about the seventy percent? Is this a victory? Is this the kind of thing we have to think of as a victory? Is that what it's come to? I just hope this isn't the end of the discussion, here. I mean, we've got a heck of a long way to go. And you have to think about what happens to conscience now."

She smiled and touched my shoulder lightly. "Can we change the subject to something happy? Please? I have to tell you. I taught a great lesson today." The day before, she told me, she and the children had read a story about a deaf child, and it had inspired an idea for a lesson.

Around the time the lawyers were holding their press conference, Ms. Luddy had run to the music teacher and asked if she might borrow a snare drum. She hurried back to the classroom with the drum and set it off to the side, nestled in its shiny silver fold-up stand. She blew up balloons—yellow, red, blue, pink. She threw them on the floor.

The kids filed in. She told them to sit down on the floor. She gave each kid a balloon. They shouted anxious questions: What were they supposed to do with the balloons? What was up with the drum?

"Close your eyes," she told them. "Hold on to your balloon. Be as quiet as you can be."

All eyes closed.

Ms. Luddy beat the drum with all her strength, as loudly as she could.

"What did you feel?" she asked.

"Shaking!" one student shouted.

"Vibration!" said another.

She did it again.

That, Ms. Luddy had explained, was how deaf children enjoyed a musical performance. "They experience music by holding on to a balloon and feeling the vibrations."

"That helped them understand on a very deep level. To stand in another person's shoes, to see, feel the world through that person's experience," Ms. Luddy told me. "Talk about powerful."

"I hoped someone would come into my classroom and ask, 'Are they going to read a paragraph about balloons and underline the main idea?'"

She knew many eyes were on her at school this year after her Teacher of the Year award and after Jeremy and Shasa's class had dazzled everyone with high CMT numbers. Her new kids? "They're a different story," she said. "Some of them barely read on a first-grade level."

"And math? This is third grade, and I'm talking about kids who have trouble with basic math. Simple addition. We are going to be working hard, is all I'll say." In the coming months she'd be drill sergeant as well as teacher.

Meanwhile, Simpson-Waverly was in the running for the prestigious Blue Ribbon award from the U.S. Department of Education, which recognized schools with high test scores. Ms. Luddy was dubious about the honor.

She looked at the clock. It was after 5 p.m. She'd been at Waverly since 7 a.m. She grabbed her canvas bag, crammed with SFA lesson plans and record sheets, which she'd have to finish before going to sleep and turn in the following day. Many of Tony Amato's programs had survived his dramatic departure.

She headed for the door, then saw the balloons. About a dozen, abandoned by the kids, drifted along the carpet. Ms. Luddy tossed her coat and bag back onto a chair. She grabbed kid-safe scissors in her right hand and marched toward the balloons. She cradled one tight in the crook of her left arm and raised her right arm high. The scissors hovered.

"People are going to think it's gunshots," she said. "It's going to be loud. Should I?"

She had to. If she didn't, the balloons would drive the children and her nuts the next morning. Kids would fight over them, make them squeak, float, pop. They'd rub the balloons gleefully in their hair, then stick them to their sweaters. They'd ask about static electricity, but there would be no time for static electricity.

She stabbed a yellow one. Bang.

She popped a red one. Then more: Bang. Bang. Bang.

Shriveled scraps of blue, yellow, red, and pink latex scattered across the floor. Ms. Luddy inched along, stooped, and collected each one. She tossed them into the green trash can.

Outside her door, the most mild-mannered of the custodians stood, broom in hand, utterly still by a garbage barrel. He stared at her.

"Oh, did you think those were gunshots?" Ms. Luddy teased. "Did I scare you?"

"Well, I didn't know what . . . ," he began.

"No gunshots," she said, smiling sweetly and pushing the elevator button. "It was just me. Just Ms. Luddy popping balloons."

"Balloons?" The custodian looked pleasantly surprised. "Balloons, hey?"

She stepped into the elevator.

"They're all popped now," Ms. Luddy shouted, poking her head out from the elevator. "They're all gone. Good night, now!"

Jeremy

IN SPRING 2003, two months after the *Sheff* settlement, Jeremy plugged away at his new fifth-grade work. He never complained except when he said that his teacher "gave all of us the answers on the science quizzes," which, he went on to say, she then returned to the office to demonstrate that the children had learned science.

"I'm just guessing here, okay? But my guess is that this is not a very good way to learn science," Jeremy said. Several classmates confirmed the science-quiz event and, like Jeremy, expressed confusion. None thought to protest.

Jeremy also began exercising indoors after homework.

"Just moving my legs around a little and some push-ups, move my arms and things," he announced proudly. "I don't want people calling me 'fat boy' my whole life."

The CMT loomed on the horizon of his life. He'd take it again in sixth grade. But meanwhile, concrete evidence of accomplishment surfaced in the Otero home. Papers came home with "Good Job!" scrawled on them. And in the corner of Jeremy's living room sat a barely used, shiny red mountain bike.

"Where'd you get that?" I asked Nina. "Did you buy this?"

"No. I didn't buy this. You kidding? It's from the test," Nina said. "Raymon. He do good on the test. They give him the bike. Weird, eh?"

Raymon, Jeremy's brother, had reached the "mastery" level on the sixth-grade test in all three subjects — reading, writing, math. So Raymon and some other high-scoring Simpson-Waverly students won bikes donated by a local retailer. Nina and Anna, however, had reluctantly told Raymon that he couldn't ride it.

"Gangs," Jeremy explained. "Out there." He pointed to the window. "It's really getting really bad." So there would be no more bike riding. But Nina and Anna kept some hope alive.

"This year for them, it's good in school still," Nina said. "For Jeremy, fifth grade now, and he doin' good and not in no trouble. And Raymon, he make my mother proud. He doin' real good on tests, on everything. So, nope. No trouble from them."

PART EIGHT

You Just Have to Do What You Can

"It's little Anxious," he said to himself, "to be a Very Small Animal Entirely Surrounded by Water. Christopher Robin and Pooh could escape by Climbing Trees, and Kanga could escape by Jumping, and Rabbit could escape by Burrowing, and Owl could escape by Flying, and Eeyore could escape by—by making a Loud Noise Until Rescued, and here am I, surrounded by water and I can't do *anything*."

— Piglet, in A. A. Milne, *Winnie-the-Pooh*

Graduation Day

I N JUNE 2004, eight months after the Bush administration
did award Simpson-Waverly School a Blue Ribbon and honor
it as one of six national "models in urban education," James Thompson
stepped onstage to preside over the sixth-grade graduation ceremony.

The former members of Ms. Luddy's third- and fourth-grade classes
had dressed up in their Sunday best and wore their noblest expres-
sions. They stood in a line, just behind James Thompson, regarding
the assembly of parents, guardians, grandmothers, brothers, and sisters
below.

James Thompson stretched his arm out theatrically in proud presentation. These children, here, he explained, had scored remarkably well
on the CMT back in fourth grade. Those scores had impressed the
Blue Ribbon judges from the U.S. Department of Education. "Much
of our achievement and recognition are the result of the hard work of
these children," Thompson intoned.

Moms and dads, grandparents, and foster parents applauded and hollered out their kids' names. Ear-piercing whistles and thumping claps
flew toward the graduates. The children stood tall, stoic, stage smiles
plastered on their faces. No one giggled, not even Rashida.

Rashida, in a classic lime green shift and heels, looked stunning.
Kayla, hair drawn into a bun, smiled wide. She'd polished her shoes.
Martin's mother had replaced his signature bright white T-shirt with

a starched dress shirt, blue suit, and striped tie. He looked like a little man, expectant, with eyes that still wandered. Jeremy, in a white button-down shirt, played a folksy tune on the drums.

The school district's director of social work, Winston Johnson, who'd grown up in Hartford and gone to Weaver High School, spoke. He told the crowd that the graduating youngsters needed caring grown-ups to "scrutinize their friends" and "preach, preach, preach, preach, preach, preach, preach." Johnson recited Douglas Malloch's sentimental old standard, "Be the Best of Whatever You Are." He'd memorized the verses while he was a student in Hartford, decades earlier:

> If you can't be a pine on the top of the hill,
> Be a scrub in the valley—but be the best little scrub by
>   the side of the rill;
> Be a bush, if you can't be a tree.
> If you can't be a bush, be a bit of grass,
> And some highway happier make;
> If you can't be a muskie, then just be a bass—
> But the liveliest bass in the lake!
> We can't all be captains; we've got to be crew . . .

Who'd dare take issue with this humble inspiration? Even Martin Luther King Jr. had recited parts of it in a speech just months before his assassination. But listening to it, I had to wonder how that same message would play at a suburban graduation.

What about passion? What about power, vision, high accomplishment, even fame? Power increases personal freedom. Wealth buys material objects, but also security in old age, comfort for one's children, healthier food, a safe neighborhood, knowledge. If Rashida, say, became the best cashier some chain store in Hartford ever had, she'd still have to work a second job to feed her kids. Couldn't this poem be interpreted as advising kids to settle? In sixth grade?

Martin had the discipline, creativity, will, and independent spirit to become an artist. Shasa cherished the hope of one day healing others as a doctor. She'd done everything exactly right so far—the science-fair victory, the intense engagement with every (infrequent) classroom experiment. Patrick barely knew it, but he wrote beautifully, with a tender, soulful sensibility. His sophisticated humor and precise articulation of the absurd were pretty nearly adult already. Rashida was unfocused and antagonistic—but so was I at eleven. She was also a zealous advocate against injustice. Given half a chance, equal educational opportunity, and some firsthand knowledge of life beyond the North End, she could become a great sociologist or perhaps a fiery civil rights lawyer.

But Winston Johnson probably chose the correct poem if we were to consider not the graduating children's capabilities, nor their hopes at this point in their lives, but their real-world odds. Perhaps he was telling them a horrible truth, just sugarcoated with rhyme. Too much optimism can set you up for heartbreak. As a social worker in Hartford, Winston Johnson had surely seen his share.

Postgraduation

S IX OF SIMPSON-WAVERLY's most experienced teachers — no doubt important variables in Waverly's test scores — retired at the end of the 2003–4 school year. Thompson, himself another key variable, also retired. In 2005, Ms. Luddy planned to continue teaching third and fourth graders in her second-floor classroom for years to come. As this book goes to press in 2006, she is still there.

Before James Thompson retired, he released his school from some of the CMT mandates that had most likely helped push up test scores and win Bush's Blue Ribbon at great cost to other sorts of learning. In September 2004, Waverly became a "classical magnet" school. Teachers commenced using a teaching model focused on the classics, designed to help students think more critically and reflectively. Ms. Luddy enthusiastically attended training seminars that emphasized group discussions, analytic skills, and moral decision making. Thompson told me just before he retired that he hoped teachers and administrators would convert Simpson-Waverly into an "interdistrict *Sheff*" school, attracting a rainbow of students from Greater Hartford.

He was hopeful but realistic. "To really make it work, we need much more of a commitment from higher levels, financial and otherwise. I'm not sure about the leadership at this point. You just have to do what you can."

Thompson, though, felt the new curriculum might "open up minds" as well as doors. Training in the classics, he told me, might afford some Waverly students easier transition to a selective "classical" program at Quirk Middle School. And kids who then did well at Quirk could move on up to a rigorous classical program at Hartford Public High.

"That's something," he said. "It's a path."

But in March 2005 Simpson-Waverly's latest round of test scores came out. The glory days were over. A paltry 21 percent of fourth graders met the state's reading goal—an astounding 35-percentage-point drop from when Jeremy's class had taken the test three years earlier, in 2001. And 21 percent of Waverly's fourth graders met the state goal in math—putting Simpson-Waverly 6 percentage points below even the low Hartford average. The 45 percent who met the goal in writing, though still about 10 percentage points better than the city average, represented a decline of 35 percentage points from Jeremy's class in 2001.

"It's hard to know what happened exactly," Ms. Luddy told me. "No one's talking miracle school anymore, though. That's for sure." Onlookers speculated that Thompson's departure and the retirement of all those experienced teachers did it. But by the time the numbers hit the *Courant,* the staff members at the shining star Simpson-Waverly were embroiled in racially based infighting. It had all started after the city's new school superintendent, Robert Henry, who is black and Hispanic, replaced James Thompson with a white principal. The white principal in turn replaced retiring black teachers with white ones. The wisdom and finer-grained details of the personnel decisions aside, from Ms. Luddy's perspective the controversy broke down along racial lines and quickly dominated life there.

Meanwhile, test scores at the University of Hartford Magnet School, which remained racially integrated and grew even more popular, continued their slow, steady rise. Nearly 50 percent of students met the state's goal in reading there in 2004 and 45 percent met the goal in writing. About 27 percent met the goal in math. The school's multiple-intelligences approach stayed intact, the students still went on many field trips each year, and recess hadn't been interrupted.

In August 2004, the *Sheff* plaintiffs again revived the case. They filed a motion in New Britain Superior Court, charging that the state had failed to comply with the settlement agreement it had signed in good faith 18 months before. A few hours after the filing, reporters squeezed into a tiny meeting room in Wes Horton's Hartford office for a press conference.

Horton and Elizabeth Sheff sat side by side, microphones in their faces. Wes Horton, still perky and now 62 years old, wore a conservative blue suit. He'd tucked one of those trademark yellow silk handkerchiefs into the breast pocket. A brass sailboat model, colorful, costly fresh flowers, and framed posters of Hartford decorated his shelves and walls. Elizabeth Sheff looked somber and testy. A single fine braid dangled in front of her eyes. Her nose ring twinkled. Such an odd pair, these two. And yet, over the years that the case had dragged on, each had learned to amuse the other. For all his heartiness and skill, Wes Horton couldn't pass himself off as an angry or even quotable rebel for the cause. And Elizabeth didn't go in for formality, proper procedure, or even smiling if she didn't damn well feel like it. They balanced — an uncalculated integration, a cross-racial, cross-class embodiment of what virtue the fight itself might generate.

Wes Horton kept it simple. The settlement agreement had stipulated that 2,400 Hartford students be enrolled in desegregated magnet schools by September 2004. But state officials had projected that only 862 Hartford students would be enrolled by then. What's more, the officials had told him that they couldn't reach another stipulated benchmark, putting 4,800 students in eight new schools by 2007. It wasn't for lack of interest from either urban or suburban families. Parents had signed 6,000 of their kids onto magnet school waiting lists. In September 2004, nearly 3,000 children's names languished on the waiting list just for Cheryl Kloczko's University of Hartford Magnet School.

Elizabeth Sheff didn't mess around. She had no trouble venting in public. The tally, she said, was "shameful and awful."

Then a reporter asked Wes Horton, "Given how long this has taken and how difficult this has been—I mean, it's been going on for a long time, so how long do you continue, I mean?" The crowd tittered. Sixteen years, and sometimes it seemed that so little had changed.

"Well"—Wes Horton grinned—"this is important, and so I'm prepared to stick with it for the rest of my natural life, if I have to." The reporters laughed and Wes Horton's happy face belied his seriousness. He turned to Elizabeth Sheff.

"Is that how you feel, Elizabeth?" he asked.

"Amen," she answered. "Yes, I do."

By early 2006, Sheff and Horton were indeed sticking with the case, even months after state superior court judge Susan Peck said during a hearing on the plaintiffs' motion that she was unlikely to rule in the plaintiffs' favor. (State lawyers, during the same hearing, argued that state education officials had decided it was wiser to increase new school enrollments gradually.) The plaintiffs shelved their motion before Judge Peck officially ruled, even though the numbers indicated that the state indeed had not complied with the agreement's requirement to enroll 1,200 more Hartford students in desegregated schools by the 2005–6 school year. (By 2005–6, only 500 new city students had enrolled in desegregated schools since the agreement took effect.) The names of 6,822 students—from the city and the suburbs—sat on waiting lists for interdistrict magnet schools in the Hartford region. The plaintiffs' lawyers expected to sit down soon with state officials to begin negotiations for a second agreement—the 2003 settlement would expire in the 2006–7 school year—that might increase the number of children in desegregated schools.

"Obviously, you look at the numbers on the waiting list and you can

see that there's a whole lot more demand to fill," said the young LDF
lawyer Chinh Le, who took over for Dennis Parker and Derek Douglas.
"And that's with no marketing or advertising. With the right kind of
marketing, I think you could create even more demand."

By 2006, Dennis Parker had moved on from LDF. He headed up
the civil rights division for New York attorney general Eliot Spitzer.
Parker's protégé, Derek Douglas, had become associate director for economic policy for the Center for American Progress, a progressive think
tank in Washington, D.C. Phil Tegeler became executive director at
Poverty and Race Research Action Council, a nonprofit research group
in Washington, D.C. Wes Horton, Martha Stone, Chinh Le, and lawyers from the American Civil Liberties Union kept *Sheff* alive.

IN 2004, JOHN BRITTAIN had made a surprise proclamation
to a *Hartford Courant* columnist. He'd confessed to "a rather personal
radical rethinking about integration." "The resources, time, money and
effort such as we put into *Sheff v. O'Neill*," he'd said, "we should really
invest in trying to improve educational achievement even in all one-
race, non-white schools." His fellow colleagues were dispirited—some
were personally hurt—by his statement, but Brittain's actual position
proved more nuanced.

The columnist hadn't gotten anything wrong. John Brittain had, he'd
confirmed to me, uttered the quoted words. But no newspaper column
could have caught the decades of disappointment, resignation, and,
perhaps, self-protective optimism embodied in Brittain's statements for
the record.

As it turned out, John Brittain wasn't giving up. Less than a month
after his comments, he stood at the podium before the Education
Foundation of Harris County in Texas and delivered a keynote address
marking the 50th anniversary of *Brown v. Board of Education*. He'd
concluded by asking the big question:

Can a child of color enrolled in a school district with extreme racial and ethnic segregation, high concentration of poverty, insufficient financial support, and low academic achievement rates obtain an equal educational opportunity? . . . Theoretically yes, the schoolchild can obtain an equal education, because all children can learn and many poor children, but not most, rise above their adverse conditions to achieve at least the minimum passing academic standard. Yet I note there are not successful poor and racially imbalanced school districts *as a whole* meeting the state's expected standard of achievement, and given the history of race and education in this country, the practical answer to my questions is NO. Therefore it leads me to inevitably continue to support some form of . . . the integrationist remedy.

John Brittain's position, after a brief glitch, was more or less what it had always been. In fact, he took his final words from Judge Ellen Peters's decision in *Sheff*: "Economists and business leaders say that our state's economic well-being is dependent on more well-educated citizens. And they point to the urban poor as an integral part of our future economic strength . . . So it is not just that their future depends on the state; the state's future depends on them."

John Brittain's professional life had long revolved around a central integrationist vision, and he still believed that the country should follow the same insight. But in 2004, he'd turned 60. And after all the losses and setbacks, it was time, he said, to spend his energy pursuing other related causes—affordable housing in the suburbs, after-school programs for poor kids, funding to give school districts a prayer of meeting the requirements of the No Child Left Behind Act, academic support programs at colleges for graduates of inferior high schools.

In March 2005, John Brittain left his job at the Thurgood Marshall

School of Law and moved northward, again, to become chief counsel and senior deputy of the Washington-based Lawyers' Committee for Civil Rights—the same organization he'd worked for just out of law school. He planned to teach too, possibly at his alma mater, Howard Law School.

THAT SAME MONTH, a U.S. District Court judge sentenced the former governor of Connecticut, John Rowland, to one year in federal prison. Just before Christmas, Rowland had pleaded guilty in federal court to a charge of "stealing honest service." He'd accepted gifts from employees and contractors who'd gotten lucrative jobs from the state. Rowland moved out of the elegant governor's mansion and into a modest, three-bedroom ranch house in West Hartford. The Adriaen's Landing downtown development project continues to rise along the river, the shamed governor's legacy to Hartford.

IN APRIL 2005, Tony Amato resigned abruptly as superintendent in New Orleans, following a meeting where, according to a *Times-Picayune* reporter, "Amato's management was a consistent target of parents, board members and state legislators in the audience." The reporter, Brian Thevenot, wrote, "That was a far cry from eight months ago, when Amato enjoyed the support of politicians statewide, who pushed a law granting him unprecedented authority, and of voters, who trounced his enemies on the School Board at the polls." Thevenot continued, "When he arrived two years ago, Amato mesmerized audiences with inspired speeches and grand promises . . ."
Tony Amato lasted in New Orleans two years and two months.

THE MURDERS AND SHOOTINGS in the North End went right on happening. Politicians' promises of more police officers for the neighborhood grew more common, especially after a young mother was shot and killed while holding a bottle of milk for her baby about four years after little Takira got shot on her pink scooter.

IN THE 2004–5 school year, T.J. won a place in the Hartford Magnet Middle School, an interdistrict school created because of *Sheff*. He was the only one of Ms. Luddy's students to benefit from the *Sheff* case.

Aisha, Kayla, Keesha, Rashida, Jinaya, April, Barbara, Dominique, and Shasa went to Fox Middle School. Fox, that year, failed to make "adequate yearly progress" under the No Child Left Behind Act.

Martin went to South Middle School, in the southern section of Hartford. South Middle that year also failed to make "adequate yearly progress" under the No Child Left Behind Act. The entire school district of Hartford, Connecticut, in fact, that year failed to make "adequate yearly progress" under the No Child Left Behind Act.

Hamilton, Naia, and Owen moved out of the Northeast neighborhood.

Jeremy and five others from Ms. Luddy's old class tried but failed to win lottery places in *Sheff*-created middle schools. Patrick's grandmother, meanwhile, tried to get him into a suburban middle school. Because Patrick's half sister lived in suburban Windsor and attended public school there, his grandmother hoped administrators would let him in too. She even figured out a way to get him the few miles across the city line each day. But officials denied Patrick special permission. He joined the others at Fox Middle School.

"What I want is to stay on track," Patrick told me, looking down at his shoes. "You know, the way you saw me in Ms. Luddy's?"

"Do you want to go to Fox?" I asked.

"There you goin' with that 'want' again," he retorted playfully. "Want? No. I don't want. I don't have a choice, do I?"

Jeremy's older brother, Raymon, entered eighth grade at Fox Middle School in September 2004. Raymon had placed well in his graduating class two years before at Simpson-Waverly. His test scores had been high; his homework record, nearly perfect. In sixth grade, he'd read far above eighth-grade level. But during his seventh-grade year at Fox,

Raymon had complained of lockdowns at the school. He'd imagined they were inspired by administrators' fears that neighborhood crime would seep into the building. So they'd locked classrooms and halted movement within the building. That term, *lockdown,* of course, came from prison vernacular. By fall of seventh grade, Raymon told me he "hated" Fox.

"It sucks there," he'd said. "That's all there is to it and all I want to say."

Raymon had never seemed lighthearted, but he appeared glummer after beginning middle school. By winter of seventh grade, he'd been suspended for fighting. I'd watched his aunt Nina try, but she could not get Raymon to do homework or even admit he had any.

"The thing with Raymon and school? It make me sad, real sad," Nina said. "He was doin' real good before, you know. He was! The teachers said. I don't know what gonna happen now with him. I don't know. I try to talk to him, tell him he gotta start doin' good again for his own good, for his life, you know? I call the school and they say they can't do nothin' if he ain't gonna do his work. And that's true, you know. What they gonna do? I talk to him every day. But he don't listen and he don't believe in nothing about school no more."

WITH A BIT of logistical help from Ms. Luddy and from me, in spring 2004 Jeremy won admission, with a generous scholarship, to Watkinson School, a private, progressive coeducational middle and high school on the Hartford side of the border with West Hartford. Watkinson, with small classes and an innovative curriculum in math, science, social studies, literature, and the arts, enrolled a racially diverse student body from across Greater Hartford.

Over the summer, Jeremy lost himself completely in a book Watkinson's teachers had assigned for summer reading, *Growing Wings* by Laurel Winter. On the first day of school in September 2004, Jeremy rose at 6 a.m. and caught the city bus to Watkinson. He was an hour early and the first student to arrive. In the beginning, he held his own academically among his more privileged fellow students and made friends easily. But by February it became clear that an inadequate background in math—despite those high CMT scores—was holding him back. Finishing his homework in the cramped apartment became a challenge. Jeremy struggled, worried, and sought extra help from his teachers, who also opened a classroom where he could finish his homework in the early morning hours before school began. By late 2005, in eighth grade, with his math performance improving, he excelled in Spanish, appreciated the books assigned in English, enjoyed his friends, and had fun acting in drama class. He still thought a lot about what he wants to be when he grows up.

"See, okay, well. I know I used to say scientist. And I still want to study more science. Like in school and everything. I mean, it's not that I lost my interests in those things. But I changed my mind, I guess, and I think this is because of Ms. Luddy, because she is right now an important role model in my life. I'd like to have a life like her life, and you can see the way she helps kids stay on track and stuff. Ms. Luddy does a lot of good stuff every day for kids, and I could follow that kind of example. So I guess that's why I say teacher. To set an example. What do you think? Do you think I'd make a good example?"

AFTERWORD:

The Beloved Community?

SINCE THE FIRST *Sheff* trial ended in 1993, scholars across the nation have quietly produced evidence rather decisively documenting the harms of segregation and the benefits of policies and programs that connect racially and economically isolated families to the mainstream. Were John Brittain and Wes Horton only now starting to argue *Sheff v. O'Neill* in trial court, they might very well be able to make a surer, simpler case.

Before considering this research, it's useful to acknowledge that "desegregation" represents not merely a "policy" or set of political choices but an aspiration, a moral vision of an inclusive, cohesive society. School desegregation, in particular, is not and never was sold by its advocates merely as the most effective "treatment" for increasing test scores. Evidence, however, does strongly suggest that reducing concentrated poverty—segregation's ever-present attendant—might in fact contribute to higher achievement.

There is indeed one crucial truth that's often subsumed in the legal battles, in the reports of research findings from universities. It is so basic a principle to educators in racially mixed schools and to involved, informed civil rights lawyers that it usually goes unargued: Desegregation and integration aren't synonymous. Desegregation, the condition the *Sheff* lawyers tried to bring about, is a precursor, a process sought in part through legal enforcement. Desegregation may be brought forth by laws.

But good does not inevitably flow from it. Mere desegregation may, as Martin Luther King Jr. said, create a society "where men are physically desegregated and spiritually segregated, where elbows are together and hearts apart. It gives us social togetherness and spiritual apartness," and it can leave racial minorities, King warned, "with a stagnant equality of sameness rather than a constructive equality of oneness."

Integration, in the best sense far exceeding "assimilation," is a richer coming together. In an integrated school—of the sort Cheryl Kloczko's University of Hartford Magnet School and Timothy Nee's Montessori Magnet School aimed to be—more than demographics looked good. No student stood unconnected to the whole. Teachers imparted to children that each was vital to others. Climbing past desegregation to integration takes more than a court judgment. It takes open hearts, open minds, and open attitudes—qualities the best adults struggle to gain and most five-year-olds have in abundance.

Schools such as UHMS work to carry children toward what Martin Luther King called his own "ultimate goal"—fostering the "beloved community in America . . . genuine intergroup and interpersonal living—integration." By 2005, UHMS had achieved something rarer than improved test scores. Though challenges remained for Kloczko and her teachers, the *Sheff*-inspired UHMS was busy intentionally, purposefully bridging a racial, economic, and ethnic divide a century in the making. It wasn't a "white school." It wasn't a "black school" or a "Puerto Rican" or a "Latino" school. It was not an urban school. It was not a suburban school. It was finally just a school.

But administrators in America have increasingly been pushed to regard only bottom-line results. And certainly, a style of accountability that might help prevent educational neglect of the nation's most vulnerable students is a crucial policy. But desegregation's "success," if it can even be measured quantitatively, should be considered over the long term as well, weighing the experience's effect upon adult lives, opportunities, points of view, educational attainment, social mobility. In the decade-plus since the first *Sheff* trial, it's been confirmed, through social science, though scantly publicized, that desegregated schooling correlates strongly with many long-term benefits for racial minority students.

The large body of contemporary scholarship demonstrating the benefits of reducing segregation and concentrated poverty is far too intricate and vast to examine comprehensively here. But some newer findings stand out.

In 1994, just two years after the *Sheff* trial began, Professors Amy Stuart Wells and Robert Crain of Columbia University's Teachers College reviewed decades of studies on longer-term outcomes of desegregated schooling. Wells and Crain wrote in their conclusion, "Beginning with the aspirations of high school students and ending with tangible results of black adults' social networks and participation in the work force, our analysis has attempted to trace the path of perpetual segregation and isolation, pointing out the various junctures at which the cycle can be broken by black students who have access to information about better education and occupational opportunities and who are less fearful of whites."

Ten years later, in 2004, Amy Stuart Wells and her colleagues released findings from a qualitative interview study of more than 500 adult graduates of desegregated high schools. "Our central finding is that school desegregation fundamentally changed the people who lived through it," Wells wrote. "Desegregation made the vast majority of the students who attended these schools less racially prejudiced and more comfortable around people of different backgrounds."

In a rigorous statistical study, desegregation in Texas schools was strongly associated with higher achievement among black students and had no statistically significant effect upon whites. This led the study authors to recommend more housing desegregation programs so black families could move from isolated, high-poverty neighborhoods into more diverse schools.

MEANWHILE, A GROWING BODY of research indicates that students from low-income families simply do better academically in predominantly middle-class schools. (Studies also show that the same is true of middle-class students.) Findings such as these have led the Century Foundation, a nonprofit, nonpartisan research think tank, to consistently argue that "the best way to improve education would be to give every American schoolchild the chance to attend a middle-class public school." (Former Connecticut governor Lowell Weicker, a *Sheff* supporter, who is also a former Republican U.S. senator, chaired the Century Foundation panel that made the recommendation.)

It appears that an increasing, though still quite small, number of school officials agree with the Century Foundation's conclusion. In 2000, officials in the 101,000-student Wake County, North Carolina, district adopted a combined racial and economic integration plan. Under the policy, each school enrollment would be between 15 and 45 percent minority, and no school would have more than 40 percent poor students. There has been no rigorous statistical study of district policy, but school officials have publicly speculated that increased test scores may stem, at least in part, from a reduction in concentrated poverty. At the end of the 20th century, several other school districts began experimenting with economic integration, either in combination with racial integration plans or as an alternative to race-based policies. These include St. Lucie, Florida; San Francisco; Cambridge, Massachusetts; Greenville, South Carolina; and Brandywine, Delaware, among others.

A study of elementary school students in Madison–Dane County, Wisconsin, found that for each 1 percent increase in middle-class enrollment, low-income students improved .64 percentage points in reading and .72 percentage points in math. For the typical low-income student, this would mean that moving from a school with 45 percent middle-class classmates to one with 85 percent middle-class classmates would mean "a 20 to 32 percentage point improvement" in the low-income student's test scores. Researchers in Denver, Colorado, in Maryland, and in Escambia, Florida, report positive relationships between a student's attendance at a middle-class school and his or her achievement.

Despite the small successes, economic school segregation, like racial segregation, is on the rise, according to the Century Foundation's Richard Kahlenberg, the intellectual father of the economic integration movement. One Century Foundation study projects that economic segregation will increase in all but six states between 2000 and 2025.

BUT AS IT TURNS OUT, the political constituency inclined to favor racially diverse learning environments may be larger than was once assumed. The tall pile of "friend of the court" briefs collected by the University of Michigan in two closely watched affirmative action cases that came before the U.S. Supreme Court in 2003 suggests this. In the companion cases *Grutter v. Bollinger* and *Gratz v. Bollinger,* plaintiffs challenged the constitutionality of affirmative action plans at the University of Michigan's law school and undergraduate college, respectively.

In June 2003, the U.S. Supreme Court ruled that "diversity" is indeed a "compelling interest" in higher education. The Court said that race is one of several factors admissions officers may indeed constitutionally take into account to achieve a racially diverse student body.

The high-profile decisions inspired wrangling among academics and advocates. But some of the most compelling arguments in favor of creating diversity came from traditionally conservative corners of big business and the military. Sixty-five Fortune 500 companies filed an amicus curiae brief in favor of the University of Michigan and its affirmative action policies. Twenty-nine prominent, high-ranking former military officers signed a brief cataloging the cohesive effects of desegregation in the military and the benefits of policies that attract diverse populations to training academies. The list of retired and former officers included Robert "Bud" McFarlane (national security adviser under

Ronald Reagan) and Norman Schwarzkopf (the four-star general who commanded the Allied Forces during the Gulf War).

The full legal and educational implications of the Michigan decisions haven't played out yet because the U.S. Supreme Court still has to rule on the question of whether the logic in *Grutter* is applicable to K–12 education. In the summer of 2004, in the first post-*Grutter* ruling on K–12 school desegregation, a federal court in Kentucky upheld a desegregation plan in Jefferson County, in which officials had voluntarily considered race in school assignment decisions in order to achieve diverse student bodies. The Kentucky case, *McFarland v. Jefferson County Public Schools*, attracted no national publicity. But lawyers at the NAACP Legal Defense Fund toasted the decision as a fresh expression of the *Brown* dream.

"Integrated schools, better academic performance, appreciation for our diverse heritage and stronger, more competitive public schools are consistent with the central values and themes of American culture," Chief Judge John G. Heyburn II wrote in the Kentucky case. The plan to achieve diversity, Heyburn wrote, served numerous compelling interests. Integration, the court concluded, had led to educational benefits for students of all races over two and a half decades, helping students overcome the adverse effects of concentrated poverty.

And in June 2005, the First U.S. Circuit Court of Appeals ruled that the school district in the city of Lynn, north of Boston, had a "compelling interest" in the educational benefits of racial diversity. The ruling allowed Lynn to continue use of its voluntary desegregation plan, under which students could transfer out of their assigned school zone if the move would contribute to desegregation.

"We're living, and our children will live, in an increasingly diverse society, and the sooner that our children learn to work and interact with children who are different—by background, by culture, by race—our children are going to be better off and we'll all be better off," Massachusetts attorney general Thomas Reilly, who supported Lynn's plan, told reporters following the ruling. (The attorneys general of New York, Maine, Iowa, and Utah also filed briefs supporting Lynn.)

At this writing, in January 2006, it remains to be seen whether a U.S. Supreme Court refreshed by several new Bush appointees will pull the nation away from these judicial affirmations.

WE CAN FIND SOME of the best evidence for the benefits of lessening the concentrations of poverty in studies not of "school desegregation" but of housing programs that share *Sheff*'s principal aim of connection. "Mobility" and "deconcentration" are catchall terms for housing programs and policies that attempt to break up pockets of extreme neighborhood poverty by dispersing the very poor more evenly throughout a metropolitan region. Until recently, this notion was one of those rare policies helped along by both political parties. Jack Kemp, the housing secretary under George H. W. Bush, for example, was a strong advocate, and Henry Cisneros, the head of HUD during Bill Clinton's first term, built strongly upon his Republican predecessor's momentum.

For liberals such as Cisneros, the attraction of housing mobility is obvious. Such programs contain within them the acknowledgment that racism and discrimination, in tandem with government policies and incentives, created ghettos in the first place. Helping people move out of those ghettos levels a playing field, remediating what many historians and sociologists call an unfair contest that confers unearned advantage to suburban whites.

Mobility programs, though, also contain elements that have historically appealed to conservatives. In most cases, mobility translates into little more than giving people vouchers and encouragement to move to better neighborhoods and thus is a "hands off" policy that relies on the market and consumer choice. And while it's hardly cheap—vouchers usually cover 70 percent of a recipient's government established "fair market rent," and the most effective programs include professional counseling—the strategy costs far less than building and maintaining and policing vast housing projects. Mobility also seeks to shield the next generation from influences that social conservatives have long viewed as ghetto-based pathologies: teen pregnancy, quitting school, drug dealing.

Mobility became a favored cross-party policy beginning in the 1980s, after poverty researchers devised an accountant's definition for concentrated poverty: census tracts where more than 40 percent of the residents are poor. This threshold acknowledged a kind of submersion in the dominion of poverty. This was the point at which poverty's symptoms—crime, drug dealing, teen pregnancy, overburdened, low-performing schools—showed up at overwhelming levels. The determining feature of life in such places, sociologists told us, was dearth of opportunity—most obviously of opportunity to secure decent education and jobs—and, more abstractly, a palpable apartness from the connections and exposure to mainstream society.

The case against concentrated poverty was strong—and credible to policymakers on both sides early in George H. W. Bush's term. The question was still what to do about it.

The results from the nation's first large-scale housing mobility program, Gautreaux, in Chicago, signaled a hopeful direction. The Gautreaux program—which sprang from a court order following litigation against the city's housing authority—funded moves by poor, black families out of public housing and into lower-poverty neighborhoods where no more than 30 percent of the residents were also black. The results from Gautreaux were spectacular compared to nearly every other anti-poverty program. And they surprised researchers: The Gautreaux children were much less likely to drop out of high school than their peers who hadn't moved, much more likely to be in college-prep classes, and much more likely to attend college. The improvement among kids who'd transferred from chaotic, overwhelmed urban schools to smoother-functioning suburban schools was particularly striking.

In the late 1980s and the early 1990s, these findings flowed sensibly from the academic policy wonks in Chicago to policymakers and officials in other cities and to civil rights groups. Following Gautreaux, residents of public housing, often represented by national civil rights groups, sued their local housing authorities and the U.S. Department of Housing and Urban Development. Though each case was a little different, generally the plaintiffs' argument was similar to what the Gautreaux plaintiffs' argument had been in 1966: Local housing officials, in tandem with HUD, had sited housing projects in minority neighborhoods, thereby concentrating poverty and knowingly creating and compounding racial segregation.

As complex litigation tends to, the lawsuits had dragged on in the courts. But Cisneros, who came into office with Bill Clinton in 1994, settled 17 of them. And as a result, local officials, working with HUD, put in place mobility programs that allowed willing poor families to get out of housing projects and into those less segregated, less poor, less violent, less unhealthy neighborhoods.

The federal government made another significant move in 1994, implementing the experimental Moving to Opportunity demonstration project. Putting MTO into gear strongly signaled that the government was taking mobility and poverty deconcentration seriously. In practical terms, MTO was tiny—it involved 4,600 families. Its purpose clearly wasn't wide-scale social justice, but the further accumulation of knowledge. MTO was the first and largest federally funded randomized experiment—termed a "demonstration"—to determine the effects of diffusing high-poverty neighborhoods. Public housing residents in five selected cities—Boston, New York, Los Angeles, Chicago, and Baltimore—volunteered to take part in MTO. Each was randomly assigned to one of three groups. The experimental group received housing vouchers they could use only in census tracts where less than 10 percent of residents were poor. Specially trained counselors helped these families find housing in often exclusionary and costly private markets.

The counselors answered questions and addressed tenants' fears about moving to a new community. A second "comparison" group received no counseling and got housing vouchers they could use anywhere, not just in low-poverty neighborhoods. A third control group stayed in the projects.

HUD commissioned a 10-year evaluation of MTO. (The final evaluation was originally slated to start in 2004, but the funding for it has not been forthcoming from George W. Bush's HUD.) Interim evaluation results—released in 2003—were encouraging. So far, researchers report that the families that moved were more likely to live in far better quality housing and to have far less exposure to violence and crime. Mothers were more likely to have positive perceptions of the safety of their children's schools. The most dramatic improvements were in mental and physical health—including a drop in obesity rates and depression. Young girls benefited amazingly following their moves and were far less likely to engage in what researchers call "risky behaviors." Boys fared far less well, and in some cases did worse, however, and some researchers are currently trying to figure out why.

And as such research progressed, David Rusk, a former mayor of Albuquerque, continued publishing a series of related, classic urban-planning bibles. The first, *Cities Without Suburbs,* demonstrated that dozens of American cities such as Hartford—the isolated municipalities hemmed in by old boundaries and untouchable suburban prosperity—were doomed to continued poverty and racial segregation unless higher levels of government helped forge political, social, and economic alliances with suburban neighbors. Along with 23 other American cities, Hartford sat in Rusk's ominous table 2.20: "Cities Past the Point of No Return." At the intractable center of the urban problems, Rusk argued, sits a level of racial and economic segregation likely to generate a possibly permanent underclass. Rusk listed ways to halt the downward urban spiral. Decoding his hopeful but practical list required fluency in the sort of policy-wonk matters that glaze over lay folks' eyes. None of the recommendations was terribly dramatic. Each, though, was sensible: revenue sharing between the city and its suburbs, more Gautreaux-like housing programs to promote racial integration, policies to limit suburban growth, coordinated public transportation.

"The most effective preventive medicine would be to merge immediately the core city and the surrounding county in a unified government," Rusk wrote in 1993. He offered clear advice for policymakers: "relieve [cities] of the burden of being home to so many of their metro areas' poorest . . . households. All communities in the whole region must shoulder the burden of . . . poverty on a 'fair share' basis." In "highly complex, fragmented metropolitan areas," Rusk acknowledged, cities and suburbs were unlikely voluntarily to begin sharing either benefits or burdens. In particular, Rusk noted, "the very thought that poor people, that is, poor Black or Hispanic people, should be integrated into middle-class neighborhoods, traumatizes local politics. Effective public action to open metropolitan societies to the integration of minority poor must flow from the federal and state governments."

In other words, state and federal governments should enact policies and programs that encourage the cooperation, the integration, if you will, of municipalities to the larger metropolitan region. The approach isn't unheard of. In fact, a coalition of religious and civil rights groups have been pushing for exactly these sorts of changes in Greater Hartford. But at this writing, housing-mobility programs across the country have been threatened by budget cuts and small administrative changes that make it more, not less, difficult for poor families to get out of segregated neighborhoods.

And in Connecticut itself—still the nation's wealthiest state—the very problems that inspired the *Sheff* case continued. In September 2004, researchers at the Rockefeller Institute of Government in Albany, New York, ranked the purported "rising star," Hartford, seventh among

American cities with the highest "hardship." They'd based their findings upon rates in unemployment, the proportion of residents on government assistance, high school graduation rates, household income, and the percentage of households below the poverty level. According to the report, American cities in similar straits include Detroit, Miami, Gary, Cleveland, Buffalo, Jersey City, Newark, Providence, St. Louis, Philadelphia, Chicago, Milwaukee, Fresno, Santa Ana, and Rochester, N.Y.

The report concluded, "Each of these cities reflect the well-worn pattern of older urban areas . . . landlocked with inflexible boundaries, losing population share relative to their surrounding metropolitan areas, characterized by high levels of residential segregation, facing considerable challenges in poverty levels as well as limited educational attainment."

Meanwhile, the *Sheff* lawyers labored on, often under conservatives' impressions that they were social engineers set on forcing families into schools they did not wish to attend. Phil Tegeler, perhaps the most understated of all the *Sheff* attorneys, stated that irony well: "This entire region has been socially engineered. Saying that we're the social engineers implies that segregation is natural. And the entire history of this country teaches us that isn't the case," he said. "All we've been trying to do for all these years is to give people a choice. A choice for families who want their kids in quality, integrated schools . . . Children should be able to go to a school that prepares them well for life in the United States in the twenty-first century. That's all we ever hoped for. That's all. I haven't lost faith yet."

ACKNOWLEDGMENTS

I'M FOREVER GRATEFUL to everyone who agreed to appear in this book, especially Lois Luddy, who opened up her amazing classroom community to me. The children of room E4 opened my heart and mind in new ways and enriched my life. James Thompson, Simpson-Waverly's principal, had nothing to gain by allowing me access to his school. But he spoke to me openly and trusted I'd see the myriad complexities inherent in his job and the culture of the school he led. I learned much from him. I hope this book honors his lessons.

The plaintiff lawyers and the case's lead plaintiff, Elizabeth Sheff, were always generous with time, wit, and wisdom. I owe a great debt to Phil Tegeler, who spent many hours detailing history and fishing out documents for me. His knowledge and analyses contributed greatly to the shape of this book, especially part 2. Wes Horton reviewed an early draft of the manuscript with lawyerly precision. I'm thankful for his time and care. Chloe Horton, a retired teacher in Hartford, offered many insights and helpful suggestions. John Brittain endured many hours of interviews over three years. He was open, patient, and always fun to talk to.

In Hartford, thanks also to Susan Pennybacker, Eugene Leach, and Elizabeth Rose at Trinity College and to Jack Hasegawa and Joan Martin from the State Board of Education. Kathy McKula kindly provided me access to the Hartford Courant Library and archives. *Hartford*

Courant reporters Bob Frahm and Rick Green provided early and useful observations. The staff at the Hartford Public Library and Connecticut State Library were indispensable, always helpful. Hernan LaFontaine and Mary Carroll granted me early and informative interviews that helped provide context for the book. At the *Hartford Courant,* I have benefited from the excellent work of many reporters and columnists, but especially from that of Bob Frahm, Rick Green, Helen Ubinas, Rachel Gottlieb, Mike Swift, and Matt Burgard.

I am quite sure that this book would never have been published had it not been for the tenacity, grace, and conviction of my agent, Geri Thoma. Choosing Geri as my agent is undoubtedly the best decision I've made in my writing life. She stood by this book during a time when it would have been more sensible to abandon it.

I owe tremendous thanks as well to everyone at Algonquin Books in New York, but especially to my incredibly talented, spirited editor, Antonia Fusco. She worked on this book with great care, artfulness, and enthusiasm. I feel so incredibly lucky to have landed on her desk at just the right time. Thanks also to Elisabeth Scharlatt, Rachel Careau, Brunson Hoole, and Dove Pedlosky.

To Nancy and Guerry Eaton—thank you for gifts that are far too long to even begin to list here. Special thanks to my amazing in-laws, Sidney and Esther Kramer—to Sidney for his exacting, helpful legal work, and to both of them for their love and interest, and for championing my work over the years.

So many friends helped me through this project over the years: Susan Crawford; Meredith, Matthew, Rosie, and Maddie Daly (for friendship, Hartford housing, and home-cooked meals); Jacqui Deegan; Ann Donlan; Arthur Giangrande; Jay Heubert; Jen Jellison; Elissa Kleinman; Nadia Leal; Robin Leonard; Everly Macario; Gary Orfield; Sean Ploen; Laureline and Paul Ruano-Bourbalain; Barbara Siegfriedt (for the longest, deep friendship of my life and Harvard storage space); Jim Sparrow; Jon Strymish; Takesato and Hisako Watanabe; Joan and

Bob Weiss; and Howard Zinn. Special appreciation to Jina Moore, Martha Synnott, and Dasha Kusa—the mighty women of the third floor at the Nieman Foundation. I'm thankful for the Newton group, who provide support and inspiring conversation about art, life, work, and motherhood and fulfill a more elemental need—cool girlfriends to hang with: Louise Corrigan, Margaret Covert, Jeanine Cowen, Barbara Seal, and Sara Whitman.

I could not have finished this book without the support, love, heroic patience, wise counsel, and daily companionship of my husband and first editor, Mark W. Kramer. He edited this manuscript brilliantly. But more important, he fell in love with Hartford, Jeremy, *Sheff,* and Ms. Luddy, right along with me. Had he not accompanied me on this long journey, there would be much less of a book and much less of a life.

NOTES

Part One. Jeremy

4   *America's second-poorest big city* Hartford's poverty rate is 30.6 percent. The U.S. Census Bureau defines "big" or "large" cities as those with 100,000 residents or more. See Alemayehu Bishaw and John Iceland, *Poverty, 1999,* Census 2000 Brief (May 2003), 7, table 5, "Places of 100,000 or More with the Highest Poverty Rates: 1999." Brownsville, Texas, was the nation's poorest big city, with a poverty rate of 36 percent. After Hartford, Laredo, Texas (29 percent poverty rate), and Providence, Rhode Island (29 percent poverty rate), were the nation's third- and fourth-poorest cities according to the 2000 U.S. Census.

6   *41 percent of its children* U.S. Bureau of the Census, *Census 2000 Summary File 3 (SF 3) - Sample Data,* "GCT-P14. Income and Poverty in 1999: 2000," Geographic Area: Connecticut—Place and County Subdivision, http://factfinder.census.gov. Specifically, 41.3 percent of the city's children were poor.

6   *poorest city in the wealthiest state* Hartford is Connecticut's poorest city. Connecticut is the nation's wealthiest state, as measured by its per capita income, which was $43,173 in 2003 according to the Connecticut Department of Economic and Community Development. Also, Connecticut's 2000 median family income of $65,121 was the highest in the country.

U.S. Bureau of the Census, http://quickfacts.census.gov/qfd/states/09000 .html. See also U.S. Department of Commerce, Bureau of Economic Analysis, Survey of Current Business, www.bea.doc.gov/bea/regional/spi/. As measured by gross domestic product, the United States is the wealthiest nation in the world. In 2005, the International Monetary Fund listed the nation's GDP at $12,438,873, and the World Bank estimated the GDP at $11,667,515. See also http://en.wikipedia.org/wiki/List_of_countries_by _GDP_%28nominal%29.

13   *align curriculum with testing standards*   *No Child Left Behind Act of 2001*, Public Law 107-110, 115 stat. 1439, 1643, 1646.

17   *would meet the state standard*   Connecticut State Department of Education, *CMT Comparison Report for 2001–2003*   (Hartford, 2003).

17   *dead-last in math, science, and reading*   Connecticut State Department of Education, *CAPT Comparison Report for 2001–2003*   (Hartford, 2003).

18   *only 3 percent would in math*   Connecticut State Department of Education, *CAPT Comparison Report for 2001–2004*   (Hartford, 2004).

21   *slipped to just plain poor*   For a sociology of low-wage work among the poor, see Katherine Newman, *No Shame in My Game: The Working Poor in the Inner City* (New York: Knopf, 1999).

28   *health and emotional problems*   For an original discussion about the causes and structure of health problems in the urban ghetto, see Helen Epstein, "Ghetto Miasma: Enough to Make You Sick?" *New York Times Magazine*, October 12, 2003.

Part Two. How We Got Here in the First Place

35   *"fastest shrinking" big cities*   Hartford's population dropped by 15,618 people between 1990 and 2000, placing it among the nation's five fastest-shrinking cities that have a population of 100,000 people or more. This was a 13 percent decline. Other shrinking cities included Flint, Michigan; Gary, Indiana; St. Louis; and Baltimore. See Mike Swift, "City Regains 2,500 People," *Hartford Courant*, November 29, 2001. It is important to note, however, that generally, cities improved on many measures from 1990 to 2000. However, the improvements do not apply to ghetto neighborhoods of concentrated

poverty and highly racially segregated cities in the Northeast and Midwest especially. These places are more likely to have high levels of what scholars have called "hardship." Cities did not improve as rapidly, on as many measures, or as substantially as their suburbs did during this period. During the 1990s, the population of America's largest cities grew by 8.1 percent; growth during the 1980s was just 6 percent. According to Brookings Institution analysis, however, the population expansion was largely due to an increase in Hispanic and Asian immigration. Suburbs during the 1990s experienced population growth of 17 percent. For further information, refer to Bruce Katz, "Bridging the Racial Divide" (presentation at the Wiener Center for Social Policy, John F. Kennedy School of Government, Harvard University, April 1999). See also Lisa M. Montiel, Richard P. Nathan, and David J. Wright, *An Update on Urban Hardship* (Albany, NY: Nelson A. Rockefeller Institute of Government, 2004); and Anne Power and William Julius Wilson, *Social Exclusion and the Future of Cities,* CASE Paper 35, Centre for Analysis of Social Exclusion, London School of Economics, February 2000. For a thoughtful commentary, see R. J. Sampson, "The Embeddedness of Child and Adolescent Development: A Community-Level Perspective on Urban Violence," in *Violence and Childhood in the Inner City,* ed. J. McCord (New York: Cambridge University Press, 1997), 61–64.

44 *north from Virginia and Maryland* Barbara Beeching, "The Primus Papers: An Introduction to Hartford's Nineteenth Century Black Community" (master's thesis, Trinity College, Hartford, 1995). Beeching writes, "The 1860 Hartford City Director listed 15 insurance companies, 18 banks, 6 book publishers, 18 hotels."

44 *stayed downtown* Ibid., 25. An "African" school closed in 1868 when the system was desegregated. It stood in an area just outside what is now downtown. Glenn Weaver and Michael Swift, *Hartford: Connecticut's Capital* (Sun Valley, CA: American Historical Press, 2003), 91.

44 *back of the line and grew poorer* Terry Golway, *The Irish in America* (New York: Hyperion, 1997). This was a well-documented trend nationally as well. See Sidney M. Willhelm, *Who Needs the Negro?* (Cambridge, MA: Schenkman, 1970). See also Robert Malloy, *"Cast Down Your Bucket Where You Are": Black Americans on Immigration,* CIS Paper no. 10, Center on Immigration Studies, Washington, DC, June 1996.

44   *21,000 workers*   Weaver and Swift, *Hartford,* 102.

44   *bought out black owners*   Weaver and Swift, *Hartford,* 103–5, 96.

45   *cramped quarters*   Several historians and journalists have documented this problem. Wilbert J. LeMelle, "Skepticism and Cautious Optimism in the Minority Community of Greater Hartford," report to the Greater Hartford Chamber of Commerce, Hartford, 1964. See also Robert Rotberg, "Where Can a Negro Live? A Study of Housing Discrimination in Hartford," *Hartford Courant,* August 18, 1956; and Rotberg, "Report on Housing Bares Grim Picture," *Hartford Times,* September 13, 1956.

45   *blacks lived elsewhere*   Weaver and Swift, *Hartford,* 90–92.

45   *Downtown sidewalks grew more crowded*   Wilson H. Faude, *Images of America: Hartford, Vols. 1 and 2* (Dover, NH: Arcadia Publishing, 1996).

45   *America's wealthiest cities*   Weaver and Swift, *Hartford.* See also Hartford Post, *Hartford in 1912. Story of the Capitol City. Present and Prospective. Its Resources, Achievements, Opportunities and Ambitions* (Hartford, CT: Hartford Post Publishing Company, 1912), 180, 229.

46   *rural blacks to Northern cities*   Carole Marks, *Farewell—We're Good and Gone: The Great Black Migration* (Bloomington: University of Indiana Press, 1989). See also Emmett J. Scott, *Negro Migration during the War* (New York: Oxford University Press, 1920); Joan Jacobs, "The Creation of North Hartford: Genesis of an African American Community, 1860 to 1925" (paper, Hartford Studies Project, Trinity College, Hartford, 1998); and, generally, Nicholas Lemann, *The Great Black Migration and How It Changed America* (New York: Knopf, 1991).

46   *nearly tripled from 1900 to 1920*   Jacobs, "Creation of North Hartford." See also Ralph Pearson, "Interracial Conflict in Twentieth Century Connecticut Cities: The Demographic Factor," *Connecticut History* 17 (January 1976): 1–14.

46   *"race problem on its hands"*   Scott, *Negro Migration,* 142. Scott wrote, "Hartford was one of the industrial areas to which large numbers of the migrating negroes went. The housing problem became acute and the chief efforts of those endeavoring to better the conditions of migrants was along this line" (141).

47   *shut out of union jobs*   Jacobs, "Creation of North Hartford." See also National Urban League, Department of Research and Community Projects,

"A Review of the Social and Economic Condition of the Negro Population of Hartford, Connecticut," report to the Council of Social Agencies of Greater Hartford and the Hartford Negro Citizens' Council, September–October 1944.

47 *Johnson wrote* Charles S. Johnson, *The Negro Population of Hartford, Connecticut* (New York: National Urban League, 1921), 131.

47 *"values in that neighborhood"* Rose Helper, *Racial Policies and Practices of Real Estate Brokers* (Minneapolis: University of Minnesota Press, 1969), 201. See also Douglas Massey and Nancy Denton, *American Apartheid* (Cambridge, MA: Harvard University Press, 1993), 36.

47 *40-square-block area in North Hartford* "Survey of City Buildings," *Hartford Times*, April 11, 1941.

47 *as housing discrimination continued* Helper, *Racial Policies*; Massey and Denton, *American Apartheid*; and Gregory Squires, "The Indelible Color Line: The Persistence of Housing Segregation," *American Prospect* 10, no. 42 (January 1999). Squires, a professor at the University of Wisconsin at Milwaukee, is considered a leading expert in the field of housing discrimination. In his *American Prospect* article, Squires writes, "Though overt racism has diminished greatly over the last 30 years, most American cities remain deeply segregated. A host of other problems, such as the lack of both public services and private enterprise in inner-city black neighborhoods, have persisted in part because of this segregation. The challenge today is no longer to thwart individual white racists . . . Rather we must address the legacy of nearly a century of institutional practices that embedded racial and ethnic ghettos deep in our urban demography. Specifically, the practices of mortgage lenders and property insurers may have done more to shape housing patterns than bald racism ever did."

47 *7 percent of the city's population* Pearson, "Interracial Conflict."

48 *jobs for Puerto Rican farmworkers* Ruth Glasser, *Aqui Me Quedo: Puerto Ricans in Connecticut* (Hartford: Connecticut Humanities Council, 1997).

48 *couldn't provide work* Glasser, *Aqui Me Quedo*. See also James Dietz, *Economic History of Puerto Rico* (Princeton, NJ: Princeton University Press, 1986); and Cruz, *Identity and Power*.

48 *spread leaflets enticing workers* Glasser, *Aqui Me Quedo*. See also Connecticut Historical Society, "Nuestras Historias/Our Histories. Working

in Connecticut" (oral history), http://www.chs.org/nuestrashistorias; Craig M. Pearson, "'Too Little for Too Many' Brings Puerto Rican Migrants to the State," *Hartford Courant*, May 2, 1954; Craig M. Pearson, "Last Migration Brings 12,000 Puerto Ricans to Connecticut, Revives Old Problems," *Hartford Courant*, April 25, 1954; and Daniel Gottlieb, "Puerto Ricans Like It Here; They're Crowded but Optimistic," *Hartford Times*, September 13, 1958.

48   *6,000 Puerto Ricans had come*   Cruz, *Identity and Power,* 49.

48   *greatest concentration in any American city*   U.S. Department of Commerce, Bureau of the Census, *County and City Data Book* (Washington, DC: GPO, 1994). See also Glasser, *Aqui Me Quedo.*

49   *subsidies encouraged it*   Section 202 of the Housing Act of 1959. The program is authorized under the Housing Act of 1959; Section 210 of the Housing and Community Development Act of 1974, Public Law 86-372 (12 *U.S. Code* 1701q, 73 *Stat.* 654, 667); the National Affordable Housing Act, Public Law 101-625 (42 *U.S. Code* 12701); the Housing and Community Development Act of 1992 (Public Law 102-550); the Rescissions Act (Public Law 104-19); and the American Homeownership and Economic Opportunity Act of 2000 (Public Law 106-569). Program regulations are in 24 CFR Part 891. To learn more about the Section 202 program, see *Supportive Housing for the Elderly* (HUD Handbook 4571.3) and *Supportive Housing for the Elderly—Conditional Commitment—Final* (HUD Handbook 4571.5). The U.S. Department of Housing and Urban Development provides interest-free capital advances to private, nonprofit sponsors to finance the development of supportive housing for the elderly.

49   *"vicious rent gougers"*   Jose E. Cruz, *Identity and Power: Puerto Rican Politics and the Challenge of Ethnicity* (Philadelphia: Temple University Press, 1998), 26.

49   *"no place else he may go"*   Robert Rotberg wrote a detailed seven-part series on the problem of housing segregation in the Greater Hartford region. The series ran in the *Hartford Courant* beginning August 18, 1956.

50   *housing was inside Hartford*   *Housing: Background, Facts and Projections 1970–2000* (Hartford, CT: Capital Regional Planning Agency, 1969).

50   *"safe and sustainable"*   Author interview with James Thompson, June 20, 2000.

50   *mix of white and nonwhite*   Enrollment reports for individual schools were not kept by race and/or ethnicity during these years, but information on racial mix was obtained from interviews with Weaver High School graduates James Thompson and Alan Green. Compilation of census figures also generally suggests such enrollment patterns. See U.S. Bureau of the Census, *U.S. Census of Population: 1950, Census Tract Statistics, Hartford, Connecticut, and Adjacent Area, 1950 Population Census Report, Volume III, Chapter 23; U.S. Census of Population: 1960, General Characteristics of the Population, by Census Tracts: 1960;* and *1970 Census of Population and Housing, Census Tracts, Hartford, Connecticut, Standard Metropolitan Statistical Area and Adjacent Area* (Washington, DC).

50   *"finding it up on Westland Street"*   Author interview with Alan Green, June 21, 2000.

51   *moved* out   Herbert F. Janick, *A Diverse People: Connecticut, 1914 to the Present* (Chester, CT: Pequot, 1975). See also Ivan Kuzyk, *A Hartford Primer and Field Guide* (Hartford, CT: Trinity College, Cities Data Center, 2001).

51   *80 percent of the city's population*   U.S. Bureau of the Census, Census 2000, Table DP-1, "Profile of General Demographic Characteristics: 2000," Geographic Area: Hartford town, Hartford County, Connecticut. 121,578 people live in the city of Hartford, according to the U.S. Census of 2000.

51   *41 percent of the city's population*   Cruz, *Identity and Power*, 154.

51   *many other great Northern cities*   Connecticut Department of Education, *Estimated Data for % of Students Eligible for Free and Reduced Lunch*, 2003 (Hartford, 2003). School officials acknowledge that the percentage of children eligible for free lunch is likely higher than this. U.S. Department of Education, Office of Education Research, National Center of Education Statistics, "Characteristics of the 100 Largest Public Elementary and Secondary School Districts in the United States, 2000–2001," 2002, http://www.nces.ed.gov/pubs2002.

52   *72 percent of the students are poor*   Calculations by author. Compiled from data from Connecticut Department of Education and the Hartford Public Schools, *Enrollment Reports for* 2000 (Hartford, 2000).

The question of whether racial segregation is increasing in America and its public schools in particular depends entirely upon which racial groups one chooses to measure and compare. And it's true that racial minorities are slowly diversifying some suburbs. This demographic shift has been widely publicized but has barely had an impact on the bigger picture. As Georgetown law professor Sheryll Cashin notes in her 2004 book, *The Failures of Integration: How Race and Class are Undermining the American Dream* (New York: Public Affairs, 2004): "One might think that this coloring of suburbia would reflect progress during integration. But . . . significant declines in the segregation of suburbs are occurring only in areas with small minority populations." Sheryll Cashin adds, "At the current rate of improvement, in forty years . . . blacks will be just as segregated as moderately segregated Latinos are today" (89). As for those Latinos, while they are generally less segregated than blacks overall, their segregation rates declined, Cashin and others note, mostly in places where they are a tiny portion (less than 2 percent) of the population. Asian kids are the minority group least likely to be isolated from whites and other minority groups and most likely to go to school with black, brown, and white kids. Blacks are our most segregated racial minority group. Specifically, about half of America's black residents live in areas where about 75 percent or more blacks would have to move out in order for the group to be evenly distributed. See also *Ethnic Diversity Grows, Neighborhood Integration Lags Behind* (Albany: Lewis Mumford Center of the State University of New York at Albany, December 18, 2001); and John Logan, *Separate and Unequal: The Neighborhood Gap for Blacks and Hispanics in Metropolitan America* (Albany, NY: Lewis Mumford Center for Comparative Urban and Regional Research, 2003).

52   *segregation is increasingly intense*   Cashin, *Failures,* 88.

52   *to 7.9 million in 2000*   Paul Jargowsky, *Stunning Progress, Hidden Problems: The Dramatic Decline of Concentrated Poverty in the 1990s,* Living Cities Census Series (Washington, DC: Brookings Institution, May 2003); and Alexander Polikoff, "Racial Inequality and the Black Ghetto," *Poverty & Race* 13, no. 6 (November–December 2004).

52   *increase from 1970 levels*   Cashin, *Failures;* Jargowsky, *Stunning Progress;* Polikoff, "Racial Inequality."

52   *doubled, from about 1,300 in 1970*   Polikoff, "Racial Inequality."

52   *"deterioration of our separated condition"*   Cashin, *Failures*, 97.

52   *2.3 million white residents*   Cashin, *Failures*, 91.

53   *80 percent of his or her classmates*   Gary Orfield and Chungmei Lee, *Why Segregation Matters: Poverty and Educational Inequality* (Cambridge, MA: Civil Rights Project at Harvard University, January 2005).

53   *multiethnic American reality*   Orfield and Lee, *Why Segregation*. See also Gary Orfield and Chungmei Lee, Brown *at 50: King's Dream or Plessy's Nightmare?* (Cambridge, MA: Civil Rights Project at Harvard University, January 2004); Erica Frankenberg and Chungmei Lee, *Race in American Public Schools: Rapidly Resegregating School Districts* (Cambridge, MA: Civil Rights Project at Harvard University, 2002); and David Rusk, "Trends in School Segregation," in *Divided We Fail: Coming Together through Public School Choice*, the Century Foundation Task Force on the Common School (New York: Century Foundation Press, 2002), 61–85.

     In the 2004 Civil Rights Project report Brown *at 50*, Orfield and Lee's conclusions are worth noting in some detail: "U.S. schools are becoming more segregated in all regions for both African American and Latino students." Specifically, they report: "In many districts where court-ordered desegregation was ended in the past decade, there has been a major increase in segregation . . . Central cities of large metropolitan areas are the epicenter segregation [*sic*]; segregation is also severe in smaller central cities and in the suburban rings of large metropolitan areas . . . There has been a substantial slippage toward segregation in most of the states that were highly desegregated in 1991. American public schools are now only 60 percent white nationwide." However, except in the South and Southwest, most white students have little contact with minority students.

53   *10 percent down payment*   See Kenneth T. Jackson, *Crabgrass Frontier: The Suburbanization of the United States* (New York: Oxford University Press, 1985). See also Massey and Denton, *American Apartheid*; and Helper, *Racial Policies*, for discussion of such practices on the national level.

53   *houses common to urban areas*   These practices have been well documented on the national level. See, for example, Helper, *Racial Policies*; Jackson, *Crabgrass Frontier*; and Massey and Denton, *American Apartheid*. In Greater Hartford, the practices have been best documented in reports

by a now-defunct nonprofit advocacy group called Education/Instruccion (on file with author). As noted elsewhere, independent investigations by journalists have uncovered similar discriminatory practices. As for Hartford in particular, early discrimination and blacks' lack of mobility was well documented as early as 1920 in Johnson, *Negro Population*, 7–66.

54 *making them ineligible for loans*   Massey and Denton, *American Apartheid*; Helper, *Racial Policies*; and Jackson, *Crabgrass*, 204.

54 *"sub-standard conditions"*   Citizens Committee of the North End, special issue, *The Citizen* (May, 1962): 1. See also Hartford Community Renewal Program, "Population and Housing Report," 1965, 11.

55 *21 percent of employment*   Louise B. Simmons, *Organizing in Hard Times: Labor and Neighborhoods in Hartford* (Philadelphia: Temple University Press, 1994), 3.

55 *"these type of people into town"*   George Nagy, "Regional Housing Authority Idea Meets Overwhelming Opposition," *Hartford Times*, April 17, 1967.

55 *"come to be called the 'Negro revolt'"*   "Social Study Report," study conducted for Town Meeting for Tomorrow by the Greater Hartford Chamber of Commerce (report delivered at Greater Hartford's Conference on Metropolitan Cooperation and Development, Hartford, 1965). See also Norman Elkin, "Regional Problems and Public Opinion in Greater Hartford. Town Meeting for Tomorrow" (paper delivered at Greater Hartford's Conference on Metropolitan Cooperation and Development, Hartford, 1965).

56 *equal access to union jobs*   Theodore Driscoll, "Black Caucus Outlines Charges Before Panel," *Hartford Courant*, September 22, 1967.

56 *looting, burning, and marching*   Theodore Driscoll, "Causes of Riots Cited at NAACP," *Hartford Courant*, July 15, 1967; Theodore Driscoll, "Policeman Hurt, Stores Damaged: Mayor Listens to Grievances," *Hartford Courant*, July 14, 1967; and Theodore Driscoll, "Police Set, Reinforce Strength: Crews Remove Debris of Riots," *Hartford Courant*, September 21, 1967.

56 *five days and nights*   Donald Spivey, "Point of Contention: A Historical Perspective on the African-American Presence in Hartford," in *The State of Black Hartford* (Hartford, CT: Urban League of Greater Hartford, June 1994). See also Mark Paznikos, "Life in the Model City: 20 Years after the Clay Hill Riots," *Hartford Courant*, May 1, 1988; Barbara Carlson, "Victims

at Stowe Village Angry and Bewildered," *Hartford Courant,* September 6, 1969; Theodore Driscoll, "City Manager Gets Emergency Tower," *Hartford Courant,* September 3, 1969; and Theodore Driscoll, "Arrests Pass 500 Mark as 3-Day Curfew Ends: Disorders Result in 4 Shootings," *Hartford Courant,* September 6, 1969.

56 *adequately address the problem*   For example, the act limited the ability of the Department of Housing and Urban Development to initiate investigations. Also, damages in personal lawsuits were limited to $1,000. For more information, see George Lipsitz, *The Possessive Investment in Whiteness* (Philadelphia: Temple University Press, 1998).

56 *"white male customers"*   Michele Ingrassia, "Home Financing Biased: Study," *Hartford Times,* May 21, 1974.

57 *"I throw listings for Hartford homes away"*   Education/Instruccion, *Redlining* (Hartford, 1976) (on file with author). According to EI transcripts, when a white tester asked about the possibility of living in Bloomfield (a racially mixed inner-ring suburb), the agent continued, "We all like to believe we're not prejudiced, but with kids—do you want to be the only white walking down the street?" But black testers were steered to Bloomfield by the same agent: "I know you'll just love the Bloomfield area," the agent said.

57 *market more effectively to prospective minority home buyers*   Bruce Kaufman, "7 Firms Sign Anti Bias Decree," *Hartford Courant,* July 26, 1974.

57 *if they could get insurance*   Education/Instruccion, *Redlining.*

In 1996, Michael Sacks of Trinity College in Hartford conducted a research review that suggested that the problem of attaining adequate insurance in depressed urban areas may be worsening. See Michael Sacks, *Property Insurance and Redlining in the Inner City,* prepared for Citizens for Action in New Britain, Trinity Center for Neighborhoods, Hartford, 1996. More generally, see Gregory Squires, ed., *Insurance Redlining: Divestment, Reinvestment, and the Evolving Role of Financial Institutions* (Washington, DC: Urban Institute Press, 1997). For information on insurance redlining, see also Gregory Squires and William Velez, "Insurance Redlining and the Transformation of an Urban Metropolis," *Urban Affairs Quarterly* 23 (September 1987): 217–32; and Gregory D. Squires, William Velez, and Karl Tauber, "Insurance Redlining: Agency Location and the Process of Urban Disinvestment," *Urban Affairs Quarterly* 26 (June 1991): 567–88. A journalistic account of the continuing problem nationally is Mark Feld-stein, "Insurance Redlining: Hitting the Poor Where They Live," *The Nation*, April 4, 1994, 12.

57   *91 percent suburban*   Education/Instruccion, *Redlining*. Similarly, according to EI's data, Charter Oak Bank collected 83 percent of its deposits (about $23 million) from the city in 1975, but during that same period, 75 percent of its mortgage loan dollars went to suburban communities. The Hartford National Bank financed 11 mortgages in its fourth quarter of 1975 from the Hartford City Employees Pension Fund. All the loans went to the suburbs, including eight in West Hartford. Hartford National, getting about $1.02 billion in city-based deposits, made a return investment to the city of $116,000. (This is a ratio of nearly 10,000 to 1.)

58   *mortgages went to suburbanites*   Education/Instruccion, *Report 10* (Hartford, 1976) (on file with author).

58   *an east-west highway, Interstate 84*   Connecticut Highway Department, *Connecticut Highway Needs* (n.p., 1967). See also Connecticut Department of Transportation, *Managing Travel in Connecticut: 100 Years of Progress* (Newington, CT, 1995).

58   *in getting suburban jobs*   Andrew J. Gold, "Economic Interdependence in the Greater Hartford Region—City and Suburbs," in *Hartford, the City and the Region: Past, Present, Future; A Collection of Essays*, ed. Sondra Astor Stave (West Hartford, CT: University of Hartford, 1979). The farther out the suburb, the less likely a Hartford resident would have a job there, Gold found. Gold's analysis showed that each loss of 1,000 jobs from Hartford that left the region would "mean an initial loss of 610 jobs for suburbanites." But Gold also showed that "each 1,000 new jobs in the developing outer ring will mean only 50 new jobs for Hartford residents."

59   *"that provided their education"*   Nicholas R. Carbone, guest editorial, in Stave, *Hartford*, 21. Carbone worked as a consultant on urban and suburban disparities at the University of Hartford during the period he served as deputy mayor.

59   *reviews on multifamily housing*   Suburban Action Institute, *The Status of Zoning in Connecticut. A Report of the Connecticut Commission on Human Rights and Opportunities* (Hartford: State of Connecticut Commission on Human Rights and Opportunities, May 1978), 17.

60 *"between whites and minorities"* Suburban Action Institute, *Status*, 3.

60 *"I made charts"* Author interview with Nicholas Carbone, May 30, 2001.

60 *"for persons of lower incomes"* Housing and Community Redevelopment Act of 1974, S. 3066, 93rd Cong., 2nd sess. (1974) 101c) (6).

60 *wanted more parks* Hartford v. Glastonbury, 561 F.2d 1032.

60 *frankly wrote, "o"* Lawrence Fellows, "Hartford Battles 7 of Its Suburbs in Court," *New York Times*, November 17, 1975. The towns were Enfield, Farmington, Glastonbury, Vernon, West Hartford, and Windsor Locks.

61 *Hartford lost* Hartford v. Glastonbury, 561 F.2d 1032; *Hartford v. Hills*, 408 F. Supp. 889 (Dconn, 1976). See also William J. Sullivan, untitled paper (University of Connecticut School of Law, 1989), on file with the Connecticut Civil Liberties Union, Hartford.

61 *housing stock was there* In the 1990s, the city had 8,050 units of subsidized housing suitable for families (two or more bedrooms). By contrast, 21 surrounding suburban communities, taken together, had only 2,073 units. In Avon, just 2.6 percent of the housing stock was subsidized. The suburban towns of Avon, Canton, South Windsor, Granby, East Windsor, Ellington, and Suffield offered no subsidized housing for families in the early 1990s. Some of these towns did offer some subsidized housing units, but they were usually for elderly residents. Compiled from data found in Connecticut Department of Economic and Community Development, *Connecticut Town Profiles* (Hartford, November 2001).

61 *11 of 13 chain supermarkets* Kenneth J. Neubeck and Richard E. Ratcliff, "Urban Democracy and the Power of Corporate Capital: Struggles over Downtown Growth and Neighborhood Stagnation in Hartford, Connecticut," in *Business Elites and Urban Development*, ed. Scott Cummings (Albany: State University of New York Press, 1988), 299–332. See also Kirk Johnson, "Hartford, Its Boom Over, Sees Downtown Decaying," *New York Times*, August 22, 1990.

61 *"these types of people"* Larry Williams, "Mayor Grant of West Hartford Apologizes to Puerto Ricans," *Hartford Times*, October 25, 1973.

61 *"down payment on a house"* Ibid.

61 *"often rejected on site"* Connecticut Commission on Human Rights and Opportunities, *Housing Discrimination and Opportunities in the State of Connecticut* (Hartford, April 1986).

62   *based upon the testers' race*   Larry Williams and Lyn Bixby, "O'Neill Orders Probe of Real Estate Agencies," *Hartford Courant,* May 24, 1989.

62   *lost 17,000 . . . nearly 15,000*   SOCDS Census Data: *Output for Hartford, Connecticut,* 2001, http://socds.huduser.org/scripts/odbic.exe/census/industry.htm. See also Connecticut Policy and Economic Council (CPEC), *The Metro Hartford Region at a Crossroads* (Hartford, September 2002); and U.S. Department of Labor, Bureau of Labor Statistics Data, *Hartford LMA,* 2002, http://data.bls.gov/serlet/SurveyOutputServlet.

62   *have bachelor's degrees*   U.S. Bureau of the Census, Census 2000.

62   *have high school diplomas*   U.S. Bureau of the Census, Census 2000.

62   *left Hartford between 1990 and 2000*   According to the U.S. Census, in 1970 more than 80 percent of the county's black population still lived in the city of Hartford. Blacks in 1990 appear to have migrated to close-in suburbs, including East Hartford, Manchester, Windsor, and to a lesser extent West Hartford. Mike Swift, "City Loses Blacks to Suburbs," *Hartford Courant,* March 21, 2001. About one in three of the region's Latinos live in the suburbs—a slight increase over the 21 percent who lived there in 1990, according to the U.S. Bureau of the Census.

62   BLACKS TO SUBURBS   Swift, "City Loses Blacks."

62   *black population dropped*   U.S. Bureau of the Census. Also, author interview with Gerald Maine, Principal Planner, City of Hartford, September 6, 2002.

Swift, "City Loses Blacks." According to Swift's analysis, in 1990, fewer than one in three black residents in the county lived in the suburbs. In 2000, 46 percent lived in the suburbs. The balance lived in Hartford or in the small city of New Britain, according to Swift.

62   *to run against each other*   Matthew Daly, "State's House Lines Redrawn: Hartford, Other Cities to Lose Districts," *Hartford Courant,* November 30, 2001.

63   *reconstructed her face*   Tina Brown, "This Is Takira: She Awakened a City to the Reality of Violence. She Is 7," *Hartford Courant,* July 11, 2001; Tom Condon, "A Little Girl's Face Should Force the City to Rethink Its Priorities," *Hartford Courant,* July 13, 2001; and Tom Puleo, Matt Burgard, and Eric M. Weiss, "Allies to Join City's Crime Fight: Governor Offers State, Federal Help," *Hartford Courant,* July 13, 2001.

63   *"We're going to play hardball"* Puleo, Burgard, and Weiss, "Allies to Join."

63   *brought state police back* For example, Matt Burgard, "Stricken Family Ponders Lost Son's Path," *Hartford Courant*, November 15, 2002; Chris Harris, "Mortal Street Problems," *Hartford Advocate*, February 21, 2002; Matt Burgard, "Police Seek 2 Shooting Suspects: Warrant Obtained in Random Killing," *Hartford Courant*, March 13, 2002; News Briefs, "Shooting Victim's Condition Improves," *Hartford Courant*, February 18, 2002; Matt Burgard, "Popular Man, 24, Shot to Death," *Hartford Courant*, March 7, 2002; Matt Burgard, "Another Son Killed on Street: 21-Year-Old Victim Called a Quiet Kid," *Hartford Courant*, January 15, 2002; Gregory Seay, "Man Shot Dead May Have Been Robbery Victim," *Hartford Courant*, February 3, 2002; and Matt Burgard, "Protesters Seek Better Policing," *Hartford Courant*, February 7, 2002.

63   *pedaling a bike near his house* Burgard, "Suspected Gunman Named: Police Seek 19-Year-Old in Shooting of Boy," *Hartford Courant*, July 16, 2003.

64   *low-wage service positions* See, for example, Mike Swift, "As Adriaen's Rises, So Does Public Bill," *Hartford Courant*, February 2, 2004.

64   *shop, hang out, talk, trade tips* For scholarly discussions of this phenomenon and of the power of social networks in shaping opportunity, habits, expectations, and economic success, see, most notably, Ronald Burt, *Structural Holes: The Social Structure of Competition* (Cambridge, MA: Harvard University Press, 1992); Mark Granovetter, "The Strength of Weak Ties," *American Journal of Sociology* 78, no. 6 (1973): 1360–80; C. W. Perdue, J. F. Dovidio, M. B. Gurtman, and R. B. Tyler, "Us and Them: Social Categorization and the Process of Intergroup Bias," *Journal of Personality and Social Psychology* 59 (1990): 475–86; Leo Brajkovich, "Sources of Social Structure in a Start-up Organization: Work Networks, Work Activities, and Job Status," *Social Networks* 16 (1994): 191–212; Mark S. Mizruchi, "Cohesion, Equivalence, and Similarity of Behavior: A Theoretical and Empirical Assessment," *Social Networks* 15 (1993): 275–307; Trond Petersen, Ishak Saporta, and Marc-David Seidel, "Offering a Job: Meritocracy and Social Networks," *American Journal of Sociology* 106, no. 3 (2000): 762–816; Roberto Fernandez and Nancy Weinberg, "Sifting and

Sorting: Personal Contacts and Hiring in a Retail Bank," *American Sociological Review* 62, no. 6 (1997): 883–902.

66 *a pretty big psychological leap*   The urban sociologist William Julius Wilson has argued that traditional quantitative studies that attempt to explain the causes of persistent inequality are inherently limited because they fail to take into account the impact of structured inequality on the perceptions, ideas, interactions, and actions of groups of human beings. Quantitative frameworks, while useful in many ways, are not, Wilson writes, "designed to capture the impact of relational, organizational, and collective processes that embody the social structure of inequality. Included among these processes are the institutional influences on mobility and opportunity; the operation and organization of schools; the mechanisms of residential racial segregation and social isolation in poor neighborhoods; categorical forms of discrimination in hiring, promotions, and other avenues of mobility." Quoted from W. J. Wilson, "The Role of the Environment in the Black-White Test Score Gap," in *The Black-White Test-Score Gap*, ed. C. Jencks and M. Phillips (Washington, DC: Brookings Institution Press, 1998), 508. On a related methodological matter, see also Charles Tilly, *Durable Inequality* (Los Angeles: University of California Press, 1998). Tilly outlines the long, complex process by which social inequality is created and maintained. Also, generally, see William Julius Wilson, *The Truly Disadvantaged: The Inner City, the Underclass, and Public Policy* (Chicago: University of Chicago Press, 1987).

Part Three. A Feeling That We Can Do Better

73 *litigated high-profile cases*   Later, Reid would write an influential brief in the 1978 U.S. Supreme Court case *University of California Regents v. Bakke*, which upheld affirmative action. J. Clay Smith, "Herbert O. Reid, Sr.: A Teacher of the Houstonian Tradition," in *The Footsteps of Giants: The Roots and Wings of the Howard Lawyer* (Washington, DC: Howard University, 2003), http://www.law.howard.edu/alumni/legalgiants/huslgiantdec2k.htm. See also Genna Rae McNeil, *Groundwork: Charles*

Hamilton Houston and the Struggle for Civil Rights (Philadelphia: University of Pennsylvania Press, 1983).

78 *"widespread existence" of racially segregated schools* As cited by Plaintiff's Post Trial Brief, *Milo Sheff, et al. v. William A. O'Neill,* Superior Court Judicial District of Hartford/New Britain, April 19, 1993.

79 *transfers of minority children to suburban schools* Schools for Hartford (Cambridge, MA: Center for Field Studies, Harvard Graduate School of Education, 1965). See also Plaintiff's Post Trial Brief, 65. In the brief, the plaintiffs argue, "The Harvard Report projected increasing racial concentrations in the Hartford Schools in future years if strong steps were not taken to promote integration. Like many reports in later years, the Harvard Report also explicitly focused on the problem of high poverty concentration in the Hartford Schools. The Harvard Report also described the educational harms that result from segregation. The Harvard Report contained a feasible interdistrict proposal that would have significantly alleviated the growing problems of school segregation at the time it was proposed."

79 *grown to several thousand kids* Author interview with Mary Carroll, founding director of Project Concern, June 7, 2001. See also Edward Iwanicki and Robert Gable, "Selection of Students for Project Concern" (internal report, Project Concern Program, Hartford, 1979); and Edward Iwanicki and Robert Gable, "Final Evaluation Report, 1978–1979" (internal report, Project Concern Program, Hartford, 1979) (on file with author).

79 *nearly 30,000 students* Connecticut State Board of Education, *Condition of Public Elementary and Secondary Education in Connecticut* (Hartford, 1977).

79 *Windsor and West Hartford* Lumpkin v. Meskill, U.S. District Court, District of Connecticut, Civil Action no. 13,716 (1973). In *Lumpkin,* plaintiffs' causes of action included the following: "The laws of the State of Connecticut have established each town in the State as a school district, placing control of each school district in the town in which the school district is located and requiring children to attend school within the district in which they reside. Numerous schools within the town of Hartford have a minority group population in excess of 90 percent. As a result of the geography, business location, and minority group population distribution

and makeup within the town of Hartford it is impossible to integrate these schools within the school district of the Town of Hartford in an educationally sound manner. The laws of the State of Connecticut establishing the school districts of Hartford and its contiguous towns erect unnatural legal barriers to the desegregation of the Hartford School District and its individual schools, more particularly, those schools which have a minority group enrollment in excess of 90 percent."

80   *"metropolitan areas of this nation"*   Brief Amicus Curiae of City of Hartford, Connecticut, in Support of Respondent Bradley, *Milliken v. Bradley,* no. 73-434, Supreme Court of the United States (1973).

81   *"I dissent"*   *Milliken v. Bradley,* 418 U.S. 717 (1974).

83   *three Supreme Court justices*   In 2003, 22 percent of the nation's active federal judges had been appointed by Reagan. Another 22 percent had been appointed by George W. Bush Sr. during his four years in office. Bill Clinton would even up the score, however. In 2003, 44 percent of active federal judges were Clinton appointees. See Vincent Bugliosi, *The Betrayal of America: How the Supreme Court Undermined the Constitution and Chose Our President* (New York: Thunder's Mouth Press, 2001). See also Henry Abraham, *Justices, Presidents, and Senators: A History of the U.S. Supreme Court Appointments from Washington to Clinton* (New York: Rowman and Littlefield, 1999).

84   *in the U.S. Supreme Court case*   *McCleskey v. Kemp,* 481 U.S. 279 (1987). See Randall L. Kennedy, "*McCleskey v. Kemp*: Race, Capital Punishment, and the Supreme Court," *Harvard Law Review* 101 (1988): 1388–1443.

84   *perpetrators with black victims*   David Baldus won the Harry Kalven Prize for Distinguished Scholarship from the Law and Society Association for his studies used and ultimately dismissed by the majority of the U.S. Supreme Court in the *McCleskey* case. Much of the work is included in David Baldus et al., "Arbitrariness and Discrimination in the Administration of the Death Penalty: A Challenge to State Supreme Courts," *Stetson Law Review* 15 (1986): 133, 159–69, 163–64. Richard Dieter of the Death Penalty Information Center in Washington, DC, points out that two more recent statistical analyses confirm Baldus's original findings. See Richard Dieter, *The Death Penalty in Black and White: Who Lives, Who Dies, Who Decides* (Washington, DC: Death Penalty Information Center, 1998), http://www.deathpenaltyinfo.org/article.php?scid=45&did2539#20.

84 *"underlie the entire criminal justice system"* McCleskey v. Kemp, 481 U.S. 279 (1987), 314.

85 *into poverty* "Ronald Reagan: An Inventory of Spoken Word Audio Recordings in the Vincent Voice Library," Michigan State University, http://www.lib.msu.edu. 35.3 million Americans were living in poverty in 1983, which was an 18-year high, representing 15.2 percent of the population. See http://www.census.gov/hhes/www/saipe/nontechdoc/fluct.html. See also Sheldon Danziger and Peter Gottschalk, "The Impact of Budget Cuts and Economic Conditions on Poverty," *Journal of Policy Analysis and Management* 4 (Summer 1985): 586–93.

85 *Jackson's views, not his* Bugliosi, *The Betrayal.*

86 *Democratic politics in New York* http://www.roberthjackson.org/theman 2-2-2-4.

86 *interracial dating* Bob Jones University v. United States, 461 U.S. 574. For commentary, see Derrick Jackson, "The Court That Throttled Democracy," *Boston Globe*, December 13, 2000. See also Bugliosi, *Betrayal.*

87 *"made desegregation work"* Frye Gaillard, *The Dream Long Deferred* (Chapel Hill: University of North Carolina Press, 1988). See also Alison Morantz, "Desegregation at Risk: Threat and Reaffirmation in Charlotte," in *Dismantling Desegregation: The Quiet Reversal of* Brown v. Board of Education, ed. Gary Orfield and Susan E. Eaton (New York: New Press, 1996).

87 *uncomfortable silence* Gaillard, *Dream.* See also Morantz, "Desegregation at Risk," 179. In the mid-1980s, however, a Christian fundamentalist won election to the school board with a "neighborhood schools" platform. A later study would suggest that Charlotte's new arrivals—affluent Northern transplants—feared racial integration would lower school quality. This helped to fuel the movement to dismantle the city's desegregation plan in the early 1990s. See Roslyn Mickelson and Carol A. Ray, "Fear of Falling from Grace: The Middle Class, Downward Mobility, and School Desegregation," *Research in Sociology of Education and Socialization* 10 (1994): 207–38.

88 *"but equal" requirement* San Antonio Independent School District v. Rodriguez, 411 U.S. 1 (1973). On Justice Douglas's comments about the crippling effect of *Rodriguez* paired with *Milliken*, see also Richard Kluger, *Simple Justice* (New York: Vintage, 1977), 772.

88 *"an Achievable Goal"* Julius Chambers, "Adequate Education for All," *Harvard Civil Rights–Civil Liberties Law Review* 22, no. 1 (1987): 11–32.

90   *earliest school finance equity cases*   Horton v. Meskill, 172 Conn. 615, 376 A.2d 359 (1977).

91   *education-funding system*   In 2000, another lawsuit charged that the state had not complied with the ruling and that glaring annual per-pupil expenditures remained as a result. But the lawsuit, *Johnson v. Rowland*, later died for lack of funding. In its decision in *Horton v. Meskill*, the court had focused on two articles within the constitution: Article 1 in its first section creates a "fundamental right" to education. Connecticut's constitution had the standard "equal protection clause" declaring that "no state shall . . . deny to any person within its jurisdiction the equal protection of the laws." Considered in tandem, the court ruled, the articles amount to a promise of "equal educational opportunity."

96   "'*divided educational facilities*'"   Connecticut State Department of Education, *Report on Racial/Ethnic Equity and Desegregation in Connecticut's Public Schools* (Hartford, January 1988).

96   "*an ivory tower*"   Robert Frahm and Jacqueline Cutler, "2 Lawmakers Attack Desegregation Plan," *Hartford Courant*, December 24, 1987.

96   "*rein him in*"   Frahm and Cutler, "Lawmakers Attack."

97   "*want to achieve*"   Frahm and Cutler, "Lawmakers Attack."

97   *action on school integration*   Plaintiff's Post Trial Brief, *Sheff v. O'Neill*, 78. Also, author interview with Gerry Tirozzi, October 30, 2000; author interview with Jack Hasegawa, November 3, 2000; author interview with Philip Tegeler, November 8, 2000; and author interview with John Brittain, November 9, 2000.

97   "*big, big monster*"   Frahm and Cutler, "Lawmakers Attack."

103   "*best offered*" *for her children*   Author interview with Marianne Lado (née Engleman), January 12, 2001; author interview with Mary Carroll, June 7, 2000. Also, interview notes from Lado's interview with Marge Little on July 8, 1988, were made available to the author. On file with the NAACP Legal Defense and Education Fund and with the author. Mary Carroll was present at the interview. In 1988, Marge Little was a paraprofessional with Project Concern.

104   "*learn how to deal with other people*"   Ibid.

105   *that she'd had to forsake*   Author interview with Mary Carroll, June 7, 2000.

107   *did that poorly* Connecticut State Department of Education, *Grade 4 Mastery Test Results: Summary and Interpretations* (Hartford, 1988); Connecticut State Department of Education, *Grade 6 Mastery Test Results: Summary and Interpretations* (Hartford, 1988); Connecticut State Department of Education, *Grade 8 Mastery Test Results: Summary and Interpretations* (Hartford, 1988). Also, author interviews with Elizabeth Sheff, Jack Boger, and John Brittain.

Part Four. Trials

128   *kids' fates after graduation* In 2003, members of the board of trustees finally took issue with misleading statistics that claimed that upwards of 80 percent of Hartford's graduates had gone on to four-year colleges. See Rachel Gottlieb, "School Board Struggles to Find Reality," *Hartford Courant,* December 17, 2003.

129   *lowest-paying jobs* Braddock based his general conclusions about the longer-term effects of segregation and desegregation upon numerous statistical studies he'd conducted himself, as well as upon reviews he'd conducted of similar work by other scholars. In one study, Braddock found that black students who had attended predominantly white schools were more than twice as likely to choose a predominantly white college as blacks who attended high schools that were more than 75 percent black. The racial composition of a black student's high school, he found, has the greatest impact among many factors—including grades and even proximity to home—on whether a student will choose a predominantly white college. See J. H. Braddock, "The Perpetuation of Segregation across Levels of Education: A Behavioral Assessment of the Contact-Hypotheis," *Sociology of Education* 53 (1980): 178–86. Similarly, in a 1989 study, Braddock and a colleague, James McPartland, found that previously desegregated blacks were far more likely to be working in racially mixed settings. The two researchers also found that minority applicants from segregated communities and schools may be discriminated against because their recommendations and references (from segregated institutions) carry less weight than do recommendations or references provided by white candidates. They

concluded, "Due to segregation of schools and communities, white employers may be less familiar with a black school, a black clergy, or a black firm that a minority individual may use for sponsorship of his or her job candidacy, or white employers may feel more suspect of information provided by minorities due to stigma and stereotypes attached to minority sources." See "Social-Psychological Processes That Perpetuate Racial Segregation: The Relationship between School and Employment Desegregation," *Journal of Black Studies* 19, no. 3 (1989): 267–89. Also noteworthy are J. H. Braddock, R. L. Crain, J. M. McPartland, and R. L. Dawkins, "Applicant Race and Job Placement Decisions: A National Survey Experiment," *International Journal of Sociology and Social Policy* 6, no. 1 (1986): 3–24; and J. H. Braddock and J. M. McPartland, "How Minorities Continue to Be Excluded from Equal Employment Opportunities: Research on Labor Market and Institutional Barriers," *Journal of Social Issues* 43, no. 1 (1987): 5–39.

135   *came to action*   The eventual law required regional committees to devise proposed plans, which, unlike the governor's original proposal, had to be approved by numerous local government entities. The plans would not have been binding, even if passed. But most of the proposed plans failed to pass even at the local levels. Connecticut Public Act 93-263.

139   *attended were also poor*   Her particular methods—called hierarchical linear modeling—partialled out the effects of family poverty and long-term poverty, so that she could quite safely conclude, after controlling for multiple factors, that schools with high concentrations of poverty are, in themselves, harmful for student achievement and tend to slow the rate of learning. A typical child who is poor and attends a school where more than 50 percent of the children are also poor, Kennedy found, would suffer an achievement decline as a result. To be exact, between grades two and four, such a child, on average, would lose a full 30 percent of the progress a typical nonpoor child in a nonpoor school would gain during these two years.

142   *"History, Law, and Myth"*   Christopher Collier, "New England Specter: Town and State in Connecticut History, Law, and Myth," *Connecticut Historical Society Bulletin* 60 (1995): 1–3. See also "Sleeping with Ghosts: Myth and Public Policy in Connecticut, 1634–1991," *New England Quarterly: A Historical Review of New England Life and Letters* 65, no. 2 (June

1992): 179–207. For further discussion, see Timothy Hollister, "The Myth and Reality of Home Rule Powers in Connecticut," *Connecticut Bar Journal* 59 (December 1985): 389–97.

143   *slip across the lines*   For an insightful exploration of these matters concerning Connecticut in particular, see also Kathryn McDermott, *Controlling Public Education: Localism Versus Equity* (Lawrence: University of Kansas Press, 1999).

148   *not worth fighting for anymore*   See Gary Orfield and Susan E. Eaton, *Dismantling.* See also, Susan E. Eaton, *The Other Boston Busing Story: What's Won and Lost Across the Boundary Line* (New Haven, CT: Yale University Press, 2001).

148   Sheff-*related matters in the state*   Darryl L. McMiller, "Public Opinion and School Desegregation in Hartford, Connecticut," *Equity and Excellence in Education* 33, no. 2 (2000): 68–79.

148   *72 percent answered yes*   Nationally, a 1999 CNN poll found that more than two-thirds of the American people believed racial integration had "helped improve" the quality of education for black students. Mark Gillespie, "Americans Want Integrated Schools, but Oppose School Busing," Gallup News Service Poll Release, Gallup Organization, Princeton, NJ, September 27, 1999. That said, as one would expect, few people polled in 1999 liked the idea or even the word *busing.* Specifically, Gillespie of Gallup News Service writes, "Nearly six out of ten Americans believe more should be done to integrate the nation's classrooms. However the vast majority would prefer to accomplish school integration through methods other than busing." Nearly 70 percent of those polled said integration has improved the quality of education received by black students. About half of those polled said it has improved the education of white students. (In 1990, 56 percent of Connecticut residents surveyed were opposed to busing according to McMiller, "Public Opinion." But when a pollster introduced the possibility of other options—magnet schools, voluntary transfers—the approval ratings increased. Nearly 70 percent in Connecticut agreed with the statement, "If more children went to racially mixed schools, we would have less of a problem with racial prejudice.")

149   *cause further segregation*   One could consider this argument differently. Consider first the desegregation rates in the previously isolated Wilmington,

Delaware, when it was a stand-alone school district, with a student population that was about 90 percent black and majority poor. At best, the portion of whites in the average black student's school could not have been
more than 10 percent. Then the Wilmington district, following a lawsuit,
was merged with the larger, more heavily white county district under a
city-wide desegregation plan. Thus, under desegregation, the proportion
of white students to black students, after incorporation with the suburbs,
would at least in most cases *be far higher than 10 percent.* So even if the district lost some white students county-wide, Wilmington students were still
learning in more racially diverse schools. Orfield and Eaton, *Dismantling.*

150 *never even flirted with mandatory desegregation* Orfield and Eaton, *Dismantling,* chapter 1.

151 *Armor's predictions never came true* Rodney Ho, "After the Buses," *Vir-
ginian Pilot and Ledger Star,* January 17, 1993. See also Vivian Ikpa, "The
Effects of Changes in School Characteristics Resulting from the Elimina-
tion of Mandated Busing for Integration upon the Academic Achievement
of African-American Students," *Educational Research Quarterly* 17, no. 1
(1990): 19–29; Leslie Carr and Donald Zeigler, "White Flight and White
Return in Norfolk: A Test of Predictions," *Sociology of Education* 63 (1990):
272–82; and Orfield and Eaton, *Dismantling,* chapter 5.

151 *deliberate return to segregated schools* *Riddick v. School Board of the City
of Norfolk, Virginia,* 784 F.2d 521 (4th Cir. 1986). Orfield and Eaton, *Dismantling,* chapter 5.

151 *"Hartford is doing quite a good job"* According to his testimony, Armor's
multiple regression analysis found that if one were to take a community's
socioeconomic status, percentage of single-parent families, and poverty
level into account, the minority kids in Hartford were getting the test
scores that one would predict. The college-going rates were about what
you'd expect too, he said. That the test scores and the college-going rates
were higher in the suburbs, Armor concluded, was a function of the higher
socioeconomic status in those communities. Segregation had nothing to do
with it. And black children, he'd concluded after looking at the working-
class and poor town of East Hartford, a system he termed "desegregated,"
did just about as poorly there as they did in Hartford.

156 *native of Massachusetts* Kluger, *Simple Justice,* 73.

162　*"behalf of our schoolchildren"*　Chris Sheridan, "Ruling in Landmark School Case," *Hartford Courant*, April 13, 1995.

162　*protesting the ruling*　Richard Weizel, "Aftermath of a School Ruling: Rallies and an Appeal," *New York Times*, May 7, 1995.

162　*"constitutional rights violated"*　Weizel, "Aftermath."

163　*"struggle is perseverance"*　Sheridan, "Ruling."

163　*"under the rug"*　Sheridan, "Ruling."

Part Five. Back to School

190　*story about Hartford's turnaround*　Kate Zernike, "A Hard-Nosed Teachers' Union Backs Changes, and Schools Gain," *New York Times*, July 31, 2001.

191　*"Texas miracle"*　Walter Haney, "The Myth of the Texas Miracle in Education," *Education Policy Analysis Archives* 8, no. 41 (August 19, 2000). See also Stephen P. Klein, Laura S. Hamilton, Daniel F. McCaffrey, and Brian M. Stecher, *What Do Test Scores in Texas Tell Us?* RAND Issue Paper, October 24, 2000; and Diana Jean Schemo and Ford Fessenden, "A Miracle Revisited: Measuring Success; Gains in Houston Schools: How Real Are They?" *New York Times*, December 3, 2003.

191　*Houston's school superintendent then*　"The Texas Miracle," *60 Minutes*, CBS News, August 25, 2005, http://www.cbsnews.com/stories/2004/01/06/60II/main591676.shtml; Michael Winerip, "The 'Zero Dropout' Miracle: Alas! Alack! A Texas Tall Tale," *New York Times*, August 13, 2003; and Schemo and Fessenden, "Miracle Revisited."

191　*as much as 48 percentage points*　Winerip, "'Zero Dropout' Miracle"; "Texas Miracle," *60 Minutes*; Diana Jean Schemo, "For Houston Schools, College Claims Exceed Reality," *New York Times*, August 28, 2003; Wendy Grossman, "Making (Up) the Grade: This HISD Program Teaches a Big Lesson; Don't Question What the District Touts," *Houston Press*, April 6, 2000; Catherine and Capellaro, "Blowing the Whistle on the Texas Miracle: An Interview with Robert Kimball," *Rethinking Schools* 19, no. 1 (Fall 2004): 1.

191　*improved markedly during Bush's tenure*　Haney, "Myth"; Klein et al.,

What Do Test Scores. The RAND report compared performance on the Texas exams with performance on the national test known as the NAEP. The NAEP results showed far larger and widening gaps, for example, between the performance of white and minority students, while the gaps on the Texas test appeared far smaller.

191   *punishment for low student achievement*   Samuel Casey Carter, *No Excuses: Lessons from 21 High-Performing, High-Poverty Schools* (Washington, DC: Heritage Foundation, April 1, 2000).

191   *explain away low achievement*   Abigail Thernstrom and Stephan Thernstrom, *No Excuses: Closing the Racial Gap in Learning* (New York: Simon and Schuster, 2003), 169–89.

192   *smoking does not cause cancer*   Richard Rothstein, *Class and Schools: Using Social, Economic, and Educational Reform to Close the Black-White Achievement Gap* (Washington, DC, Economic Policy Institute, 2004), 61–83.

201   *creation of a panel*   Some members Rowland chose, and others were selected by high-ranking legislators.

201   *city schools better?*   Author interview with Jack Hasegawa, chief of staff for EIP panel, Hartford, Connecticut, October 4, 2001. Also, author interview with Gordon Bruno, executive director of the Connecticut Center for School Change, Hartford, Connecticut, May 10, 2000. Bruno and his staff also compiled exhaustive notes on the EIP meetings. The notes were made available to the author. Interview with Philip Tegeler, July 7, 2000. Tegeler attended several meetings. See also Robert Frahm, "Sheff Panel Continues to Struggle with Focus: Group Sharply Split on How to Proceed," *Hartford Courant,* December 12, 1996; Robert Frahm, "Sheff Panel to Hear Solutions Favored by Plaintiffs," *Hartford Courant,* November 20, 1996; Robert Frahm, "Sheff Panel Takes Up Issue of Parents' Role," *Hartford Courant,* October 24, 1996; Robert Frahm, "More Preschool Programs a Key Goal of Sheff Panel," *Hartford Courant,* December 4, 1996; and Rick Green, "Sheff Panel to Consider a Broad Range of Educational Changes," *Hartford Courant,* October 10, 1996.

201   *schools in the area be regionalized*   Yvonne Duncan and Jerry Brown, "Outline of Plan to Present to Legislature" (outline presented to Educational Improvement Panel and contained in a memo to Theodore S. Sergi, commissioner of education, December 2, 1996) (made available to author).

201 *options for urban children* The *Sheff* Plaintiffs, *Improving Our Schools: Guidelines for an Effective Plan for Quality Integrated Schools* (Hartford, November 1996) (on file with author). The recommendations were presented in 28 single-spaced pages and offered not only program suggestions but recommendations for monitoring and proposed standards for effectiveness.

202 *category was "Reducing Racial Isolation"* Educational Improvement Panel, *Report to the Governor and General Assembly*, Hartford, January 22, 1997.

202 *"educational interests"* Public Acts 97-290; 97-4; and 97-259. See also, for example, Rick Green, "State Defends Efforts to Integrate Schools," *Hartford Courant*, September 12, 1998.

202 *ordered to change anything* Fred Musante, "Remedies Elusive in Sheff Case," *New York Times*, July 6, 1997.

203 *bringing together urban and suburban youngsters* In 1998–99, the state spent $15.6 million on interdistrict magnet schools, $10.9 million on interdistrict cooperative grants, and $3.1 million for Open Choice. Information included in Judith Lohman and Alan Shepard, Sheff v. O'Neill *Response—K-12 Programs,* Office of Legislative Research Report, Connecticut General Assembly, February 8, 2002.

203 *school districts, including Hartford* Connecticut Public Act 97-259 as amended by Connecticut Public Act 97-11, Special Session of the Connecticut General Assembly, June 18, 1997.

203 *state-appointed board of trustees* An Act Concerning the Hartford Public Schools, Special Act No. 97-4, section 1, Connecticut General Assembly, http://www.cga.state.ct.us/ps97/Act/sa/1997SA-00004-R00SB-01200-SA.htm.

203 *"groundbreaking" . . . "less than token"* For example, the comments of State Senator Thomas Gaffey, member of the Legislator's Education Committee, Public Hearing, Legislative Office Building, Hartford, February 26, 2001. Author interview with John Brittain, by telephone, May 5, 2000.

204 *enrolled about 1,175 children* X03 CV 89-00855882S Plaintiff's Post-Hearing Brief, Superior Court, Complex Litigation Docket at Middletown, December 3, 1998, 41. See also Robert Frahm, "Critics: Choice Plan Is Failing; School Segregation Has Worsened in Hartford Since the Sheff Ruling," *Hartford Courant*, September 9, 1998.

204 *able to enroll in those schools* Enrollment in such schools in New Haven was far more substantial, in part because many of those schools existed

prior to the *Sheff* ruling. In 2001, 1,923 students—1,563 of them racial minority kids—attended interdistrict magnet schools in New Haven. Judith Lohman, *Minority Students Attending Interdistrict Magnet Schools,* Office of Legislative Research Report, Connecticut General Assembly, July 26, 2002.

204   *pull out at any time without penalty*   X03 CV 89-00855882S Plaintiff's Post-Hearing Brief, Superior Court, Complex Litigation Docket at Middletown, December 3, 1998, 33.

204   *in his closing statement*   *Sheff* Final Argument, given by Wesley Horton, Middletown, Connecticut, December 7, 1998 (document on file with author).

205   *state recorded notably large gaps*   U.S. Department of Education, Office of Educational Research and Improvement, National Center for Education Statistics, *The NAEP 1998 Reading Report Card for the Nation and the States,* NCES 1999-500, by P. L. Donahue, K. E. Voelkl, J. R. Campbell, and J. Mazzeo (Washington, DC: 1999). See also http://www.nea.org/goodnews/ct01.html.

206   *superintendent stays put*   See, for example, Council of Great City Schools, *Urban Indicator* 5, no. 2 (March 2000); and *National School Boards Association CUBE [Council of Urban Boards of Education] Survey Report: Superintendent Tenure* (Alexandria, VA: National School Boards Association, January 2002).

210   *was 52.3*   Author interview with Anthony Amato, Hartford, January 24, 2001; Connecticut State Department of Education, *Strategic School Profile, 1999–2000, Hartford School District* (Hartford, 2000).

210   *magazine, American Teacher*   "All Aboard for Reform: By Reaching Out to Parents and the Community, the Hartford Federation Has Helped Bring About a Shared Vision of School Improvement," *American Teacher,* September 2000, 1.

210   *gains in urban school districts*   American Federation of Teachers, "Doing What Works: Improving Big City School Districts," Educational Issues Policy Brief no. 12, October 2000.

210   *reported Hartford's test-score improvements*   Robert Johnston, "Test Scores Rising in City Districts, AFT Says," *Education Week,* October 25, 2000, 3.

210   SCHOOLS SHOW PROGRESS   Jeff Archer, "Under Amato, Hartford Schools Show Progress," *Education Week,* March 1, 2001, 1.

210 *"significant increases in test scores"* American Federation of Teachers, press release, September 21, 2001.

210 *"school reform models"* American Federation of Teachers, press release, October 15, 2001.

217 *"pictures in your mind"* Anthony Amato, *Spring Power School, Grade 3, Hartford Public Schools, Literacy Enhancement and Test Sophistication Program* (Hartford, n.d.), 2.

219 *"READ MORE"* DRP *Student's Practice Book, Level 4.1* (Hartford Public Schools, n.d.), 1.

219 *"intensive business-like pace"* Anthony Amato, *Literacy Enhancement and Test Sophistication Program Teacher's Resource Guide,* September–October 2000, 41, 42, 57.

219 *"mathematical understanding"* Anthony S. Amato, "Connecticut Mastery Test (CMT): What Every Parent Should Know!" (Hartford Public Schools, n.d.), 31.

220 *"editing and revising"* Ibid., 24.

229 *or by Slavin himself* For example, see N. A. Madden, R. E. Slavin, N. L. Karweit, L. Dolan, and B. A. Wasik, "Success for All: Longitudinal Effects of a Restructuring Program for Inner-City Elementary Schools," *American Educational Research Journal* 30, no. 1 (1993): 127–48 (EJ 463 408). See also S. M. Ross, L. J. Smith, R. E. Slavin, and N. A. Madden, "Improving the Academic Success of Disadvantaged Children: An Examination of Success for All," *Psychology in the Schools* 34, no. 2 (1997): 171–80 (EJ 551 696).

229 *better than similar children not in SFA* Richard Venezky, "An Evaluation of Success for All: Final Report to the France and Merrick Foundation" (paper, University of Delaware, Newark, DE, May 1994). Venezky notes (12), "The sample of students tested in the SFA schools significantly outperforms those tested in control schools in reading and language arts." See Madden et al., "Success for All: Longitudinal Effects." The American Institutes for Research, an independent Washington, D.C.–based evaluator, in 1999 rated Success for All as one of three school reform models that had research findings to back up their effectiveness. See *An Educator's Guide to School Reform* (Washington, DC: American Institutes for Research, 1999).

229 *every Hartford elementary school but one* Kennelly School stuck with Direct Instruction because teachers had adopted it several years earlier.

229 *SFA's market share* Debra Viadero, "Reform Programs Backed by Research Find Fewer Takers," *Education Week*, April 21, 2004, 1; and Kathleen Kennedy Manso, "Leading Commercial Series Don't Satisfy Gold Standard," *Education Week*, September 15, 2004, 6.

230 *Hartford paid about $4.3 million* Author interview with Anthony Amato, August 3, 2001; and author interview with Jacqueline Hardy, director of public information for the Hartford Public Schools, July 9, 2000.

231 *"before the Last 15 Minutes"* "Success for All, Six Day Schedule, Wings," (distributed to SFA teachers, Hartford Public Schools, n.d.) (on file with author).

233 *that did not use SFA* But in an updated 2004 "State Report" on its Web site, SFA Foundation again cites Hartford as making "substantially greater gains" on the reading portion of the CMT than Connecticut students generally. The Web site promotion claims that Hartford's SFA schools gained 5.3 percentage points overall, compared with the state as a whole's 1.5 percentage points. However, according to Connecticut State Department of Education data, Hartford's gains (excluding the elementary school that doesn't use Success for All) actually amount to a roughly 3.6-percentage-point gain in reading from 1998 to 2002. Among urban districts, the largest gain wasn't in Hartford, but in nearby Waterbury. Calculations by author.

233 *"implementation" of their program* Debra Viadero, "Miami Study Critiques Success for All," *Education Week*, January 27, 1999, 1. See also Laura Elder, "Popular Reading Program Leaving Kids Behind," *Galveston County Daily News*, November 28, 2003; and Jay Mathews, "Success for Some: Critics of a Controversial Method for Teaching Poor Children Claim Its Benefits Are Overrated; The Question Is, What's the Alternative?" *Washington Post*, July 21, 2002.

240 *teacher turnover and teacher burnout* R. M. Ingersoll, *A Different Approach to Solving the Teacher Shortage Problem* (Seattle: Center for the Study of Teaching and Policy, January 2001); Debra Viadero, "Researcher Skewers Explanations Behind Teacher Shortages," *Education Week*, April 10, 2002, 1; David Hoff, "Urban Districts Employing More Aggressive Hiring Tactics," *Education Week*, October 3, 2001, 1; and National Center for

Education Statistics, *Projection of Education Statistics to 2011* (Washington, DC: U.S. Department of Education, 2001).

240   *to get good at their jobs*   Cynthia Prince, *The Challenge of Attracting Good Teachers and Principals to Struggling Schools* (Arlington, VA: American Association of School Administrators, January 2002). In her comprehensive report, Prince finds, "After three years, 29 percent of beginning teachers are no longer teaching, and after five years, 39 percent have left the profession. The odds are even worse among teachers in urban schools. Within five years, half will no longer be teaching." Also, Prince reports, "Novice teachers with three years of classroom experience or less are twice as likely to be assigned to high-minority, high-poverty schools." For a journalistic account of the problem, see K. Grossman, B. Beaupre, and R. Rossi, "Poorest Kids Often Wind Up with the Weakest Teachers," *Chicago Sun-Times*, September 7, 2001.

241   *terminated EAI contracts*   Rick Green, "EAI's Challenge: Making a Profit with City Schools," *Hartford Courant*, July 8, 1994; Rick Green, "Student Scores, Accounting Method Issue for EAI: Test Results Show Decline at Company-Run Schools," *Hartford Courant*, October 19, 1994; and Rick Green, "Debate Over EAI Tearing City's Soul," *Hartford Courant*, May 21, 1995.

243   *in San Francisco*   Rachel Gottlieb, "Wanderlust for Amato," *Hartford Courant*, March 24, 2000.

243   *in Portland, Oregon*   Rachel Gottlieb, "Amato Says He's Ready to Go," *Hartford Courant*, March 2, 2002.

Part Six. The Suburbs

260   *$93,900, the lowest*   "Quality of Life Index, Changes in Median Home Values," *Connecticut Economy,* Summer 2002. See also Priscilla Canny and Douglas Hall, "Housing: Home Ownership in Connecticut," *Connecticut Voices for Children Census Connections* 1, no. 2 (September 2003).

266   *glance at balance sheets*   For an insightful, original, and lively discussion on this question, see James Ryan, "Schools, Race and Money," *Yale Law Journal* 109 (1999): 249–316.

267   *enrolls a wealthier student body*   *Education Finance Litigation: History, Issues and Current Status* (Washington, DC: National Center on Education
Finance, 2003), http://:www.ncsl.org/programs/educ/NCEF.htm. (Note
the difference between equity legislation and adequacy legislation. Equity legislation, such as Connecticut's *Horton v. Meskill,* was favored in
the 1970s; adequacy legislation, which establishes funding standards often
based on many variables, such as poverty concentration, became more
common in the late 1980s.) See Kevin Carey, *The Funding Gap: Low-
Income and Minority Students Still Receive Fewer Dollars in Many States*
(Washington, DC: Education Trust, October 2003).

287   Oklahoma v. Dowell   *Board of Education of Oklahoma v. Dowell,* 498 U.S.
237 (1991).

287   Freeman v. Pitts   *Freeman v. Pitts,* 503 U.S. 467 (1992).

287   Missouri v. Jenkins   *Missouri v. Jenkins,* 115 U.S. 2038 (1995).

287   *dismantle them legally*   Gary Orfield and Susan E. Eaton, eds., *Dismantling Desegregation: The Quiet Reversal of* Brown v. Board of Education
(New York: New Press, 1996).

287   *more segregated schools*   Orfield and Eaton, *Dismantling;* and Gary Orfield
and Chungmei Lee, Brown *at 50: King's Dream or Plessy's Nightmare?* (Cambridge, MA: Civil Rights Project at Harvard University, January 2004).

287   *30 percent by 2001*   Orfield and Lee, Brown *at 50,* 19, table 7. Orfield and
Lee note, "During the period from 1968–1999 there was a very dramatic
drop in the percentage of black students in intensely segregated schools in
all regions except the Northeast and a very substantial increase in the percent of black students in majority white schools in the Southern and Border states, where most of the segregation orders were being implemented.
Since 1988, with strong opposition to desegregation from the courts and inaction or opposition by executive agencies, segregation has increased substantially in all regions on both measures except in the Northeast where
there was never significant desegregation efforts."

288   Texas Law School   *Hopwood v. Texas,* 78 F.3d 932, 962 (5th Cir. 1996).
See also Deirdre Shesgreen, "Post-*Hopwood* Jitters? GU Nixes Minority
Clerkships," *Legal Times,* Sept. 30, 1996, 1.

288   Grutter v. Bollinger et. al   No. 02—241. Argued April 1, 2003; decided
June 23, 2003.

288 *went to Thurgood Marshall* Author interview with John Brittain, by telephone, November 10, 2003, and February 10, 2000. See also Lydia Lum, "State Law Schools Enroll More Blacks, but 90 Percent Go to TSU," *Houston Chronicle,* November 2, 1999.

310 *brusque management style* Mark Pazniokas and Rachel Gottlieb, "Mayor Gave Amato a Choice: Faced with City's Lost Confidence, Superintendent Chose to Resign," *Hartford Courant,* October 7, 2002.

311 *pass those at a 10th-grade level* Rachel Gottlieb, "Many City Grads Not Up to the Test: Police Department's Civil Service Exam Spotlights a Failure of Hartford's Schools," *Hartford Courant,* October 17, 2000.

311 *on all four portions* Connecticut State Department of Education, *Strategic School Profile 2002–03, Hartford Public School District* (Hartford, 2003).

311 *fourth-grade reading scores* Robert Frahm, "State Will No Longer Rank Schools by CMT's," *Hartford Courant,* February 5, 2003; and Robert Frahm, "Learning Gaps Persist in State: Mastery Tests Scores Edge Up, but Blacks, Hispanics, Poor Lag Behind," *Hartford Courant,* March 6, 2002.

311 *met the state's reading goal* http://www.csde.state.ct.us/public/der/ssp/dist0203/dist041.pdf. See also Frahm, "State Will No Longer."

311 *$200,000-a-year job* Rachel Gottlieb and Robert A. Frahm, "Amato Gives In to Pressure: Superintendent Reads Writing on Wall, Leaves with Ample Severance Package," *Hartford Courant,* October 29, 2001.

312 *"more than 40 applicants"* Aesha Rasheed, "Schools Chief Tailor-Made for Tough Test: Amato Specializes in Turnaround Jobs," *Times-Picayune,* February 18, 2003.

Part Eight. You Just Have to Do What You Can

329 *"models in urban education"* Robert Frahm, "A School Believes," *Hartford Courant,* April 27, 2003; U.S. Department of Education, "Paige Announces First List of No Child Left Behind Blue Ribbon Schools," press release, Washington, DC, September 17, 2003; and U.S. Department of Education, "Learning from Six High Poverty, High Achieving Blue Ribbon Schools," Washington, DC, http://www.ed.gov/programs/nclbbrs/2003/profiles.

333   *decline of 35 percentage points*   Connecticut State Department of Education, *Connecticut Mastery Test, Third Generation, Summary Performance Results, Grades 4, 6 and 8, 2000–2004, Report by Content Area* (Hartford, 2004), http://www.cmtreports.com. To be consistent, the calculations from both years (2001 and 2004) include only students not in special education. The results for both years would be lower if students enrolled in special education were taken into account.

333   *45 percent met the goal in writing*   Connecticut State Department of Education, *CMT State by School Reports* (Hartford, 2005), http://www.cmtreports.com.

337   *"future depends on them"*   *Sheff v. O'Neill*, 1290, quoting *Abbott v. Burke*, 575 A.2d (1990).

338   *one year in federal prison*   Matt Apuzzo and John Christofferson, "Former Gov. Rowland Gets a Year in Prison for Graft," Associated Press, March 18, 2005.

338   *ranch house in West Hartford*   Christopher Keating, Edmund H. Mahony, and Katie Melone, "Rowlands Leave Mansion for Private Life," *Hartford Courant*, July 1, 2004.

338   *legacy to Hartford*   Lisa Chedekel, "Broken Promise: John Rowland's Legacy As a Builder of Cities Is Lost in a Scandalous Collapse," *Hartford Courant*, June 22, 2004.

338   *lasted . . . two years and two months*   Brian Thevenot, "Besieged Amato Calls It Quits," *Times-Picayune*, April 13, 2005.

338   *promises of more police officers*   Matt Burgard, "Mother Killed: City Adds Patrols," *Hartford Courant*, June 23, 2005.

Appendix. The Beloved Community?

344   *"equality of oneness"*   Martin Luther King Jr., "An Analysis of the Ethical Demands of Integration" (address delivered at the Nashville Consultation, December 28, 1962), http://www.kingpapers.stanford.edu. See also Kenneth L. Smith and Ira Zepp Jr., *Search for the Beloved Community: The Thinking of Martin Luther King* (Valley Forge, PA: Judson Press, 1974).

345   *to examine comprehensively here*   Amy Wells, "Re-examining Social Sci-

ence Research on School Desegregation: Long-Term versus Short-Term Effects," *Teachers College Record* 96, no. 4 (1996): 691–706. Also, on the impact of a racially diverse student body upon college-going and high school graduation, see an excellent study, Michael A. Boozer, Alan B. Krueger, and Shari Wolkon, "Race and School Quality Since *Brown v. Board of Education,*" in *Brookings Papers on Economic Activity: Microeconomics* (Washington, DC: Brookings Institution Press, 1992), 269–338. See also M. Dawkins and Jomills Braddock, "The Continuing Significance of De-segregation: School Racial Composition and African American Inclusion in American Society," *Journal of Negro Education* 63, no. 3 (1994): 394–405. For a thought-provoking and original analysis about the relationship between disproportionately black schools and the achievement of black students, see Eric Hanushek, John Kain, and Steven Rivkin, "New Evidence about *Brown v. Board of Education:* The Complex Effects of School Racial Composition on Achievement" (NBER Working Paper w8741, January 2002). An earlier version of this paper was presented at the Brookings Conference on Empirics of Social Interactions, Washington, DC, January, 2000. For an excellent historic overview and fascinating contemporary examination of the need to consider social disadvantage in school achievement, see Richard Rothstein, *Class and Schools: Using Social, Economic, and Educational Reform to Close the Black-White Achievement Gap* (Washington, DC: Economic Policy Institute, 2004).

345   *outcomes of desegregated schooling* Amy Stuart Wells and Robert L. Crain, "Perpetuation Theory and the Long Term Effects of School Desegregation," *Review of Educational Research* 64, no. 4 (1994): 531–55.

345   *"less fearful of whites"* Ibid., 552.

345   *"comfortable around people of different backgrounds"* Amy Stuart Wells, Jennifer Jellison Holme, Anita Tijerina Revilla, and Awo Korantemaa Atanda, "How Desegregation Changed Us: The Effects of Racially Mixed Schools on Students and Society," in *In Search of Brown* (Cambridge, MA: Harvard University Press, forthcoming). My own 2001 study of adult African Americans who'd participated in a voluntary urban-to-suburban desegregation program reveals similar sentiments. The vast majority of past participants reported many tangible, life-shaping benefits of prior desegregation. And nearly all said they'd repeat their desegregated experience even

after admitting to not insubstantial challenges in adjusting and fitting in, both at home and at school. See Susan E. Eaton, *The Other Boston Busing Story: What's Won and Lost Across the Boundary Line* (New Haven, CT: Yale University Press, 2001).

346 *do better academically in predominantly middle-class schools* For an excellent overview, see Richard D. Kahlenberg, *Economic School Integration: An Update*, Century Foundation, Issue Brief Series, September 18, 2002. See also Century Foundation Task Force on the Common School, *Divided We Fail: Coming Together through Public School Choice* (New York: Century Foundation Press, 2002); and David Rusk, "Classmates Count: A Study of the Interrelationship between Socioeconomic Background and Standardized Test Scores of 4th Grade Pupils in the Madison-Dane County Public Schools" (mimeograph, July 5, 2002), cited in Kahlenberg, *Economic School Integration*.

346 *"a 20 to 32 percentage point improvement"* Kahlenberg, *Economic School Integration*.

347 *in Denver, Colorado, in Maryland, and in Escambia, Florida* Kahlenberg, *Economic School Integration*.

347 *increase in all but six states* David Rusk, "Trends in School Segregation," background paper for the Century Foundation Task Force on the Common School, *Divided We Fail*, cited in Kahlenberg, *Economic School Integration*.

347 *achieve a racially diverse student body* In the law school case, *Grutter*, however, the Court ruled that the current admissions plan at Michigan was not "narrowly tailored" to meet the constitutionality test.

348 *adverse effects of concentrated poverty* *McFarland v. Jefferson County Public Schools*, U.S. District Court, Western District of Kentucky at Louisville, Civil Action No. 3:02CV-620-H, Memorandum Opinion (2004).

348 *move would contribute to desegregation* *Comfort v. Lynn School Committee*, 283 F. Supp. 2d. 328.

349 *told reporters following the ruling* Denise Lavoie, "Appeals Court Upholds Lynn Desegregation Plan," Associated Press, June 16, 2005.

350 *40 percent of the residents are poor* Paul Jargowsky, *Stunning Progress, Hidden Problems: The Dramatic Decline of Concentrated Poverty in the 1990s*, Living Cities Census Series (Washington, DC: Brookings Institution, May 2003).

350   *was particularly striking*   Leonard Rubinowitz and James Rosenbaum, *Crossing the Class and Color Lines: From Public Housing to White Suburbia* (Chicago: University of Chicago Press, 2000). See also Margery Turner and Dolores Acevedo-Garcia, "Why Housing Mobility? The Research Evidence Today," *Poverty & Race* 14, no. 1 (January–February 2005).

351   *creating and compounding racial segregation*   Philip Tegeler and Shelley White, "Monitoring Housing Desegregation Litigation Settlements," *Poverty & Race* 8, no. 5 (September–October 1999).

352   *"risky behaviors"*   Turner and Acevedo-Garcia, "Why Housing Mobility?"

353   *"from the federal and state governments"*   David Rusk, *Cities Without Suburbs* (Washington, DC: Woodrow Wilson Center Press, distributed by Johns Hopkins University Press, 1995), 127–32.

354   *"as well as limited educational attainment"*   Tom Puleo, "Urban Report Has Familiar Ring for City: Hartford Ranks in Worst 10 National 'Hardship' Study," *Hartford Courant*, September 5, 2004.